Nathan Trotter

PHILADELPHIA MERCHANT

– 1787–1853 –

BY

ELVA TOOKER

ARNO PRESS

A NEW YORK TIMES COMPANY

New York • 1972

Reprint Edition 1972 by Arno Press Inc.

Copyright © 1955 by the President and Fellows
of Harvard College
Reprinted by permission of Harvard University Press

Reprinted from a copy in The State Historical Society
of Wisconsin Library

Technology and Society
ISBN for complete set: 0-405-04680-4
See last pages of this volume for titles.

Manufactured in the United States of America

Library of Congress Cataloging in Publication Data

Tooker, Elva.
    Nathan Trotter, Philadelphia merchant, 1787-1853.

    (Technology and society)
    Original ed. issued as v. 18 of Harvard studies in
business history.
    Includes bibliographical references.
    1. Trotter, Nathan, 1787-1853. 2. Philadelphia--
Commerce. I. Series. II. Series: Harvard studies
in business history, 18.
[HF3163.P5T7 1972]   380.1'092'4 [B]   72-5080
ISBN 0-405-04729-0

TECHNOLOGY AND SOCIETY

TECHNOLOGY AND SOCIETY

Advisory Editor
DANIEL J. BOORSTIN, author of
The Americans and Director of
The National Museum of History
and Technology, Smithsonian Institution

HARVARD STUDIES IN BUSINESS HISTORY

XVIII

Edited by
HENRIETTA M. LARSON
Associate Professor of Business History
and
THOMAS R. NAVIN
Assistant Professor of Business History
Graduate School of Business Administration
George F. Baker Foundation
Harvard University

Nathan Trotter

PHILADELPHIA MERCHANT

– 1787–1853 –

BY

ELVA TOOKER

Formerly Research Assistant in Business History
Graduate School of Business Administration
George F. Baker Foundation
Harvard University

HARVARD UNIVERSITY PRESS

Cambridge, Massachusetts

1955

TO MY MOTHER

Contents

PART IV

Epilogue

Appendixes

Illustrations

CONTENTS

Tables

Charts and Maps

Editors' Introduction

WHEN Norman Sydney Buck published in 1925 his distinguished work on the organization of Anglo-American trade (1800–1850), he used as his principal source the reports of various committees of the Parliament of Great Britain. In his bibliographical note he commented that another source of great significance would have been the business records of firms or individuals engaged in foreign trade. Especially would a study of an American firm's records have been rewarding since it would have approached the subject from the private side rather than the government, and from the American rather than the British, and would have indicated how changing patterns revealed themselves in the profit and loss experience of a particular firm. At the time, however, none of the leading American depositories of business manuscripts had in their possession any collections of value to Buck's study.

The year after Buck's book appeared, one of the largest known collections of business records dealing with the first half of the nineteenth century, the letters and accounts of Nathan Trotter & Company of Philadelphia, was presented by William Henry Trotter to Baker Library of Harvard University. In succeeding years these records were uncrated and catalogued and by 1931 were made available for use. They numbered more than 1,100 volumes of bound material and nearly 200 boxes of miscellaneous items.

Recognizing the value of these materials, Professor N. S. B. Gras, of the Harvard Graduate School of Business Administration, suggested them as a basis of study to Miss Elva Tooker, who was doing graduate work at Radcliffe and was a research assistant on a part-time basis in the business history department at the Harvard Business School.

Actual work on the Trotter study was begun under the direction of Professor Edwin F. Gay of the Harvard department of economics, and after Gay's retirement was continued under the guidance of Professor Gras. Then, in 1937, Miss Tooker returned to teaching and thereafter worked on the Trotter records only intermittently during summer holidays.

What this method of research lacked in continuity it gained in the time it allowed for thought and reflection. Over a period of years Miss Tooker developed a familiarity with her materials and a penetration of their significance that could not have been obtained in a shorter period.

The product of Miss Tooker's work is a book for specialists. It is, in a sense, a study of business practices as carried on more than a century ago. In three regards it is a pathbreaker. It contributes our first detailed description and historical analysis of a small-scale businessman at work. Nathan Trotter, though a "millionaire," made his money without increasing his organization beyond a handful of men. The contrast Miss Tooker draws between Nathan Trotter, the conservative Philadelphian, and Anson Phelps, the dynamic New Yorker and founder of Phelps, Dodge & Company, gives us an invaluable insight into the personal characteristics that distinguish the small-scale operator from the large. On the subject of foreign trade this study does for the period before the Civil War what William T. Baxter's book on *The House of Hancock* did for the period before the American Revolution. On the subject of short-term financing of American business it reveals for the first time how private capitalists, by assuming risks the banks were unable or unwilling to handle, supplemented the work of the banks and rendered financial assistance to a rapidly expanding economy that was constantly troubled by a shortage of capital.

Some of the incidental expenses of Miss Tooker's research were borne by the Harvard Business School and a summer's work was financed by a grant from the Business History Foundation of New York. But the principal costs of the research were borne by Miss Tooker herself. Publication was made possible by a grant of money to Harvard University from the Business History Foundation.

HENRIETTA M. LARSON
THOMAS R. NAVIN

Author's Preface

DOUBTLESS a Quaker and a Philadelphian—neither of which I am—would have realized the significance of much in the story of Nathan Trotter and his company which I have missed. In writing this history my chief qualification was persistence. Summers of sheer drudgery had to be spent in reading hundreds of thousands of letters and computing many statistical series.

It was eventually rewarding, however, and at times exciting to see the patterns of Nathan Trotter's character and business emerge. He came to seem all of a piece: conservative in his purchasing, selling, and accounting techniques; provincial in his investments. Only in his discounting of notes did he combine to some extent speculation with conservatism and provincialism.

In the midst of the task, I often asked myself how to justify spending time in this fashion. Aside from the desire to finish a study which I had begun, I was influenced by the conviction that sound business and economic history must be based to a greater extent on the findings of pieces of research such as this. Reducing the situation to its simplest terms, I accepted the fact that I was fashioning a future footnote in business and economic history.

In the course of my research and writing I have incurred many obligations. But for the initial suggestions and inspirational guidance of Professor N. S. B. Gras this history would not have been begun; but for the encouragement of Professor Henrietta M. Larson it would not have been continued; and but for the criticism and co-operation of Professor Thomas R. Navin it would never have been completed. To these three I am deeply grateful.

Through the influence of Professor Edwin F. Gay, my approach to the collection was statistical. During my subsequent study of the firm's history I have been grateful to him for guiding me to compile the statistical tables against which developments could be constantly checked. Profit and loss guided me in my interpretation as it guided Nathan Trotter in his operation of the business.

For the silhouette of young Nathan Trotter, for his marriage certificate, and for certain other family materials, I am obliged to Mrs. William Henry Trotter. Indeed the book itself owes a special obligation to Mrs. Trotter, for it was through her influence that the business papers of Nathan Trotter & Company were moved from the loft of the Trotter warehouse to the safety of Baker Library.

To Mr. William Trotter Newbold, I am indebted for much of the information contained in the closing pages of the Epilogue. To Mr. T. Morris Perot, III, I am grateful for permission to use material in his possession on the Sansom and Callender families.

Mr. Eric P. Newman supplied me with a Bank of Pennsylvania banknote from which the picture of Joseph Trotter was reproduced. Miss Edna Baechle not only gave time to checking the present location of many of the places on the map of Philadelphia but assured me that she enjoyed verifying my information "on foot, in the car, and at the Historical Society. It made the past come alive again."

The research on the Trotter papers has been carried on in Baker Library at the Harvard Graduate School of Business Administration. This library and the Widener Library at Harvard University were both generous in granting me the use of their facilities.

I wish to thank The Historical Society of Pennsylvania, the John Hay Library at Brown University, and the American Antiquarian Society, Worcester, Massachusetts, for permission to use their materials.

Mr. Howard Cook kindly gave me permission to use a reproduction of his etching of the warehouse of the Trotter firm made in 1926.

To Professor Henrietta M. Larson, Editor of the *Bulletin of the Business Historical Society,* I wish to express my thanks for allowing me to use substantial parts of an article of mine which appeared in the *Bulletin* under the title "A Merchant Turns to Money-Lending in Philadelphia."

A work as technical and as full of opportunities for error as this book must necessarily owe much to many hands. Miss Audrey Barrett carefully typed the final manuscript. Miss Josepha Perry read the manuscript and suggested ways to clarify the text. Miss Hilma Holton edited the manuscript; she also took charge of seeing it through the press and prepared the index.

The style of the manuscript is not so much mine as Nathan Trotter's. After years of reading the merchant's letters and his personal comments in his account books, I found myself thinking about his problems in the selfsame words he would have used under the circumstances. Often, therefore, the text contains phrases which, while not the exact words of Trotter and consequently not set aside by quotation marks, reflect the nineteenth-century manner in which the merchant spoke or wrote about his business.

ELVA TOOKER

PART I

Trotter and His Antecedents

CHAPTER I

Nathan Trotter

THE MAN AND HIS CAREER

IF one walks today not far from the Delaware River in Philadelphia, down North Front Street from Arch to Market, one sees on the right a four-story brick building with the name Nathan Trotter & Company across the front. It is not an imposing enough structure to attract a second glance; yet for over 125 years this has been the location of an importing and metal-dealing house which has often brought large profits to its owners.

It is not a simple matter to date the year when this firm got its start. Although the present title was not used until 1817, Nathan Trotter had by that time been the operating head of the firm for two years and a partner for eight. Even before that, since 1803, he had been in the employ of the firm on a salary. The firm today dates its beginnings from 1789, the year when Nathan Trotter's older brother began as an apprentice with the firm whose activities he would carry on. But if one considers this earlier firm as a direct ancestor, one can push back through an extension of business partnerships to the first half of the eighteenth century.

The man of real importance in the firm's history is Nathan Trotter. Although this study might in some respects be considered a history of a firm, it is really a biography of Nathan Trotter.

Many books have been written on the lives of businessmen and many businessmen have written their autobiographies; yet few such books actually consider a man's business. Instead they usually deal with his social and governmental activities and his philosophy of life. But a book on Nathan Trotter is necessarily a book about his business life. Aside from his family life he had no other.

It is not surprising that Trotter's name is less famous than the names of such Philadelphians as Nicholas Biddle and Matthias Baldwin. Trotter was not even well-known to his contemporaries. The author of *Memoirs and Auto-biography of Some of the Wealthy Citizens of Philadelphia* knew so little about Nathan Trotter that he valued Trotter's wealth in 1846 at $200,000, while, at a conservative estimate, it was almost three times that amount (in less than a decade after 1846, Trotter left an estate valued at practically a million dollars).

The reason for Trotter's obscurity was partly that he, a Quaker, lived simply and unostentatiously; partly, also, that the nature of his business was such that it had no particular color and did not attract the general public's attention. Trotter was a metals wholesaler and out of his metals business he made profits which he did not put into his standard of living, but which he accumulated and invested in whatever ways seemed most profitable to him.

In Trotter's time discounting personal notes was one of the most important ways a man raised funds for his business. The businessman gave his note for the face value of the amount he owed. Then his creditor, if he needed cash immediately, tried to sell the note for what he could get; tried to sell it either to a bank, a broker, or perhaps directly to a man with capital. Since the note would not yet have matured it had to be sold at a discount. These discounts made up a part of the profits of banks and of men like Trotter with idle funds to invest.

America, in the first half of the nineteenth century, was undergoing a very rapid development which meant that, in order to supply the capital necessary for business, many men lived far below their means. Nathan Trotter was one who, by producing more than he was using, accumulated wealth so that he could put large sums into those business channels where they would be most productive—most productive for society and for himself as well. He helped in accumulating the pools of capital which were needed to facilitate and advance the American Industrial Revolution.

Nathan Trotter began life on the first day of August in that hot summer of 1787 when the Constitutional Convention was meeting in Philadelphia. The country's great—Hamilton, Madison, Franklin, among others, and Washington, the presiding officer—were meeting daily, as they had been since May, to draw up a Constitution that would replace the Articles of Confederation. There remained two months of work to be done before the Constitution would be completed and almost a year of national debate before it would be adopted.

Young Trotter could be grateful in later years that the time and place of his birth so favorably combined to promote his business career. New York might have been a more advantageous place in which to be born in 1787 and might have made Trotter a different man. But Philadelphia had its special merits: the Quaker discipline, with its accent on sound economic values, took the place of a training in dynamic and energetic self-seeking, such as the young man might have acquired had he been reared in the city to the north.

As a member of Philadelphia's Quaker community, Nathan Trotter was heir to a tradition of long standing, for his ancestry extended five generations or more into the history of the City of Friends. At least as early as 1692 an ancestor named William Trotter was active in Philadelphia affairs, for in that year William signed a petition to the Colonial Assembly placing himself on record as opposed to a tax of a penny a pound on the value of "every man's estate." [1] At a later date another Trotter, named Joseph, a son of William (see genealogy, Chart I), also placed himself on record in opposition to colonial tax policy by signing the Non-importation Agreement of 25 October 1765. But none of the Trotters went so far as to join the cause of independence from England; as Quakers they were opposed to war and believed that other means should be found to resolve the dispute over taxation. In 1779 Nathan's father, Daniel Trotter, submitted to double taxation rather than declare himself a supporter of the new order by taking an oath of allegiance. [2]

Few records exist concerning Nathan's early life beyond the fact that he was the seventh child in a family of ten. His birthplace, it is known, was Elfreth's Alley, where there still are houses that were standing at the time of his birth. It is also known that he grew up on Front Street, not far from the wharves along the Delaware River. [3]

It is further recorded that death was a frequent visitor to the Trotter household. In the first nine years of Nathan's life he lost two brothers and a sister—and in the tenth he lost his mother. How the family of seven motherless children fared for the next three years is not known

though it is possible that an aunt kept house for them. It *is* known that
Nathan at the age of fourteen also lost his father and thereafter became a boarder, with his younger brother, Thomas, at the Quaker
School at Westtown—written Weston in the Trotter records.[4] Thomas
entered the school in February, 1801, and Nathan in April,[5] followed
by their two younger sisters at a later date. Since charges at the school
were moderate—board for one quarter was only $20 in 1801—it may
have been that relatives of the Trotters chose the school as a solution
of what to do with the orphaned children.

By chance there exists a journal kept by John Comly, who had
charge of the Westtown school in the years when Nathan was first
there.[6] On one occasion Comly recorded that he was "much tried in
meeting on account of a restless disposition among the boys, evincing a
great degree of thoughtlessness and unconcernedness about the important business of performing Divine worship in spirit and in truth."
One feels that Nathan was fortunate to have come under the care of
such a schoolmaster as Comly, who was moved to confide to his

Chart I

TROTTER GENEALOGY

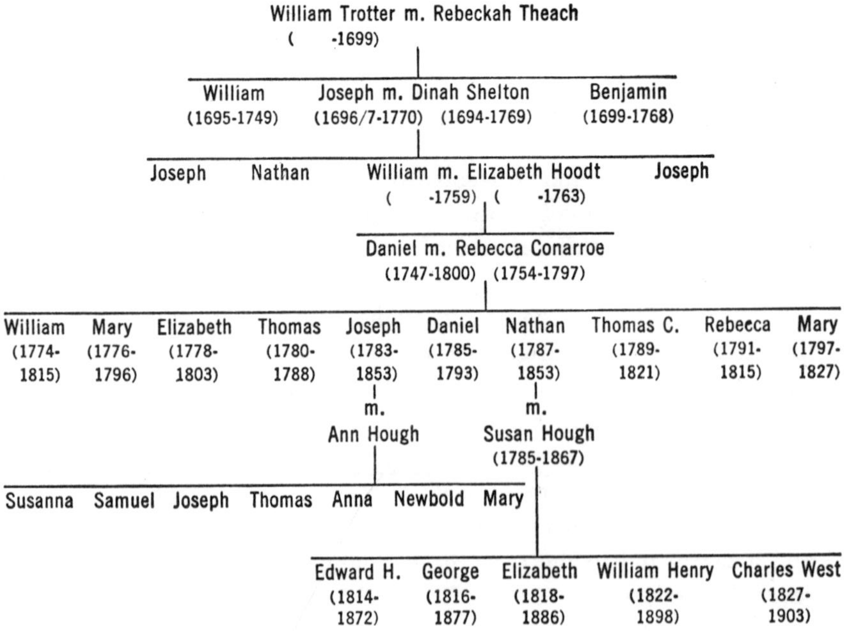

William Trotter m. Rebeckah Theach
(-1699)

William	Joseph m. Dinah Shelton		Benjamin
(1695-1749)	(1696/7-1770)	(1694-1769)	(1699-1768)

Joseph	Nathan	William m. Elizabeth Hoodt	Joseph
		(-1759) (-1763)	

Daniel m. Rebecca Conarroe
(1747-1800) (1754-1797)

William	Mary	Elizabeth	Thomas	Joseph	Daniel	Nathan	Thomas C.	Rebecca	Mary
(1774-	(1776-	(1778-	(1780-	(1783-	(1785-	(1787-	(1789-	(1791-	(1797-
1815)	1796)	1803)	1788)	1853)	1793)	1853)	1821)	1815)	1827)
				m.		m.			
				Ann Hough		Susan Hough			
						(1785-1867)			

Susanna	Samuel	Joseph	Thomas	Anna	Newbold	Mary

Edward H.	George	Elizabeth	William Henry	Charles West
(1814-	(1816-	(1818-	(1822-	(1827-
1872)	1877)	1886)	1898)	1903)

Journal: "There is great need of patience and stability in the government of children, lest the mind become agitated or soured by trifling occurrences. Preserve calmness of spirit, and act not in thy own will."

Enoch Lewis probably taught Nathan mathematics. Grammar, reading, and geography—with frequent scientific lectures—made up the rest of the course of formal study. Well-known Quakers visited the school and talked to the boys and girls. Students were required to copy such maxims as "Avoid bad company" and "Keep your own secrets," and judging by Nathan Trotter's practices the maxims had real influence.

Somewhere Nathan Trotter acquired an interest in phrasemaking and in books and poetry. In his own home there had been such books as Woolman's *Journal,* Carvel's *Travels,* Howard's *Life,* and a "Quarto" *Bible.*[7] When Nathan was a young man of twenty, he made the comparatively heavy investment of $8.05 in books which he purchased at Andrew Bayard's auction: [8] seven volumes of Rollins' *Ancient History,* six volumes of *Plutarch's Lives,* and a copy of *The Vicar of Wakefield.*

An exercise book in which Nathan worked out geometry problems is still preserved.[9] Some of the exercises were related to actual problems he met later. Under a section headed "Artificers Work" were problems on timber measure, and, as a future dealer in copper, he may have found opportunity to apply this rhymed assignment:

> Let the top and the bottom diameters be,
> In just such proportion as 5 is to 3:
> Twelve inches the depth I propos'd and no more;
> And to hold in ale gallons 7 less than a score.

Poetry which he also copied in this book was by Pope and Thomson among others. Some of it, copied when he was about twenty years old, reflects an interest in nature, contemplation, and religion. Following a section in which he recorded the death of his mother and his father, he copied "A Description of a Parish Poor House." The psychologist might question whether the young orphan was moved to accumulate wealth by fear of such a fate. At any rate, along with better poetry, he copied this awesome picture:

> There is yon house that holds the parish poor,
> Whose walls of mud scarce bear the broken door.
>
> . . . . .
>
> There children dwell who know no parents' care,
> Parents who know no children's love dwell there,
> Heart broken matrons on their joyless bed,
> Forsaken wives and mothers never wed;

Dejected widows with unheeded tears,
And crippled age with more than childhood fears
The lame, the blind, and far the happiest they,
The moping idiot, and the madman gay.
Here too the sick their final doom receive.

. . . . .

Nathan Trotter apparently had both affection and respect for West-town. Five years after he had left the school he went back with James Martin "& others" for a reunion. To make a good appearance he made expenditures "for hand[kerchiefs] gloves &c 3.31." [10] Nathan sent several of his own children to Westtown, and in the 1840's he paid the expenses of his niece's two sons at the school.

When Nathan finished his schooling at the age of sixteen, he went to work for William, his oldest brother. William was Nathan's senior by thirteen years and was already in business even before the death of their father Daniel. William had not followed the father into the chair and cabinetmaking trade. The father had early taken as an apprentice the young Ephraim Haines, whom he later admitted to a partnership in his business. In addition to becoming a partner Ephraim became a son-in-law by marrying Nathan's sister Elizabeth. It may have been that Ephraim's place in the family business effectively prevented the other sons from becoming cabinetmakers. William had been apprenticed at the age of fourteen to a Philadelphia merchant and importer named William Sansom. [11] Thus, the son of a craftsman formed a connection which was to take him and his brother Nathan into a wholly new line of business, a business which was capable of growth and expansion far beyond the business of the handicraftsman.

After a seven-year apprenticeship in the store of William Sansom, and a voyage to China as supercargo on the *Pigou*, a ship in which his employer was financially interested, young William Trotter entered business as a partner of Joseph Sansom, younger brother of his former employer.

Some time before November, 1800, William married Mary Kempton, who was not a member of the Society of Friends. For having "accomplished his marriage contrary to the Order of [Quaker] Discipline," William was "treated with by the Overseers" and, proving obstinate, was disowned by the Society. [12]

In 1803 the Sansom & Trotter partnership was dissolved and William Trotter went into business for himself to carry on the importing of goods from England—the business in which the Sansoms had been engaged. This business supported William and his wife and, in time, their seven children. It also served as a training place for William's younger brothers, Joseph and Nathan.[13] Joseph had become William's assistant in 1800, and Nathan in the year that William became an independent businessman.

Nathan's first duties must have included a certain amount of bookkeeping, for scattered here and there through William's account books, from 1803 on, are entries in the younger brother's handwriting. Beginning in 1806 Nathan assumed principal responsibility for keeping the accounts, and in that year he made his first trip to New York to buy merchandise for his brother's store. On his twenty-first birthday, 1 August 1808, he became William's salaried clerk.

Following the centuries-old practice of the sedentary merchant's helper, the young Trotter also engaged in a few business ventures on his own account. As early as 1804, he was buying linens at an auction conducted by the firm of York & Lippincott. William Trotter's daybook shows that the purchase price of $15.22 was borrowed by Nathan from his older brother and was returned six months later. But whether Nathan profited in this early venture is not clear.

Nathan's personal daybook, kept from January, 1807, shows that he also made purchases and sales of small amounts of suspenders, sandpaper, pocketbooks, skivers, nankeens, hessians, watch chains, keys, etc., and, in company with William, of damaged sheet iron and tin plate. Some of this personal business conducted by Nathan was financed with $150 borrowed from the two uncles who served as his guardians, Thomas Conarroe and Joseph Trotter. For this loan the nineteen-year-old merchant gave his note payable on demand with interest. He also sold on commission some articles for Joseph King of New York and took some small shares in ventures to the West Indies.

In addition to these mercantile activities, Nathan added to his income by keeping books for the firms of Halberstadt & Haines and Conarroe & Scott. The Haines of the above firm was Nathan's brother-in-law, Ephraim, who, after the death of Nathan's father, had become a lumber merchant in addition to carrying on his trade as a cabinet-maker.[14] The Conarroe of the firm of Conarroe & Scott was Nathan's guardian and uncle (on his mother's side). Conarroe & Scott were timber merchants and wharf builders at "Beach near high bridge" in Kensington. Since both of these firms dealt in lumber, a part of

Nathan's work for them was to estimate the amount of timber in rafts of logs.

On 1 July 1809, William formed with his brothers, Nathan and Joseph, a partnership called William Trotter & Company. This was the firm which, after the withdrawal of Joseph in 1812 and the death of William in 1815, Nathan took over and ran as his own. At times he admitted others to partnership in the business, but only as junior or silent members of the firm. His was the principal responsibility for conducting the business and to him must go the credit for making the firm the important business enterprise that it became.

Unlike so many successful businessmen, Trotter did not allow his commercial affairs to absorb his time to the exclusion of his family. It is therefore as important to an appreciation of Trotter's way of doing business to become acquainted with this man in his home as to know him in his office.

Nathan Trotter probably met his wife through his brother Joseph. In 1809 Joseph had married a girl named Ann Hough, daughter of Samuel and Susan Newbold Hough of Mount Holly, New Jersey. Within a year of the marriage Nathan was courting his new sister-in-law's older sister, Susan.

It was, however, about four years before Susan consented to marry her persistent suitor. Nathan, in his account book entitled "Memorandum of expenses arising from the purchase of sundry articles requisite for House Keeping" refers to his courting difficulties in this fashion: "the voyage commencing in the year of our Lord, 1810–11, yet owing to contrary winds, not completed till October, 1813, and even at that only effected by perseverance arising from a full evidence that the object was worth buffeting many Billows to obtain: and I advise all who embark in so good a cause to be govern'd by the dictates of their hearts."

I do not know how Susan Trotter looked beyond the fact that her daughter-in-law, Mary Jane, wrote of her in 1850, when Mrs. Trotter was sixty-five years old: "I never saw her looking better or prettier." [15] Probably Mary Jane would not have used the word "prettier" had Mrs. Trotter not been attractive. Nathan's friend John W. Rulon speaks of her as "amiable." [16]

There are a number of indications in the family correspondence that Nathan's marriage was a tranquil one and that the husband was considerate of the wife's desires. On one occasion when Nathan had sent some gentle but young horses to one of his wife's relatives for the winter, he asked that the horses be exercised moderately, since "if they should get any bad tricks or not be perfectly gentle in harness, our women would not dare to risk with them being very timid." On another occasion, when Nathan's children Elizabeth and George were in New York, Nathan wrote his son: "Mother feels concerned about their [Elizabeth and a cousin] riding horseback & thee must tell them to be careful & be satisfied without it."

Nathan Trotter had the idea, not held at law but practiced by the Sansoms and other Quakers at the time, that his wife's money was her own. Daybook entries include such items as : "Cash dr to Susan Trotter. She paid me 200 dolls a few days since, being mainly Int. recd of E. Hough and which is payable to her on demand being exclusively hers."

The private ledger account headed "Expences of Nathan Trotter & Sukey" within a few years was changed to "Expences of N. Trotter's family," a family which, including the parents, in time numbered seven. The eldest son, Edward Hough, born 27 November 1814, increased the expenses by at least $44: $20 to the doctor and $24 to the nurse. Four other children were born to Nathan and Susan: George, Elizabeth, William Henry, and Charles West.

For much of Nathan's early life, at least from the year 1800 when his father died until his marriage in 1813, the young man had no real home. Some of the time he boarded in the homes of one or the other of his older brothers, William or Joseph. Consequently it is natural to suppose that he thoroughly enjoyed a home of his own when he came to have one.

After living the first six years of his married life in rented houses, Nathan bought two lots in 1819 and built a house on the west side of North Front Street below Vine. Nathan, his family, and sometimes two apprentices lived there until 1830 when he moved to Fourth Street near Green, next door to his brother Joseph and across the street from the Fourth and Green Street Meeting House. The families of these brothers who had married sisters were intimate. Nathan once wrote his children who were abroad: "at home of evenings we assemble as usual in the yard or parlour of our or next door House, & the subject of your absence is generally Canvased."

If this Fourth Street residence was typical of the old houses still in the neighborhood, it was probably a three-story brick house with some grounds in back. Records show a payment for painting "half a

large green gate in front of dwelling" and for "glazing light in piazza."
A payment of $23.75 one year for pruning, cleaning, and dressing the
garden and planting annuals seems to indicate there was a flower garden within the enclosure.

Household bills were kept along with business accounts and from
them it appears that the Trotter family, about every other month in the
late 1830's, bought a barrel of Extra flour for $7.75. Sugar by the barrel
cost $23.62. The Philadelphia Ice Company delivered half a peck of
ice a day during the summer months and the milkman, Daniel Woolman, left three half pints regularly with now and then an extra quart.
Mocha coffee was purchased in 25 pound lots.

More stimulating liquids were also among the bills. Nathan Trotter
believed in temperance but not in complete abstinence. His fatherly
advice to Edward, when the son was about to sail for England, was not
to let the fellow passengers "induce thee to partake with them of ardent
spirits or lead thee beyond *one* generous glass of wine a day." Beer was
purchased by the half barrel from Perots for $3.00; nine gallons of
Madeira wine cost $27.00; and "1 box Claret" at $5.00 is among the accounts.

A charge of $19.00 for 1,000 "Segars" purchased of Lewis & Com-
pany prepares us for the man Trotter, comfortable in his own home,
as reflected in these words from a letter writter by Nathan to his
English business correspondent and friend, Townshend Wood: "After
you left us we steered our course home took a Cup of Souchong
and then retired to a comfortable corner near the fire and had amidst
the fumes of a good cigar many cogitations about matters and things
connected with your visit."

The wood in this fire was probably hickory purchased at Compton's
wharf between Race and Vine and the Souchong may have been prepared by the hired girl who signed the receipt with a cross when she
received her wages. Whether Sukey or the illiterate hired girl prepared
the tea, it was surely measured from an Octagon-shaped lacquered
caddy with a lock and key and S. T. "cyphered on it"—which Nathan
had once requested a supercargo to bring back for him on a return
voyage from China. And it may well have been served in one of the
"landscape & Gilt Tea china" cups of the Sinchong pattern which
Nathan's brother William had called "Cow Landscape." It is not unlikely that as Nathan smoked, and drank, and cogitated in the comfortable corner by the fire, he looked up now and then at one of the

"handsome landscape paintings costing about four dollars each" which a supercargo had procured for Nathan in Canton back in the days when the War of 1812 had just ended and trade with the Orient was first opened after he had become a householder.

The family life at Nathan and Susan Trotter's was apparently a happy one. When their son Edward went to Europe on reaching his twenty-first birthday, he wrote to his sister Elizabeth: [17]

Although pleasures and enjoyments are found in travelling there is something associated with our home superior to all and the pleasure of anticipating the return to that home forms one of the most delightful features of our wanderings. . . . Believe me Sis: the compliment thee paid me in mentioning how you missed me at home and the spirit which dictated it are duly appreciated by one whose . . . greatest pleasure will be / after the object of his visit is accomplished / to return once more to the paternal roof and enjoy the Society of those amongst whom his happiest hours have been spent. Give my love to Mother and *Little Charley* and tell him that I often think of him and shall not fail to bring Something for him.

Nathan Trotter was concerned with the pleasure and education of his children. Bring home "some pleasing little matter for our children" reads a memorandum to his supercargo friend, John W. Rulon, about to leave for the Orient.[18]

Nathan Trotter's affection for his only daughter, Elizabeth, stands out in his correspondence. When Elizabeth, a young woman of twenty-six, was on a visit, he wrote, in a fatherly and Quaker vein,[19] "It really is lonesome my dear E without thee, Mother misses thee and when you again write state the prospect and how 'the way seems to open'." Then again, six years later, while she was in Europe with her brother George and his wife, "Dearest Lizzie" received this communication, half humorous and half serious, from Edward's wife: [20]

I have one word of caution for thee do not leave thy heart behind thee, as I am sure Father would never consent to the Ocean separating you from them again. He is looking very well and watches the arrival of the Steamers anxiously. Your letters create quite an excitement among us.

Once Nathan Trotter paid his son Edward one hundred dollars for a gray mare, Luna, considered a "fine Hackney," which he bought "only with a view for Elizabeth" to ride. At the time of her marriage to John J. Thompson, in 1852, Nathan's private daybook itemizes payments amounting to $3,955.79 for furniture, mirrors, carpets, china, silverware, tinware, gas fixtures, papering, painting, and an $85 furnace

for Elizabeth's house at 138 North 9th Street which he had just purchased for her use.[21]

Edward Trotter married Mary Jane Hart and was disowned by the
Society of Friends for violating their discipline "by accomplishing his
marriage by the aid of a hireling minister." [22] Mary Jane, however,
judging from correspondence, was a happy member of the family. In
June, 1850, Nathan Trotter took Mary Jane and his granddaughter,
"little Sue," along with his wife on a ten days' business trip with four
or five directors of the Lehigh Crane Iron Works, to visit the property
of the iron works. To this Trotter combination of business and pleasure, Mary Jane had been early introduced since on her honeymoon
her husband had been asked by his father to deliver an order for
copper to the McKims on his way through Baltimore with his bride.[23]

From such information about Nathan Trotter's relationship with his
family as can be gained from the dollars-and-cents chronology, now
and then certain familiar father-son situations emerge. In May of 1838,
Nathan Trotter and his fifteeen-year-old son William Henry went to
New York by boat. Nathan wrote his other sons, Edward and George,
who were at home keeping store: "Here we are hemmed in by a
Storm—We landed yesterday about ½ p 1. Found it very cold in the
passage and had to keep pretty much in the Cabin—and I could not
point out to Wm the many interesting sights I expected." After finding
"an Eating House & satisfying hunger," Nathan and his son visited
the *Great Western*, one of the great ships of its day, a 1,321-ton four-
masted English steam paddler which had gained fame as the largest
passenger vessel built especially for the Atlantic run.[24] "She is indeed a
tremendous affair. . . . I Shd. be better reconciled going in her than
before I saw her—She lay 2 miles up the East River & afternoon was
mostly consumed in the Visit."

The business ability of his second son, George, seemed to please
Nathan. While the oldest son, Edward, was abroad Nathan was ill
several times, once with gout and once as the result of being "thrown
from the little York waggon in driving a run away Horse." Nathan
wrote Edward: "I never wanted to see thee so bad   on George
devolves great responsibilities & he discharges his duties very well."

Though he dealt with businessmen at the distant reaches of the sea
lanes, Nathan Trotter never traveled far from home. He went on
"jaunts" to his old school Westtown, or "up the North River," or to
Mount Holly, New Jersey, where he had many associations. There he

Young Nathan Trotter

William Sansom

Joseph Sansom

had courted Susan Hough; there his younger brother Thomas had gone into business and there he was a director of a local bank. He made business trips to New York and Baltimore and once, at least, he went to Washington. He went to various parts of his home state to collect debts or to "recruit his health"—to Easton or the celebrated watering place Bedford Springs. But for the most part he transacted his business from his office in Philadelphia.

Yet Nathan considered travel important as is shown in this extract from a letter which he wrote Edward, who was going abroad with his cousin Joseph.

> The more I reflect upon this visit to Europe and particularly to England the more am I convinced of the advantage it may be to you not only as regards business but in forming a proper estimate of a liberal education and making you sensible of your own deficiencies and embuing your minds with a determination to store, by observations of men and things, whatever is profitable, and subsequently if you are favored to return home safely, to confirm it to yourselves by solid reading knowing that you have made the best use of the privilege your parents have extended in thus offering you opportunities which [they] themselves never enjoyed.

The only two underlined parts of this letter of guidance to Edward were the requests of "*keep a regular a/c of all monies recd. from Mr. Wiggin and of your expenditures*" and also to "*keep a record of events.*" Nathan advised his son—some would say in accordance with the traditional tenets of the capitalist and the Quaker—that one can derive the fullest benefit from a journey only if one keeps an accurate record, "a daily memo . . . of whatever interesting or profitable has presented itself" so that later one's memories might be "refreshed and the advantage of observations be newly applied" to one's own subsequent benefit as well as to the satisfaction and pleasure of one's friends.*

This type of advice Nathan gave his children again and again. Like the repeated passage of the same law, it doubtless indicates a lack of compliance. To Elizabeth, when she was visiting cousins in Virginia, Nathan wrote: "Thee will have kept a journal no doubt, giving for the edification of your friends an accot of your sittings, and walkings, and ridings and opportunities afforded for the bettering the condition of mind and body." [25] And when Elizabeth, George, and George's wife Mary Ann were in Europe in 1850 the elder Trotter was still urging: "Keep your eyes open & note all you see in your journal."

Family and business interests occupied so much of Nathan Trotter's

---

* This letter is printed in full in Appendix 1.

time that one is inclined to ask: did he never play? There is no evidence in the manuscripts that he fished or hunted. Early in his married life he bought a chequerboard, so perhaps he and Sukey spent evenings by the fire playing chequers.

He was fond of horses. The very first year after he went into business for himself he paid $2.34 for a license to use his gig or riding chair. He occasionally mentioned the joys of sleigh riding, a relaxation even good Quakers might enjoy. In February, 1821, he wrote a customer that sleigh riding was "a mode of travelling many are fond of, in fact the tingling of the bells and the general hilarity of the company makes time pass very pleasantly. . . . I have spent several days myself in the same recreation during the sleighing." In February just ten years later he wrote Anson Phelps in this unbusinesslike phraseology:

> Winter with its icy fetter has so completely enchained us that several weeks must elapse before we can have any trade by water—the ice in the Delaware is probably 12 inches thick and forms a complete Bridge and thousands of persons of all sizes, ages & colours with multitudes of sleighs may be seen passing to & fro & forms indeed a novel spectacle which added to the great eclipse to day has given abundance to amuse and reflect on.

Nathan Trotter, the kindly, alert, shrewd man of business had a special gift for friendship. One of his intimates, John W. Rulon, was a supercargo who spent many years in Calcutta. Before setting out on one of his long absences, Rulon wrote 16 August 1836 to his friend Nathan indicating some of the strands which made up their friendship.

> I cannot leave without expressing in a few lines to thee my most heartfelt thanks for the many kindnesses shewn by thyself and amiable wife to my dear Wife & family during my former absence, and I beg now to request that you will be pleased to continue your great kindness towards them, and be assured it can never be effaced from my remembrance and with best wishes for your health prosperity and happiness.

Nathan's relationship with another businessman, Anson Phelps, was a somewhat complicated one. Anson Greene Phelps (1781–1853), Connecticut-born, had established himself in business in New York about the beginning of the War of 1812 and so prospered that at the time of his death he was a multimillionaire. In 1821 Phelps had formed a partnership with Elisha Peck which dealt in cotton and metals, Peck managing the English end of the business in Liverpool where the firm was known as Peck & Phelps.[26] In 1834 the firm became Phelps

Dodge & Company, a predecessor to what is now one of the nation's largest copper mining and smelting companies.

Nathan Trotter admired Anson Phelps'qualities and considered him "the greatest man of business in the metals." Phelps was a man of "energy & promptness," and one of his conspicuous traits was that he always gave "prompt replies to all respectfully written communications" even if pecuniary interest was "not of much consequence in the matter." [27]

Anson Phelps was also the keen competitor against the background of whose dominance we see Nathan Trotter operating for the last thirty years of his life. To the wire manufacturers, Rodenbough Stewart & Company, Trotter wrote: "Phelps & Co. we understand was putting up a wire mill. If he gets under way he will spoil the pudding for some of us   he is a wonderful man for driving business." [28] The Phelps firm, as Trotter saw it, engrossed the tin-plate trade, monopolized it "from Boston to New Orleans with a radius encircling the principal Western States and we can only fill up little vacancies in our latitude." [29]

Trotter believed that "Father P," as Phelps was called by his sons-in-law and by Trotter at times in his letters to other firms, desired "to engross all the retail if possible as well as all the wholesale trade & thro his satellites to effect that object." [30] Nathan nevertheless advised his son, Edward Trotter, when the latter was in England: "Thee will be extremely circumspect in all thy movements—Say nothing disrespectfull in any way abt. the House this Side that engross all the Tin plate trade & the[e] can learn what others Say without committing thyself   thee will visit their House in Lpool."

Phelps sent Nathan Trotter melon seeds for his garden, and the two men talked on colonizing in Africa when Phelps was in Philadelphia to attend the Colonization Meeting.[31] Nathan Trotter sympathized with Phelps in two great disasters which befell him: the falling of part of his store and the business reverses which resulted in a temporary suspension of payments.[32] Phelps wrote Trotter 7 May 1832:

Owing to a very unexpected providence in the falling of a part of our new store which caused the immediate death of 3 of our clerks and a number of workmen, and deranged every letter & paper we had . . . we do not know whether we have received a reply from our respects to you of the 2d inst. . . . We would merely observe that in our present deranged and afflicted state if it should be quite convenient we should be much obliged in receiving a remittance from you.

Trotter replied promptly with a remittance and sympathy "in your distress from the late melancholy accident," but concluded "you must bear up under it, considering that your life had been thus . . . mercifully preserved." [33]

The second disaster occurred in the depression of 1837 when Phelps Dodge & Company wrote 6 May of having, "for a time suspended payment." Trotter replied: "There is none of us above the reach of misfortune and such a State of things has indeed been sufficient to shake as with an earthquake the whole Commercial World and it is therefore not surprising that the most Solvent Houses should have bowed under it." [34]

Phelps understood Trotter and occasionally mixed joshing with serious business. "Really we begin to think that the more good bargains we give the more you will claim." However, Phelps wrote, "we have to remit upwards of £10,000 by next packet and therefore have concluded to let you have the 200 Boxes which shall be shipd without delay and if you could without inconvenience remit us the amount by return mail . . . it would be in time to help us with our remittances." [35] Phelps, of course, knew that the day would never come when, as he told Trotter, "we really think the only apology you can make is to give us your order direct for 1000 Boxes without asking the price." [36] Trotter, too, liked his little joke.[37] "Permit us to trouble you with a remittance of Two thousand dollars in a draft on the Merchants Bank," he wrote Phelps Dodge & Company on 3 September 1836 when cash was exceedingly scarce in both Philadelphia and New York.

With his English correspondents Nathan Trotter developed a genuine friendship. The regular foreign correspondence, which he personally carried on even after he left more and more routine business to his sons, included opinions on current happenings as well as business matters. The Englishmen living through a period when developments in America affected their business existence, commented tolerantly and philosophically. In 1843 the Walkers wrote: "For your sake we are glad to hear that the Anthracite Furnace you are interested in is doing so well, but we fear its success will tell against us here." Newton Keates & Company thanked Trotter for copper specimens and concluded: "We have lived to see many changes in the course of trade, &

time will doubtless bring about many more, to which we must endeavor prudently to conform. This country will continue to be a great producer of metals but we cannot expect it to supply *so large a share* of all that is consumed as it has done during the present century." [38]

When representatives of the English firms came to America, the Trotters entertained them, and when the young Trotters were in England they were entertained in turn. With Townshend Wood of Liverpool and Swansea, Nathan Trotter established a particularly friendly association. Wood was in America on three visits at least. Squirrels for Wood's children and a watch for Trotter's son George were exchanged. After the death of Nathan Trotter, his sons, at Wood's request, sent him their father's photograph. In reply Wood wrote: "This morning I had the gratification of fixing upon a place in the room in which I most frequently sit—and of hanging up there the face of that old friend whose friendship was so valuable to me, and whose kindness will never be forgot—and whose benevolent face I shall enjoy looking at so long as I live." [39]

Many of the English firms felt about Nathan Trotter as did the Walkers who wrote the young Trotters: "Altho' we had not the pleasure of a personal acquaintance with him we esteemed him as a friend." [40]

Politics appear occasionally in Trotter's correspondence, but not often. I do not know whether this indicates a lack of interest or whether the merchant was following the advice he once gave his son Edward: "Be courteous and polite to all—touch not on politics." But Andrew Jackson's administration made Trotter forget his own advice. Nathan was opposed to the President's "high handed action" in removing the deposits of public funds from the Bank of the United States. He declared, in March, 1834, that he would have sold nearly all his steel except for what he described as "the state into which our good President has brought us."

The epithet "wiseacres," which Trotter applied to Jackson and his advisers, savors of the opprobrium more recently implied in "brain trusters." He hoped no act of the wiseacres would lessen the confidence of European capitalists in American stocks and commented, in April, 1838, that the wiseacres had found that one currency for the government and another for the people would not do. To keep in touch with what the wiseacres were up to, Nathan subscribed to *The United*

States Gazette, a National-Republican anti-Jackson paper published in Philadelphia.

By the 1840's Trotter lamented the fact that men with capital and means often found themselves "badly put out, owing to the derangement of all monetary affairs." Nor, he declared, "do we look for any permanent improvement in the state of things before another year when we shall have another pilot." On 30 October 1840 Nathan wrote his customers in Cincinnati, Ohio, from which state came the Whig candidate, General William Henry Harrison: "This day Penna & Ohio must do their utmost—upon them may depend the election of Gen. H & suceeding in that we hope to have your orders for goods in our line."

Nathan Trotter and his friend Christopher Hager, a merchant of Lancaster, Pennsylvania, saw eye to eye on the political situation. "The result of the election in your county has been warmly greeted by your frds here & we sincerely desire the general result may be in unison with it," wrote Trotter to Hager, who replied: "Respecting the result of the late Election in Lancaster Co. we feel proud in saying that we did our duty. The result of the state from all we can learn is still enveloped in mystery sincerely hoping we may have carried it."

The moderate Quaker appears in this letter to Jevons Sons & Company when the election of General Harrison became certain: "You are doubtless aware of the tremendous change that has taken place in the political state of things in this country—and is it not a comment on popular Government that it should have been peacebly effected by the ballot box. We hope that moderation & prudence will govern the majority in all respects."

Although Trotter was an avowed Quaker, only a few direct statements in the records reflect religious teachings. To his son Edward he wrote, at the time of Edward's European tour: "[I wish you] every possible enjoyment and happiness however subjecting your movements to what prudence & moderation may Sanction and preserve that Conscious rectitude in all things as will ensure satisfaction." The father felt exceedingly desirous that Edward should not depart from that strict code of conduct which, as he put it, "thy own sense of propriety, and the witness within will not fail to point out."

Yet, though direct statements of belief are few, the records bristle with illustrations of Quaker influences. When Frederick B. Tolles wrote his *Meeting House and Counting House,* he was dealing with the Quaker merchant of the Colonial period, but he might just as appro-

priately have been describing Nathan Trotter, a Quaker of the nineteenth century, so far as virtues, practices, and policies are concerned.

Industry, frugality, prudence, honesty, a strong sense of order are
all exemplified. One knows well that Nathan's answer would be a
positive "no" to the Meeting query: "Are there any who launch into
business beyond what they are able to manage, and so break their
promises, in not paying their just debts in due time?" Trotter could
also stand the further test: "Are Friends careful to settle their affairs
and make their wills in time of health?" Throughout his business life
Nathan tried to have his affairs in "dying order." When cholera epi-
demics threatened, he paid bills not yet due—and, of course, got the
cash discount.

Prudence and moderation are words which appear often in his
correspondence and in his daily operations. The rectitude which he
wrote about is exemplified in his own conduct. The virtue of strict
truthfulness, leading to silence and business astuteness, was one of
Trotter's outstanding characteristics. "Keep thy affairs to thyself," he
told his son.

Few occasions appear when it might be said that Nathan Trotter
deviated from high ethical standards. One was in connection with the
government practice of adding a flat commission of 5 per cent to all
invoices and charging duty on the commission as well as on the cost
of the goods. To this practice Trotter voiced his vigorous objection,
since he was buying directly from the manufacturer. He got around
it by requesting his English correspondents to bill the tin plate osten-
sibly at such a reduction that, when the 5 per cent commission was
added, the aggregate amount was the same as before the customhouse
adopted the practice. The English firm of John & Edmund Walker
complied with this request and replied: "To remedy the addition of
5 per cent by your Custom House to our Invoices we will in future
price the invoice that goes with the Tinplates at 1s/ 6d per box below
our real price to you   if this will not suit you please advise us." [41]

A second instance of what might be regarded as a lapse from strict
Quaker principles occurred at a time when Trotter was being forced
by economic events and against his inclination to act as a commission
agent. In this instance he endeavored to conceal the fact that he was
acting for others rather than for himself.

The conflict between the drive of industry and a realization of the
transitory character of this life is possibly illustrated by two quotations

written on a scratch paper by Nathan early in his career. Along with a few figures and doodles he wrote: "Money makes the mare go," and "Who steals my purse steals trash."

Willingly or not, Trotter gave some time, though probably not very much, to matters which were not concerned with his family or profits. At least four times he served on the jury—in 1819, 1824, 1825, and 1840. This duty took time from his business and caused him much irritation. A clerk wrote, 12 March 1825: "Our N Trotter has (much in the cross we assure you) been confined all the week on the Jury, nearly all the the time on one trial, and only released for part of this day." [42]

Early in his business career, Nathan served for one year, 1817–1818, as his brother William had before him, as Guardian of the Poor. Nathan's district extended "from the South side of Vine to the North side of Arch St. & from the east side of 4th street, to the River Delaware." His Guardian accounts, which are in the Trotter collection,[43] dealt with some of the same types of people described in the verse on the Parish Poor House which Nathan had copied as a youth. There was a blind girl, a woman whose husband had deserted her and left her with children to support, and "an aged woman very lame" to whom, at her request, he gave an order of admission to the Alms House since her son's wife "used her ill." In his year as guardian he gave many orders for delivery of fractions of a cord of wood, disbursed $1,368.50, and gave 10 orders for interment and 54 for admission to the Alms House.

It was Trotter's civic duty to serve a year as Guardian of the Poor, and Trotter did his duty as he saw it, but during his lifetime he gave relatively little to charity and at his death he left his entire fortune to his wife and children.* Unlike Anson Phelps and Stephen Girard he made no effort to establish, out of his wealth, an endowment or other monument to his memory.

Among his friends and contemporaries probably no one thought of Nathan Trotter as a leader of men. He was stolid and reliable, not brilliant, effervescent, or creative. He was a manager of affairs, not an organizer of men. Though he carried on a large business he did it with a minimum of organization. Whenever he ventured outside his business it was as an assistant to others or as a participant in a program already established and operating (as in the case of the Guardianship of the Poor), not as a director or organizer of something new.

---

* See Nathan Trotter's will printed in Appendix 2.

Though Trotter rose to wealth, he never aspired to social position. One of the reasons why his wealth reached such large proportions was that, unlike many other men after attaining economic success, he did not spend his income on an increased standard of living. Trotter's life is a triumph of middle-class virtues Through industry and perseverance, through thrift and careful management, he managed to lead a prosperous, happy, and fruitful life. He himself would not have asked for more. That he did not achieve fame or recognition as a founding father of Philadelphia's commercial or industrial prosperity meant little to him. He derived his satisfaction from his work, not from what other people said about him or thought of what he did.

CHAPTER II

Family Antecedents

AS has already been intimated, Nathan Trotter's heritage flowed out of the past in two converging streams. From one source came the middle-class Philadelphia Quaker heritage of Nathan's family; from the other came the mercantile business inheritance of Nathan's older brother, William, through his association with the Sansoms. The one was as important as the other in shaping the personality and career of the young Philadelphia importer.

The simple, conservative, middle-class traditions of the Trotter family as well as their Quaker characteristics, persisted in Nathan and his brothers and continued to exercise over Trotter, the merchant, that pervasive influence which is so distinguishable in the man's business career. An inheritance from the Sansoms, through his brother William's continuation of their business, introduced young Nathan to a kind of enterprise which was not restricted, as the handicraft business of his father had been, by the nature of the local 'market. The mercantile business of the Sansoms took the world as its market and admitted to no limitations in its growth possibilities except the limitations of the businessman himself, as reflected in his talent, his energy, and his creative purposefulness. To this new sphere of business Nathan Trotter brought many attributes that came to him out of his family past. Some of these attributes were to contribute to his success; others were to put a ceiling on his accomplishments.

Information about some of Nathan's ancestors is scanty. William, the earliest of the Trotters in Philadelphia, was a "sawyer." At least so reads a quit claim release showing that he owned land on Chestnut Street.[1]

That William also was a Quaker is revealed by the Minutes of the Philadelphia Monthly Meeting of December, 1692, which record in the customary phraseology that "Mary Sibthorp and Margaret Beardsley present William Trotter and Rebeckah Theach, who declared their intentions of marriage the first time; John Kinsey and Richard Gove are appointed to inquire as to his clearness." Having declared their intentions a second time on the 31st of the first month, William and Rebeckah received the approval of the Meeting and were married the 18th of the second month—that is, the 18th of April—in 1693.[2]

We learn from the "First Tax List for Philadelphia County," drawn up in accordance with a law passed by the General Assembly and approved by the governor in 1693 "For Granting One penny p pound to King William & Queen Mary," that William Trotter was taxed 2s. 6d. on property valued at £30.[3] Six years after his marriage he died of yellow fever[4] leaving his wife and three young sons: William, Joseph, and Benjamin (see the genealogy, Chart I).

William's "eldest son and heir at law," another William, became a "husbandman" owning 100 acres in White Marsh, Philadelphia County.[5] William, Sr.'s son Benjamin was by occupation a turner or chairmaker,[6] but was also known as a "zealous Preacher amongst the Quakers . . . not more conspicuous for his Zeal and indefatigable Labour in the Gospel, than Rectitude of Life, which with a meek and humble Deportment, adorned the Doctrine he preached," to quote from his obituary.[7]

The most famous of the Philadelphia Trotters was the second son, Joseph, Nathan's great-grandfather. He it was who became a member of the Provincial Assembly and a signer of the Non-importation Agreement of 25 October 1765. This ancestor of Nathan Trotter was a cutler and as such knew and used the best steel. He also dealt in ironmongery. An advertisement which he ran in the early 1741/42 issues of Benjamin Franklin's weekly *Pennsylvania Gazette* runs: "Smith's Anvils, Vices [sic] and Files, to be SOLD by JOSEPH TROTTER, at the Sign of the Sickle and Steelyards, in Second-street, Philadelphia." In another of Joseph Trotter's infrequent advertisements, dated 1749, he listed anvils, vises, bake-irons, grindstones, and London steel, to be sold "Very cheap for ready money." Either because his place of business was well-known, or because of oversight,

Joseph did not even give his address when he placed newspaper notices.[8]

The variety of goods in which Joseph dealt is indicated by the articles listed in an advertisement which ran in *The Pennsylvania Gazette* of 3 and 10 January 1771, about two months after his death, which announced:

> At the house where JOSEPH TROTTER lately dwelt, in Second-street, the sale of a quantity of ironmongery; amongst which are files, coopers adzes and howels, bench and hand vises, smiths sledges and hammers, cross cut and whip saws, brass cocks and gimblets, H and HL hinges, and chest ditto, locks of different sorts, iron traces, bricklayers trowels, smiths rasps and grindstones, large scale beams, iron pots, kettles and skillets, and sundry other things too tedious to mention.

Since Joseph Trotter was one of the signers of the Non-importation Agreement,[9] he evidently obtained some of his goods directly from England. Other purchases were made from Philadelphians. His receipt book for the years 1725–1758 is in the Historical Society of Pennsylvania [10] and its entries include "5 gross of sickle handles" from James Cresson; "tuns of iron" from Thomas Potts and others; grindstones, German steel, weight beams, and "bushells of coalls" from local merchants. Joseph Wharton, Jeremiah Warder, and John Dillwyn are among the well-known merchants from whom he made purchases.

Second Street, Philadelphia, was the location of Joseph Trotter's residence as well as his place of business. Joseph Trotter and Dinah Shelton, both members of the Philadelphia Monthly Meetings, were married in 1718. I know nothing of Dinah's ancestry. She may have been a sister or a daughter of the Joyce Shelton who, on 26 January 1714 brought to the Philadelphia Monthly Meeting her certificate from the London Monthly Meeting dated 1713, 12, 26.[11]

Little of Joseph's home life is reflected in the surviving records. Elizabeth Sandwith Drinker entered in her journal, that interesting source of information about Philadelphians in the eighteenth century, that on 24 May 1759 she "drank Tea at Josh Trotter's." Since Elizabeth was born in the house of her grandfather Jervis, on the corner of Trotter's Alley,[12] and grew up in that neighborhood, it is likely that she saw the Trotters frequently. From Joseph Trotter's receipt book we learn that "Ye 3 of ye 11 mot 1728/9," he paid George Mifflin £14 in full " for A hoghead of rum & all other accounts to this day." And throughout the years 1738–1752, Joseph rented pasture from Jacob

Banckson. Some member of the Trotter family probably walked to the Banckson pasture twice a day to milk the cow.

In the period when Joseph Trotter was a prominent member of the Provincial Assembly, he showed enough interest in personal adornment, Quaker though he was, to purchase 32 silver coat buttons and a pair of silver buckles from a Philadelphia silversmith.[18] More typically Quaker is his contribution of £10 to the "Hospital for the Relief of the Sick for Poor of the Province and for the reception and care of Lunatics." [14]

In addition to managing his business and acting, for one year at least, as treasurer of the City of Philadelphia,[15] Joseph Trotter served in the General Assembly as a "representative of the Freemen of the Province of Pennsylvania" from the 1739–1740 session through that of 1755–1756. During these seventeen years, at the Assembly meetings in the building now known as Independence Hall, he was an active member along with such well-known Quakers as Isaac Norris, Israel Pemberton, Sr., James Pemberton, and John Kinsey. The non-Quaker, Benjamin Franklin, was at first clerk and then a member of these Assemblies. Joseph Trotter appears to have been popular as a vote getter. He stood fourth in his constituency in the election of August, 1752: only Edward Warner, Isaac Norris, and Evan Morgan had more votes and none of them had more than 20 over his total.[16]

An examination of the Assembly's records during this period [17] gives considerable information about the type of person Joseph was. First of all there is some evidence that Joseph was likely to serve on committees more closely connected with business than with literary matters. Almost never in the seventeen sessions was he appointed to a committee which was to prepare a "Draught of an answer" to the Governor's Message. Neither was he ever on the Committee of Correspondence: such men as Israel Pemberton, Isaac Norris, Thomas Leech, and Speaker John Kinsey were regularly appointed to that committee. As a businessman, Joseph Trotter was asked to serve each year on the committee to inspect and settle the "Accounts of the Incidental Charges for the Current Year." These incidental charges amounted to £1,443 in 1753 and ranged from £453..13..0 "to the members of Assembly, for their Attendance, at 6s. per Day" and £58..14..2 to Conrad Weiser "for Expences, &c. on his Journey to Albany and the Mohocks Country, in the service of the Government and for his Trouble therein," down to £5 to Mary Burden "for sweeping and airing the Statehouse &c" and £1..2..0 to "Plunket Fleeson, for a Bottom for the Speaker's Chair."

Joseph Trotter was also the sort of person selected to help prepare a bill for "the more easy and speedy Recovery of Small Debts," and for the "more easy recovery of Legacies within the Province." In addition he was appointed to inspect the laws relating to Ferries and to report thereon to the House.

In 1742 Joseph was one of the Trustees to have the "Care and oversight" of Fisher's Island and the "Negroes, and Appurtenances" thereon, and to provide a good tenant to whom the island might be leased for not over seven years. This piece of land came to be known as Providence Island where a pest house was later established. Joseph and the other Trustees must have been good stewards, for in 1744 the Assembly resolved that they be given £63 "for their Trouble and Expense in the Management of their Trust."

In addition to the trusteeship reward and his salary of 5s. and later 6s. a day, Joseph Trotter received money from the Provincial Treasury for another duty. In 1747 he was appointed a "Signer of the Twenty shilling Bills in the Room of James Mitchell, deceased." The compensation for the onerous task of signing these pieces of paper currency was 15s. a thousand.

For a number of years Joseph Trotter was one of the committee selected to "prepare and bring in a Bill for the Amendment of several Laws relating to the Poor and for the better appointing of Overseers of the Poor within the City of Philadelphia." Over half a century later his great-grandsons, William and Nathan, were to be overseers operating possibly under some of the provisions suggested by this very committee.

A judicious man, surely, would be appointed to the Committee of Grievances. Here, too, Joseph Trotter frequently served, along with Benjamin Franklin, George Ashbridge, James Wright, and Peter Worral. This committee had power to send for any "Persons, Papers, and Records" necessary for its work. When one Thomas Gravan set forth that "his wife, by Reason of some Abuses she received from the Indians" while they were in Philadelphia, died leaving him with seven small children, whom he was unable to maintain and for whose care he prayed relief, Joseph Trotter and Abraham Chapman inquired into the matter. They found no evidence "that the woman's death was occasioned by any Hurt she received from the Indians," and so the petition was dismissed.

From all these shreds of evidence we seem to see in Joseph Trotter a person of judgment and discretion. But how did he stand on the larger issues of his time? In the 1750's defense of the frontiers was an outstanding problem, and for years the predominantly Quaker Assembly had voted money for the King's use, even though some of this money was spent for armed defense. Gradually, however, as armed hostilities continued to occupy the attention of the Provincial Assembly, Joseph Trotter came to believe that his duties as a member of that body and his beliefs as a Quaker were in conflict.

One of the few occasions on which he was on a "draughting" committee was in 1748, just after the President of the Provincial Council, Anthony Palmer, had sent a message recommending that the Assembly, since it had "the sole Disposal of the Public Money . . . employ some part of it for the Service of the Public in the Protection of their Trade." The answer, prepared by Joseph Trotter and four other committee members included the statement that

it is difficult for us to express our Sentiments; the most of us, as well as many others within this Province, you know, have professed ourselves principled against the bearing of Arms; and yet, as we enjoy the Liberties of our own Consciences, we think it becomes us to leave others in the free Exercise of theirs.

On 3 April 1754, Governor James Hamilton, "apprehending the French invasion asked supplies of men and money to resist the invaders and repel Force by Force," to which Joseph Trotter joined with sixteen members of the Assembly in voting "no," while eighteen voted in favor of the grant. The next year Joseph was one of seven Assembly members opposed to "striking £60,000 in bills of credit and for granting the same to the King's use." Late in the 1755–1756 session six Quaker members of the Assembly resigned, and a year later Joseph Trotter, along with most of the other Quaker members, declined to run for office. Thus Quaker control over the Pennsylvania Assembly came to an end with the year 1756.[18]

Joseph was out of politics the remaining fifteen years of his life. Perhaps he thereafter was able to devote more of his time to business. At least he accumulated enough property [19] so that, in 1769, he was required to pay a tax to the proprietors of £51..12..0.[20]

Joseph's wife Dinah died in May, 1769. Joseph died the twenty-fifth of November the following year.[21] To Joseph and Dinah had been born a family of ten children. Among them was a Joseph who became a chairmaker, a Nathan who became a blacksmith, and a William of whom I know little except that he engaged in what was vaguely called "mercantile pursuits."

This William—Nathan's grandfather—married Elizabeth Hoodt, the daughter of a cooper. The Hoodts, like the Trotters, were an old Philadelphia Quaker family.[22] William and Elizabeth Trotter lived on the east side of Second Street, south of Market (then High Street).[23] Their children, all born in the Second Street house, numbered five sons and a daughter, of whom at least two died young. Since William himself died in 1759 and Elizabeth four years later, the children must have been placed under the care of guardians.[24]

One of the surviving sons was Daniel Trotter, the father of Nathan. Since Daniel was only twelve when his father died, it is possible that within a year or two he may have been apprenticed either to his great uncle Benjamin Trotter, the preacher and chairmaker, or to another chairmaking relative, a Joseph Trotter—probably an uncle—who lived in Mulberry Ward. This much is clear: Daniel Trotter became a chairmaker, cabinetmaker, and joiner by trade.

Daniel grew up surrounded by relatives. His uncle Nathan, the blacksmith, had a shop in Second Street between Market and Chestnut,[25] and in the square bounded by Market, Chestnut, Front, and Second Streets, lived his grandfather Joseph Trotter, his grandmother the widow Hoodt, a widow Trotter, and a Spencer Trotter.[26] Little wonder that an alley which ran west from South Second Street to Strawberry Alley was named Trotter's Alley.[27]

The list of marriage certificates of the Philadelphia Northern District Monthly Meeting included, on the 9th day of the 11th month, 1773, that of Daniel Trotter, joiner, son of William and Elizabeth Trotter, deceased, and Rebecca Conarroe, daughter of Thomas and Mary Conarroe of the Northern Liberties, the northern suburb of Philadelphia. Only the year before, Mary Conarroe and her children Rebecca, Thomas, and Antrim had transferred their Quaker certificates from the Burlington (New Jersey) Monthly Meeting to that of Philadelphia.[28] The year after his marriage Daniel Trotter was living in Mulberry Ward—probably in Elfreth's Alley.[29]

Chairmaking, particularly windsor chairmaking, had been an im-

Chart II

PHILADELPHIA STREET MAP INDICATING PLACES WITH TROTTER ASSOCIATIONS

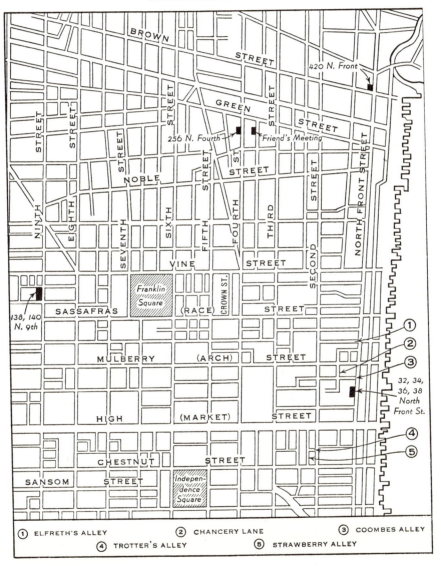

BROWN STREET

420 N. Front

GREEN STREET

256 N. Fourth   Friend's Meeting

NOBLE STREET

NINTH STREET
EIGHTH STREET
SEVENTH STREET
SIXTH STREET
FIFTH STREET
FOURTH STREET
THIRD STREET
SECOND STREET
NORTH FRONT STREET

VINE STREET

Franklin Square

138, 140 N. 9th   SASSAFRAS   (RACE)   CROWN ST.   STREET

①

MULBERRY   (ARCH)   STREET

②

③

32, 34, 36, 38 North Front St.

HIGH   (MARKET)   STREET

④

⑤

CHESTNUT   STREET

SANSOM   STREET   Independence Square

① ELFRETH'S ALLEY   ② CHANCERY LANE   ③ COOMBES ALLEY

④ TROTTER'S ALLEY   ⑤ STRAWBERRY ALLEY

portant industry in Philadelphia from the 1740's on. Before and after
the Revolution windsor chairs were "shipped in great quantities to
the other colonies, to the West Indies and even to European ports."
In the period from 1783 to 1790 over thirty-six hundred chairs were
sent from Philadelphia to Charleston alone.[30] The section of Front
Street between Arch and Race included in the 1780's many cabinet-
makers and chairmakers. One of these was Daniel Trotter, for it was
in this neighborhood that Daniel carried on his business and raised
his family.

Between 1774 and 1797 ten children were born to Daniel and Rebecca Trotter.[31] Three of the children died before the tenth child was
born: one of consumption; one, in 1793, of yellow fever; and a third,
Mary, of an unnamed disease. In recording Mary's death, Nathan
stated:

Departed this Life in Philada. the 13th of the 10th mo. 1796 about ½ past
10 oclock PM. aged 20 years and 2 mo. She had been a long time before her
death in a very poor state of health, for which she went several times to the
houses of her relations out of Town accompanied by her Mother to try what
use the country air might be, but all was of little benefit to her, who when
the close of Life drew nigh, quietly resigned her spirit to the Lord. . . .

About four months after the death of this daughter whose health must
have given great concern to her parents, Rebecca Trotter gave birth
to her last child and two weeks after that died at the age of forty-
two.[32] Daniel Trotter survived his wife but a few years. In Nathan's
manuscript book there is this entry: [33]

Daniel Trotter departed this life in Philad'a on Fourth-day the 30th. of
the 4th mo 1800 about 11 o clock P M aged 52 yrs 10 mo & 17 days—
    The death of his dear Wife was a close trial to him but being fully con-
firmed that it was her great and everlasting gain, he became resigned to the
will of Providence, whose ways are unsearchable—about this time his health
began to decline, and left him in much weakness of body, a considerable
time previous to his death—a short time before his departure he desir'd several of his family to come to his bedside and then seperately bid them affectionately farewell. He then lay in a calm and resign'd frame of mind, until
he breath'd his spirit into the hands of his maker & we now trust he has entered into those mansions of peace prepared for the righteous.

At the time of Daniel Trotter's death, in 1800, his eldest son, William, had recently married and his eldest daughter, Elizabeth Trotter
Haines, had been married only a few years. The five minor children,
Joseph, Nathan, Thomas, Rebecca, and Mary, were left under the
guardianship of their uncles, Joseph Trotter and Thomas Conarroe.

Daniel Trotter's business must have been fairly successful. In addition to supporting a family he was able to leave his children an estate of probably over twelve thousand dollars.[34] It included a house and lot in Front Street valued at $6,700 and lots and a house and shop in Elfreth's Alley valued at $1,850. Nathan's proportion of his father's personal estate was $382.91, after deduction of personal expenditures made for him by his guardians between the years 1800 and 1808.

In addition to his small patrimony, Nathan inherited a constitution that was, I believe, not especially rugged. Three of his forebears, the first and second William Trotters and his father, Daniel, died at an early age, leaving minor children to be cared for by family guardians. Later on, when Nathan's brother William, another inheritor of the family physical characteristics, died at the age of forty, Nathan assumed and for twenty-one years carried the responsibilities of guardianship of William's children.

There was also in Nathan's heritage a distinctive artisan tradition, for among his ancestors were a sawyer, a cooper, a chairmaker, and a cutler—handicraftsmen all. After the custom of the times, these men kept small shops where they sold their handiwork, along with a few allied products which they purchased for resale. Their market was local, their trade direct. When Nathan's father, Daniel, made chairs to be sent abroad, he sold them to an exporter and did not attempt to establish market contacts himself. For the most part these men probably produced to order. Their life was uncomplicated by the need to predict demand, to study market conditions, to acquaint themselves with price fluctuations in far-off lands. They probably did not trouble themselves much with the intricacies of exchange, with the regulations of the customhouse, or with the need, through forethought, to keep their capital active, liquid, and earning a return. For the most part their capital was their skills, and these skills they necessarily kept employed as steadily as they could without much planning, for their day-to-day livelihood depended on it. Thrifty, steadfast, not overly ambitious, content to rear their children as they had been reared, these were the men in whose mold Nathan Trotter's career might have been shaped had his life not been influenced by the early death of his father and the subsequent training he received in the quite different environment of the importing business which had been established by the Sansom family.

CHAPTER III

Business Antecedents

T H E Sansom family, with whose business William Trotter was associated, differed markedly from the Trotters. The Sansoms were well-to-do merchants, socially prominent, widely known, and cosmopolitan. For three generations men of the Sansom name had contributed importantly to the Philadelphia business world.

The first of the Philadelphia Sansoms was Samuel, a Quaker who arrived in the City of Friends in 1732.[1] Family records state that this Samuel had been born in London in 1707 and had been "bred to business" by a relative of his mother's, one John Croach, a London merchant.[2]

About five years after arriving in Philadelphia, Samuel Sansom placed an advertisement in *The Pennsylvania Gazette* which would seem to indicate that he had already gone far toward becoming a specialist in dry goods:[3]

JUST IMPORTED

To be Sold by Samuel Sansom, at his Store in Norris's Alley: Blankets, Ruggs, Quilts and Coverlids, Drugetts, Broad Cloths, fine London Shallons suitable, Men and Womens Stockings, worsted and cotton Caps, Musslins, Cambricks, Hollands, three fourths, seven eights and yard wide garlix, Dowlas, Princes Linnen, fine Ozenbrigs, Sheeting, check Linnen, Sail Cloth, Cotton Handkerchiefs, Buckrams, Persian, Callicoes, choice Bohea Tea, and China Ware, with Sundry other Goods, very cheap for ready Money, or reasonable Credit.

In 1736 Samuel Sansom married Sarah Johnston,[4] but the marriage was destined to be visited with grief, for only one of their seven children—Samuel, Jr., born in 1739—reached adulthood.

Chart III

SANSOM AND PEROT GENEALOGY

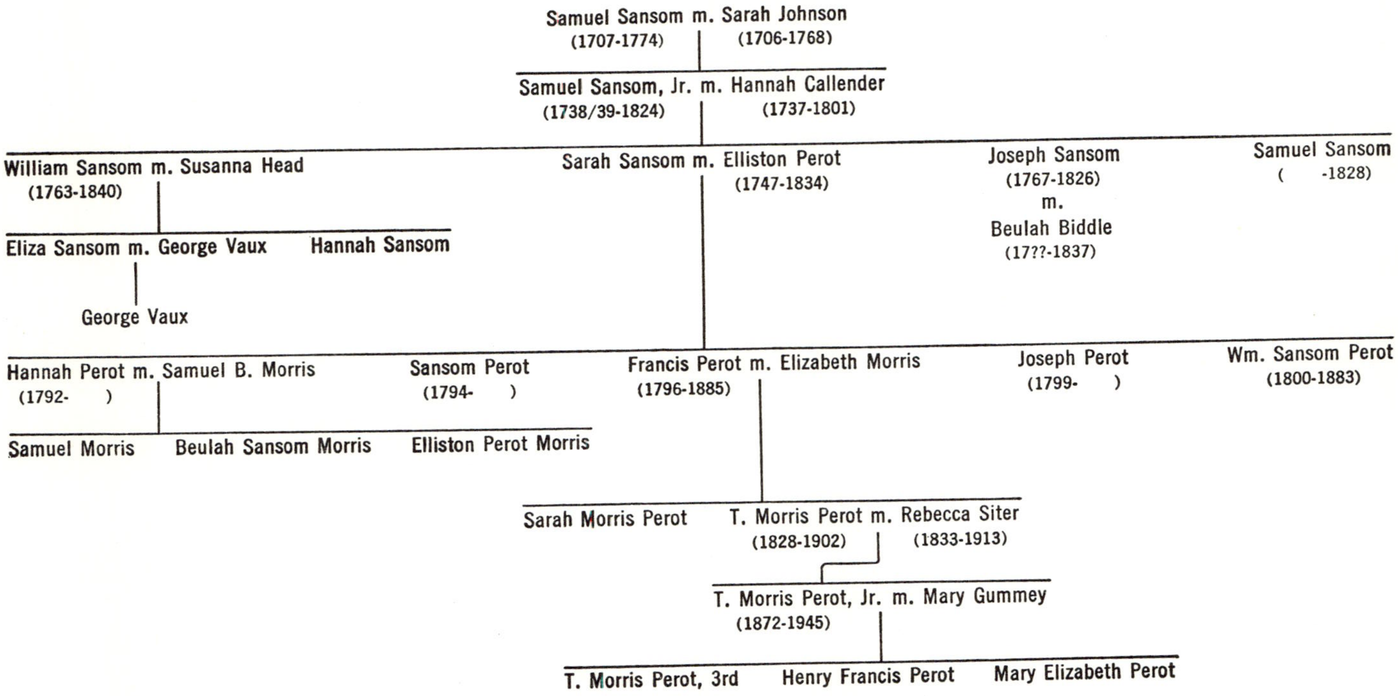

Samuel Sansom m. Sarah Johnson
(1707-1774) (1706-1768)

Samuel Sansom, Jr. m. Hannah Callender
(1738/39-1824) (1737-1801)

Sarah Sansom m. Elliston Perot   Joseph Sansom   Samuel Sansom
(1747-1834)   (1767-1826)   (-1828)
m.
Beulah Biddle
(17??-1837)

William Sansom m. Susanna Head
(1763-1840)

Eliza Sansom m. George Vaux   Hannah Sansom

George Vaux

Francis Perot m. Elizabeth Morris   Joseph Perot   Wm. Sansom Perot
(1796-1885)   (1799-)   (1800-1883)

Sansom Perot
(1794-)

Hannah Perot m. Samuel B. Morris
(1792-)

Elliston Perot Morris

Beulah Sansom Morris

Samuel Morris

Sarah Morris Perot   T. Morris Perot m. Rebecca Siter
(1828-1902)   (1833-1913)

T. Morris Perot, Jr. m. Mary Gummey
(1872-1945)

T. Morris Perot, 3rd   Henry Francis Perot   Mary Elizabeth Perot

Shortly before the birth of his son and namesake, Samuel made a business trip back to London. Preparing for his departure, Samuel placed this advertisement in the *Gazette:* [5]

ALL Persons indebted to Samuel Sansom, are desired to pay speedily, he intending for London, this Fall.

On his return to Philadelphia in the fall of 1739, Samuel bought space in the *Gazette* for a series of advertisements in which he listed in great detail the dry goods that he had brought back from London and Bristol.[6] No other merchant's advertisements were so long. Apparently Sansom was ambitious to become a large-scale enterpriser.

There are a number of indications of Sansom's prosperity. He purchased real estate in 1741 and 1743: one piece, located in a section of Philadelphia where business was active, was acquired from the descendants of William Penn at a cost of £132. .0. .11 English sterling; the other, bordering on a vacant lot, cost £50.[7] Sansom also invested in shipping. Joining such well-known merchants as Abel James and Jeremiah Warder, he became part owner of the 35-ton brigantine *Samuel,* the 90-ton Philadelphia-built ship *Liverpool,* and the 70-ton snow (a type of square-rigged vessel), *White Oak.*[8]

When Samuel Sansom, Jr., was about seven or eight years old, his father felt affluent enough to buy from a Philadelphia silversmith a waiter and three porringers.[9] The Sansoms lived on the west side of Front Street between Market and Mulberry, at least as early as 1757–1760.[10] Probably the house stood on the lot purchased in 1741.

Samuel and his wife Sarah appear frequently in the pages of Elizabeth Sandwith Drinker's journal. Sarah was one of Elizabeth Sandwith's sponsors when she declared her intentions of marriage to Henry Drinker, 28 November and 26 December 1760, and there was much social intercourse between the two families. Samuel Sansom, Jr.— "Sammy" in the Journal—read French with Elizabeth, and he and his wife, Hannah, later spent many afternoons at the Drinker's country house at Frankford and "supped" or drank tea or coffee at the Drinker home near the Sansom's on Front Street in Philadelphia.

In the 1740's and 1750's, many freight-renting importers (that is, merchants who imported their goods by hiring space on ships owned by others) were advertising imported cloth in *The Pennsylvania Gazette.* But after the extensive lists of the late 1730's and early 1740's, I have found none of Samuel Sansom's. In the absence of other evidence,

Samuel's obituary of 2 March 1774 may furnish at least a partial explanation. The obituary begins: [11]

On the 23d ult. died SAMUEL SANSOM, senior, late of this city, Merchant, in the 67th Year of his Age—He was one of those early Traders (of whom there are few Survivors) whose Opportunities for acquiring a Fortune were very great, but being of a Disposition bounded by Moderation, and strictly punctual in Complying with his engagements, he was thankful for the Enjoyment of a reasonable competency, and used to say that he had enough.

It may well be that the adverse trade conditions obtaining in the years before the Revolutionary War had been sufficiently discouraging to cause Samuel to withdraw from business. Whatever the explanation of Samuel's decision not to advertise, there is strong evidence that his business had prospered. In 1780 his estate, which included property in Southwark and in Mulberry, Upper Delaware, and High Street wards, was taxed on an assessed valuation of £92,060, a not insubstantial figure.[12]

Long before the death of Samuel Sansom, his son had started on a business career. In the fall of 1759 Samuel, Jr., and Benjamin Swett, Jr., went to London, where they remained until the next May, probably forming business connections.[13] Since young Sansom's father had come from London 27 years earlier, there may also have been Sansom relatives and family friends to visit.

In September of 1760, "Sansom & Swett, jr.," advertised for sale, at their store on Front Street between Market and Arch, cloth and hardware which they had just imported. Terms were cash or six months' credit.[14] This is the pattern of the Sansom family business: freight-renting importers of English goods with a wholesaling business on Front Street. It was later to become also the pattern of the Trotters.

Samuel Sansom, Jr., two years after he had entered the importing business, married Hannah Callender, the daughter of William Callender (1703–1763). Hannah's father was a merchant, too, indeed a very well-to-do one. Born in Speightstown, in Barbados, he had "made trading voyages to North America in family vessels, bringing over sugar, etc." [15] Later he had settled in America and had imported muscovado sugar and Barbados rum.[16] In addition he had taken a part interest in seven vessels—one of them named the *Barbadoes Factor*. Since Hannah was Callender's only surviving child, some of the merchant's wealth may have descended to his Sansom grandchildren, including ownership of "Callender's grand houses," which Watson describes in his

Annals as being located on Front Street, adjoining Elfreth's alley steps.[17]

During the 1760's, Samuel Sansom, Jr., kept newspaper readers informed that he had for sale "A NEAT assortment of merchandise, suitable for the season," at his store on the bank (east) side of Front Street above Market and a little below the Old Ferry—a landmark which everyone knew. Typically these goods were advertised as having just been imported in one of the "last ships from London." [18]

Samuel and his business may be seen through the eyes of a fellow Philadelphian in this letter written 19 May 1768 by Edward Penington to Dr. George Vaux of London. The letter dealt with the apprenticeship of the doctor's son Richard.[19]

Respected Friend
    Dr. George Vaux

I recd. thine of the 24th. 2 mo by thy Son Dickey and have endeavored to fix him in some principal House but as yet it has not been in my power, and I doubt will not.—I do not think it would be any advantage to him to [word missing?] before he is 21 Years of Age, however were I Inclinable to bind him only for four years, I should not be able to get any one to take him for so short a time to stay—Viz about 5 years & 2 months
    The only one I have heard of that wants an apprentice and is any way suitable is Saml. Sansom Junr. He is a sober man and as I am Informed does his business methodically but I am afraid has not quite business enough to keep a Lad fully Employ'd   however I expect to place Dickey with him unless Joshua Fisher & Sons Agree to take him which they have under consideration and are to give me an answer in a few days.

As it finally turned out, Dickey Vaux became a Sansom apprentice.

On 8 April 1776—less than two weeks before the clashes at Concord and Lexington—Samuel Sansom was elected to an office that was, possibly, as much a mark of social standing as a position of business responsibility. He was made treasurer of the Philadelphia Contributionship for the Insurance of Houses from Loss by Fire. During the difficult period of the Revolution and for many years after, Sansom must have performed his duties efficiently, for the minutes of the board, 2 June 1807, record among the orders drawn on the treasurer: "One in favour of James Howell for a Silver Pitcher and Stand a present to Samuel Sansom as a memorial of his disinterested Services as Treasurer to the Institution 31 years £52..1..9.[20]

Samuel and Hannah Sansom had a family of five children, four of whom survived to adulthood. In 1782, during the uncertain days of the

Revolution, Elizabeth Drinker records under the date of 22 June [21] that Samuel and his family, together with the young members of the Drinker, Downing, and other Philadelphia families, "moved out of Town where they intended residing for a time 2½ miles from ye City, at a place of theirs on Schuylkill." [22]

Of the three sons born to Samuel and Hannah Sansom, only William and Joseph became Philadelphia businessmen. None of the three left a male heir and the Sansom name died out. One of the Sansoms' two daughters, Sarah, married Elliston Perot, another Philadelphia merchant who had come from Barbados as had Sarah's grandfather Callender. The children of Elliston and Sarah Perot in their turn became Philadelphia businessmen. Thus, although the Sansom male line disappeared, the family continued, and wherever one found the family— their wives and their descendants, through daughters, unto the third and fourth generation—one found business. [23]

William Sansom (1763–1840) was a man of substantial and varied activities. Among other things he invested in securities: at one time he took $50,000 of the Loan to the Commonwealth of Pennsylvania. [24] He adventured large sums in shipments to Canton, Calcutta, and Batavia. The few records of Sansom's activities still with the Trotter papers show that he shipped $35,000 on the *Pigou* to Canton in 1796, had $34,123.71 invested in shipments from Canton in 1809, and shipped $50,000 to Canton and Calcutta in 1810.

William must also have been the most active real-estate promoter in Philadelphia in his day. When Robert Morris became bankrupt, William Sansom bought Morris' unfinished house and the square from Chestnut to Walnut between Seventh and Eighth Streets. [25] This purchase—from a man whom William Sansom considered "unfortunate & imprudent" and whose family had "seen days of great splendour and apparent happiness & wealth"—was made in December, 1797. [26] Sansom then built rows of brick houses on Walnut Street and on what was afterwards called Sansom Street, "thereby producing a uniformity in building ranges of similar houses often since imitated, but never before attempted in our city," so wrote Watson in his *Annals*. [27] Later Sansom erected about 60 houses "out Vine street beyond Tenth." [28]

A city map of Philadelphia, dated 1819, is inscribed: [29] "This plan of the city of Philadelphia and environs is respectfully inscribed to William Sansom Esqr. who has contributed more than any other citizen to embellish the same, by the number, beauty and *uniformity* of his buildings." (Italics added.) Whatever may have been said about the beauty of these buildings, there was no denying their uniformity.

By the year 1798 William Sansom was in a position to write to John Dickinson, a well-known Quaker, in these terms:[30] "As I have come forward in the theatre of Life in some measure since thee left this state it may be necessary to say that Providence hath indulged me with an ample fortune."

Not only had William Sansom acquired a fortune but he had helped guide Pennsylvania companies.[31] He was for many years an active director of the Bank of Pennsylvania. In addition he was one of the "corporators" named in the charter of the Insurance Company of the state of Pennsylvania; from 1795 to 1797 he was a director of the Insurance Company of North America; he was president of the Delaware & Schuylkill Company and of the Schuylkill & Susquehanna Navigation Company; and he was one of the managers of the Philadelphia & Lancaster Turnpike, in which company his brother-in-law Elliston Perot was also concerned.

Sansom was not devoted to business alone. He was one of the persons in the "Northward Ward" to collect in 1791 for the relief of "many industrious persons suffering from the want of employment." [32] In 1812 he was one of a committee of five appointed from the Philadelphia Monthly Meeting for the Northern District "to procure materials, engage workmen, and supervise the erection" of the Fourth and Green Street Meeting House [33]—the meetinghouse, by the way, which Nathan Trotter later attended. The historian of Pennsylvania, Robert Proud, is reported to have said that he could not have published his history "unless William Sansom had assisted him financially." [34]

Joseph Sansom (1767–1826), younger brother of William, seems to me essentially an artist, not a merchant, although he appears in the Philadelphia directories in the 1790's and early 1800's as the latter. Literature, art, education, and travel were among his interests. He visited foreign lands, wrote about his visits, and had his writings published.[35] When he set off on a journey he took along a copy of Thomson's *Seasons* in his pocket. Quotations from Thomson, Pope, and classical authors are scattered through his writings.

There is still in the possession of the Perot family a collection of silhouettes which Joseph made and entitled: "A Occasional Collection of Physiognomical Sketches chiefly North Americans, and drawn from the life, designed to preserve the characteristic features, personally,

mentally or officially Remarkable Persons and the endeared memory of
Private Friends or Public Benefactors with professional notices, &c."
The collection, made in 1790–1792, includes Joseph's brother-in-law,
Elliston Perot, and Elliston's brother John, as well as various members
of the Sansom family. The two of William and Joseph Sansom are re-
produced on page 15.

Beauty excited Joseph Sansom.[36] He once spent 24 hours in a
prison in Rome after a man on the "Nightly watch," suspicious of
Joseph's wanderings in the moonlight to see the colonnades of St.
Peter's, discovered that the artistic American did not have his passport
with him.

"San Carlo al Corse designed by Pietro da Cortona, is one of the
most beautiful Edifices in Rome," wrote Joseph. "Where the Nave opens
into the Dome, the eye is completely gratified with its aerial swell,
lighted by eight or ten Windows." The building was across from
Joseph's lodgings and he "sometimes got up before day to observe the
effect of darkness upon its distinct proportions, when faintly dissipated
by the glimmering tapers of the morning mass, which in the winter
solstice . . . [was] celebrated before day-light." [37]

Even Joseph Sansom's will had a spiritual rather than a formal business tone. It began: "I resign my soul into the hands of its merciful
creator, in humble hope that he will pardon all my Transgressions, and
blot out all my Sins, for Jesus Christ's sake, the blessed Mediator and
Redeemer." [38]

Yet this Philadelphia Quaker, interested in so many matters other
than buying and selling, had considerable influence in the establishment and character of what was later to be the business of Nathan
Trotter. It was Joseph who, in company with his brother William, first
gave employment to Nathan's older brother William; and it was also
Joseph who, in 1799, offered William a partnership in the importing
business with the understanding that William would handle the business in Philadelphia while he, Joseph, went abroad with his young wife,
Beulah Biddle, "daughter of a Jersey Farmer." [39]

Joseph and Beulah Sansom returned to the United States in 1802,
landing in New York in September. Soon after reaching Philadelphia,
Joseph set about disposing of a considerable amount of nonmetal
goods which had been ordered shipped from Europe to the account of
Sansom & Trotter in Philadelphia.[40] On 19 November 1802, a lot of
woolens, linen handkerchiefs, colored thread, and two trunks were

sent to the auctioneers Yorke & Lippincott with these instructions: "Please give a fair chance to morrow, and dispose of the following at not less than the prices affixed or thereabouts for accot of Jos Sansom." All of this lot but a piece of mixed coating was sold. However, two lots sent to the auctioneers Shannon & Polk and John Connelly were returned unsold.

At the end of the year 1802, Joseph Sansom terminated his partnership with William Trotter and took as his share of the firm's remaining assets the leather, felting, and galloons left on hand. William took the steel and sheet iron. For the next year or so Joseph continued to be listed in the directory as a merchant, with his place of business given as 411 High Street, which was at that time the location of his father's business also. But in 1804 he definitely withdrew from the importing trade and permitted William Trotter to take over his ties with English agents. Thereupon William wrote to the cloth merchant, John Waddington: "Jos. Sansom having declined the importation business, I continue it & occupy the Store in Front St." [41]

Thus began the Trotter business, independent of the Sansoms but based on countless connections which William Trotter had acquired as an apprentice with that family and as a partner of Joseph Sansom. The same type of goods was imported—leather (morocco and kid skins), textiles (bocking baize, rattinets, flannel, felting, plains or forest cloth, etc.), and metals (tin plate, sheet iron, and steel)—and from the same merchants, in London and Birmingham, Halifax and Leeds. The imports continued to come by the regular—and in the case of shipments from Hull and Bristol, frequently irregular—trading vessels. Payments as before were made in bills of exchange, purchased in Philadelphia and sent to England, or in cash, paid to the English firm's agent in Philadelphia. And, as before, the business continued to be conducted at wholesale. Of 50 Philadelphia customers in the 1799–1802 period whose occupations I can check in the directories of that city, 6 were shopkeepers, 7 were merchants, 17 were specialized merchants or storekeepers having an iron, shoe, or paper store or warehouse, 12 were handicraftsmen, 7 had paper works and might be classified as mill operators or manufacturers. Only one was possibly an ultimate consumer.

The place of business which William Trotter took over from his predecessors was 45 North Front Street, the old Sansom store. Trotter paid William Sansom rent of $600 a year for the store. What was evidently a basement warehouse or store at the back, opening on Water Street, was then subleased by Trotter to various merchants for $117.50 a year. (Several years later, about 1 October 1805, William moved next door to 47 North Front where the firm's business remained until 1833.)

The London commission merchants from whom William Trotter continued to order were Pieschell & Brogdon and Bainbridge, Ansley & Company. The Birmingham house was Capper, Perkins & Whitehouse and the Sheffield firm was a Quaker concern—Oates & Colley. Woolens were purchased from Yorkshire cloth merchants: William & John Walker in Halifax and Cookson & Waddington in Leeds.

Trotter sent his orders to London with the request that his goods be shipped on either spring or fall sailing ships. The trade rhythm between Philadelphia and England was seasonal and entries in the order books of the Trotter firm, beginning in 1803 and continuing until 1822, were grouped under "Orders for Spring" and "Orders for Fall."

The English commission merchant put orders in hand as soon as he received them, and when the goods had been made, in accordance with William Trotter's specifications, the commission merchant engaged space, agreed on freight rates, arranged for insurance, and saw the goods safely stowed aboard ship.

The early years of William Trotter's independent business career were difficult times. Napoleon was setting Europe aflame and trade was being disrupted by wars abroad and restrictive legislation at home. During 1806 and 1807 there were recurrent threats of interrupted trade with England, and on 23 October 1807 Trotter specifically requested his English agent to fill an order only in the event that the "public differences" between the United States and England should be "accommodated" so that goods could be safely shipped. During the year 1808 only two invoices reached the Trotter firm from England.

Intermittently the United States invoked nonintercourse acts against trade with England, and intermittently Trotter had his supplies from abroad cut off. Under these conditions he took especial care to have orders in the hands of his English agents so that they could be filled as soon as the "hindrances" might be removed. Occasionally his agent would send shipments during a period when the restrictions were lifted only to have the goods arrive in Philadelphia after nonimportation had been reimposed. On one occasion William received a shipment of goods aboard the *Brilliant* four months after the declaration of the War of 1812. Imports that arrived after restrictions had been reinstated usually earned Trotter a handsome return, for during periods of scarcity the demand for English goods far outran the supply.

To keep his customers supplied William Trotter found himself forced to supplement his imports with purchases from local producers. In February, 1808, he purchased tin plate and American finished leather from the well-known New York tanners Israel Corse and Jacob Lorillard, and later he bought from the New York morocco manufacturer, Jacob Mott. Both Corse and Mott were members of the Society of Friends. Trotter also purchased small amounts of American finished roans and kids in Philadelphia, but "The Swamp" of New York (the tannery district) was already playing an important part in supplying American leather demands. In addition Trotter purchased country or American steel in small amounts, evidently to fill specific orders.

The West Indies were another source of business during the troubled times from 1806 to 1812. In each of those years, except 1808, Trotter invested in one or more voyages to the non-English islands of the Caribbean: Spanish Cuba and Porto Rico, Swedish St. Bartholomew, Danish St. Thomas, and independent Hayti. One shipment was also made to Spanish La Guira in South America.

Outgoing cargoes included a miscellany of goods. Usually these cargoes were made up in concert with other merchants. They included tin plate, steel, and sheet iron contributed by Trotter, tables and chairs supplied by George Halberstadt, and cloth, hessians for coffee bags, and sugar knives furnished by Trotter's neighboring merchants, Field & Thomas. To augment their shipments, the joint venturers sometimes purchased butter, hams, lard, and flour in the local market and sent them to the West Indies where there was at the time a great demand for such commodities. In return they received principally coffee.

A good deal of this trade was done on a credit of four months—both on goods and on insurance. Probably four months was the estimated time to send goods and get returns with which to pay for them. In many respects these ventures were treated like securities. As an example, shares in these ventures were sometimes sold while the shipment was on the way, in whole or fractional parts, and even on occasion were bought back again. Sometimes the sale was at an advance on the original investment and sometimes, no doubt when the investor needed the money, at the original cost.

So far as I can judge from the incomplete records of these ventures, they were losing propositions. Many other merchants were seeking an outlet for domestic goods in the West India trade and were taking payment in coffee. As a result the coffee market in Philadelphia became depressed and yielded poor returns. Furthermore, a number of shipments were captured by the British and sold at vice-admiralty court.

William Trotter's other business interest during those difficult years, from 1806 to 1812, was in the China trade. It must be remembered that William had grown up in a Philadelphia which had just entered into the China trade with vigor. The Philadelphian Robert Morris had

Table 1

William Trotter & Company
Goods on Hand as of 31 December 1807–1813, 1815
(Per Cent of Total Inventory Value)

	1807	1808	1809	1810	1811	1812	1813	1815
Metals	52.1	71.8	77.5	47.6	37.4	50.5	58.6	98.3
Leather	32.5	10.4	12.2	43.0	18.0	1.4	...	...
Woolens	14.9	7.4	10.2	3.9	1.0	...	...	...
Oriental goods	...	10.1	...	5.3	43.3	48.0	5.7	...
Russian bristles	...	...	...	...	...	...	35.6	...

been one of the chief investors in the voyage of the *Empress of China,* the first American ship to open direct trade with China in 1784–1785. William Trotter's own investments in the China trade had begun, so far as the Trotter papers indicate, with his interest in the voyage of the ship *Pigou.* It was on this ship (in whose cargo William Sansom, Mordecai Lewis, and Jesse and Robert Waln were the largest investors) that William had sailed as supercargo to Canton in 1796, immediately after his seven-year apprenticeship with the Sansoms.[42]

In April, 1807, Trotter shipped $1,200 in specie to Calcutta, receiving a year later a shipment of piece goods and indigo. In 1811 he joined with Field & Thomas and Thomas & Kille to send $10,000 to Canton aboard the *Pekin.* For the most part, however, William's part in the China trade consisted of acting as middleman in the distribution of goods imported from the Far East by his former employer, William Sansom. During those years Trotter sold, on commission, large quantities of teas, nankeens, chinaware, and silks that Sansom had imported from Canton, together with indigo imported from India and piece goods from Calcutta.

The difficulties of procuring goods during the years of trade disruption are shown in Table 1. The table lists, by percentages, the goods which William Trotter and his firm had on hand at the end of each

year from 1807 to 1815. Beginning in 1807 with what may be considered
a typical inventory of metals, leather, and woolens, the Trotters were
forced, as the war cut off their English imports, to shift to Oriental
cloths—mowsannahs, senshews, and nankeens—and to $13,787.80 worth
of Russian bristles. Then, with the resumption of trade, Nathan Trotter,
carrying on the business alone, could concentrate on metal goods.

During most of his business career, William Trotter was aided by
his two younger brothers, Joseph and Nathan, first as assistants and
then as partners. William Trotter was beholden to the Sansoms for his
earliest business opportunities and the business which William and his
brothers carried on was in a real sense an extension of the Sansom
enterprises. It was natural, therefore, that much of what Nathan learned
about business in his early years was poured in the Sansom mold and
shaped in their mercantile way of doing things.

Buying and selling, investing and insuring, shipping to far off places
and ordering goods with exotic names in the hope of finding a market
for them at home—these were the activities which Nathan Trotter
learned to engage in during the years of his apprenticeship with his
older brother. Operating on borrowed capital or on long-term credit,
advertising goods for sale, carrying on correspondence with agents at
the ends of the ocean lanes; setting prices, running risks, suffering losses
or enjoying profits—such was the life of a merchant in early nineteenth-
century Philadelphia. It was a new kind of life for the Trotters. It offered better profits than did craftsmanship, though the ordinary Philadelphia merchant may have been financially no better off than the
average Philadelphia handicraftsman. But the opportunities in mercantile trade were greater, if made full use of, and the social prestige
was higher.

From his experience in his brother's firm, Nathan acquired an intimate knowledge of goods and sources of supply. He learned the various
methods of transportation and became schooled in careful accounting
procedures. He came to know customers and the nature of their credit
ratings. He gained experience in letter writing and in business phraseology. "Thirty days after date I promise to pay without defalcation . . ."
was a phrase that he practiced writing—over and over and over. He
learned how to invest his surplus capital, how to keep it constantly
active, always earning him a return. He acquired the habit of co-operat-
ing with neighbor merchants as a means of keeping his capital regularly
employed and as a method of spreading his risks. And he quickly saw

Philadelphia Waterfront

Joseph Trotter

the advantage of using his far-flung acquaintanceships as sources of information at a time when information was hard to come by and ever so useful in trade.

The partnership which the three brothers had formed on 1 July 1809 had terminated in 1812 when Joseph, seeing only continuing difficulties in a trading business that had to operate under wartime conditions, withdrew from the firm. He had been employed in a bank—probably the Bank of Pennsylvania—since at least June, 1810, and his interest might have inclined rather toward finance than toward trade even if the profits of trade had been adequate for three partners.

For three years after Joseph's withdrawal William and Nathan carried on the business of William Trotter & Company despite the adversity of war. By 1815 Nathan, at the age of twenty-seven, was a roundly experienced importer. He had had dealings with England, with China, and with the West Indies; he knew suppliers in New York and in Philadelphia; his contacts with customers extended far into the hinterland back of Philadelphia. Under normal circumstances he might have begun to think in terms of starting his own importing enterprise, but William was failing in health, the victim of a "pulmonary affliction," and it seemed desirable for Nathan to remain with him. At length, in February of 1815, William decided that he "desired no more concern" with business affairs and withdrew from the partnership, leaving Nathan to carry on alone. On the second day of the next month, William died.

Eight days later Nathan began a new daybook. The cover was leather, boldly printed with the letters NATHAN TROTTER. A new business had been started, in reality no more than a continuation of the old. Nathan was starting a business career that would eventually bring him fortune, if not fame. For the next thirty-five years of his life he would be the head of one of the principal metal-importing houses along the east coast of the United States.

PART II

Trotter as a Metal Merchant

CHAPTER IV

An Introduction to the Business

WHEN William Trotter died, his interest in the family business was about $20,000, much of which remained with the firm in one form or another for some time. Additional capital was provided by Joseph Trotter who rejoined the firm as a contributing but more or less inactive partner; his chief interest remained his clerkship of Pennsylvania. Nathan's contribution of capital was only slightly larger than Joseph's.

The balance sheets indicate that the amounts of capital contributed by the partners and their families fluctuated from year to year. To take the figures (Table 2) of 31 December 1816 and 1817, as an example: in those years neither Nathan nor Joseph had as much capital in the business as did the Estate of William Trotter, for whose minor children Nathan was guardian. By 1816–1817 the amount of the Estate's capital had been reduced by the transfer of funds to the use of William's children, but it still amounted to $11,000. The Estate's share of the capital received interest but did not share in the profits. The same was true of the amount belonging to the partners' younger brother, Thomas Conarroe Trotter. It should be remembered that in those days, before trust companies or other institutions supplied investment services, it was customary for a family concern to invest for the women, children, and the aged of the family.

The partnership also used, without paying interest or granting a share in the profits, $1,180 belonging to their brother-in-law, Ephraim Haines, and in 1817 over $8,500 belonging to Ann and Susan Trotter, wives of the partners. Nathan and Joseph Trotter drew very little against the earnings of their business, leaving their profits to build up the permanent capital of the firm. Year after year Joseph Trotter drew no actual cash; his bank salary, plus an occasional 10 per cent premium

Table 2

Sums Contributed to the Trotter Business by Nathan and Joseph Trotter and Their Relatives as of 31 December 1816 and 1817

	1816	*1817*
Nathan Trotter	$ 7,313.22	$ 7,676.61
Joseph Trotter	6,727.50	4,517.50
Nathan Trotter, guardian	11,000.00	11,000.00
Ann Trotter (Mrs. Joseph)	916.13	4,236.57
Susan Trotter (Mrs. Nathan)	929.94	4,317.88
Thomas C. Trotter	800.00	795.75
Ephraim Haines	1,180.50	1,180.50
	$28,867.29	$33,724.81

from the bank on that salary evidently provided him with enough to live on. Only occasionally did he draw small amounts of cash or charge a purchase of merchandise against his share of the earnings.

Nathan's withdrawals were only for family expenses. And modest sums they were for a man with a wife and three children. In 1819 he drew $3,125. For the preceding four years the average had been only $1,616. During the period from 1839 until 1852 his yearly family expenses exceeded $3,500 only twice.

This modest standard of living was in marked contrast with the growing wealth of the firm and the increase of its earning power.* On 31 July 1830 the accumulated balance of profits of the two brothers stood at more than $67,000 each, and by 30 April 1839 Nathan's account alone amounted to $111,396.10.

When Nathan's sons became partners, they too observed the practice of withdrawing only small sums each year. Eventually the capital of the firm grew much larger than the amount needed in the metal business, causing the Trotters to become, in part, investing capitalists. But that is a matter for discussion in later chapters.

* See Appendix 3 for figures on Nathan Trotter's annual expenses and accumulated balance of profits.

As an employee of the Bank of Pennsylvania, Joseph was in a position to render the Trotter business real service. He was well situated to buy bills of exchange for the firm or to check on credit ratings. Using his connections in banking circles, he frequently obtained information about the safety of a long-standing debt or advice about how best to collect it, but beyond that service he seems to have given little attention to the partnership's affairs. Only occasionally did he make entries in the daybook or write letters concerning collection of debts.

We are not surprised to learn, therefore, that some time in the early 1830's Joseph Trotter decided to withdraw from the business venture with his brother in favor of full concentration on his banking business. Joseph had become cashier of the bank in 1830 and as such had to comply with the bank's charter which read: [1]

> No president or cashier of this bank, shall be directly or indirectly concerned in the purchase or sale of [government bonds] . . . nor shall the cashier be allowed to carry on any other business than that of the bank, under the penalty of five thousand dollars.

Eventually Joseph was to become president of the bank, at a time when it was considered among the foremost financial institutions in Philadelphia, with branches in Lancaster, Easton, Pittsburgh, and Columbia. However, when Joseph retired as president in 1853, some people felt that "by his conservative policies" he had "rather got out of step with the younger generation in business and finance." [2]

Oddly enough the date of Joseph Trotter's withdrawal from the Trotter firm is difficult to determine. The accounts and correspondence are so contradictory at times that they obscure the exact dates of partnership changes. Consequently in constructing Table 3, which purports to show the partnerships under which the Trotter business was conducted, I have been forced to rely on the division of profits as an indication of partnership revision dates. The reason for this vagueness in the Trotter records is easy enough to explain. The Trotter partnerships were private arrangements among family members. They were often mutual agreements and as such did not require written contracts.

What makes the date of Joseph's withdrawal difficult to establish is a letter dated 5 July 1830 in which Nathan wrote: "Our firm has changed . . . Jos. Trotter having retired from it & Mr. Conarroe taken an interest." Yet the fact remains—and this I cannot explain—that Joseph continued to receive a share in the profits of Nathan Trotter &

Table 3

Trotter Firm's Title, Ownership, and Share of Profits
1803–1850

Title of Firm	Time	Owners	Share in Profits
William Trotter	1803–June 30, 1809	William Trotter	sole owner
William Trotter & Company	July 1, 1809–April, 1812	William Trotter	one-half
		Joseph Trotter	one-fourth
		Nathan Trotter	one-fourth
William Trotter & Company	April, 1812–April, 1813	William Trotter	two-thirds
		Nathan Trotter	one-third
William & Nathan Trotter	April, 1813–June, 1814	William Trotter	two-thirds
		Nathan Trotter	one-third
William & Nathan Trotter	June 30, 1814–February, 1815	William Trotter	one-half
		Nathan Trotter	one-half
Nathan Trotter	February, 1815–December, 1816	Nathan Trotter	one-half
		Joseph Trotter	one-half
Nathan Trotter & Company	January 1, 1817–December 31, 1832	Nathan Trotter	one-half
		Joseph Trotter	one-half
Nathan Trotter & Company	January 1, 1833–December 31, 1833	Nathan Trotter	three-fifths
		Joseph Trotter	two-fifths
Nathan Trotter & Company	January 1, 1834–December 31, 1835	Nathan Trotter	two-thirds
		Joseph Trotter	one-third
Nathan Trotter & Company	January 1, 1836–December 31, 1839	Nathan Trotter	sole owner
Nathan Trotter & Company	January 1, 1844–December 31, 1849	Nathan Trotter	one-third
		Edward Hough Trotter	one-third
		George Trotter	one-third
Nathan Trotter & Company	January 1, 1850–	Edward Hough Trotter	one-third
		George Trotter	one-third
		William Henry Trotter	one-third
		Charles West Trotter	

Source: Ledgers in the Trotter collection.

Company until 1835. Moreover, as if by way of further complication, no "Mr. Conarroe" ever became a partner in the enterprise. It may have been that Nathan contemplated admitting to partnership his cousin, Richard Conarroe, who was at that time handling much of the firm's business since Nathan was in ill health. But the accounts show that Richard continued to receive only a salary (plus a bonus or additional payment of $100 to $200 a year) and after a few years left the firm to enter a partnership with one of Nathan's former clerks. It may have been, of course, that Nathan and Joseph were resorting to some ruse or technical dodge to enable Joseph to comply with the bank's charter and yet continue to draw income from Nathan Trotter & Company. But any scheme of that nature would have been so out of character for the two brothers as to be hardly credible as an explanation.

There are a number of ways to measure the success of the Trotter business. One is to plot the company's profits as is done in Chart IV. Another is to present the sales figures and to relate the profits to total sales as in Chart VI. The second method is a better yearly indicator of Nathan Trotter's ability to buy and sell his goods advantageously. Whatever the general business conditions the percentage of profits to sales was seldom above 14 or below 7.

The net profits figure includes a great deal more than merchandising during much of the time. The firm owned stocks and real estate and put money into Oriental and West Indian adventures. They also discounted commercial paper with the firm's money and sometimes bought foreign exchange advantageously. Then, too, bad debts were not always written off annually but were occasionally written off at the close of a period of years (as in 1823) when Nathan Trotter had concluded that nothing was to be realized from certain accounts. For these reasons the net profits figure does not show how efficiently the Trotters bought and sold goods; it does, however, show the general upward trend of the firm's income from 1815 to 1849 and the cycles in between.

An examination of the profits as shown in Chart IV reveals that the years 1819–1821 and 1828–1830 were low periods. Since accumulated bad debts were written off in 1823, the profits figure for that year is misleading. There was a slight drop in profits in 1834 and 1835 and again business was not good from 1839 to 1844. The sales figure trend coincides with these fluctuations in part: 1815–1822, 1827–1831, and

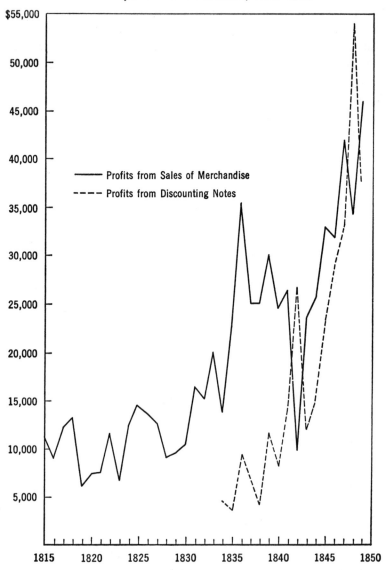

Chart IV

NATHAN TROTTER & COMPANY

Profits by Sources of Income, 1815–1849

Profits from Sales of Merchandise

Profits from Discounting Notes

1842–1843 reflect general depressions. The years 1828 and 1842, again omitting 1823, were low points.

The period of difficulty after the War of 1812, accompanying adjustments in supply and demand, as well as the depression in the late 1820's show up in all the charts. It is noteworthy that in the early years following the depression of 1837, although business in general was depressed (1837–1843) Nathan's profits did not reflect the hard times until the early 1840's, for reasons to be discussed later.

From a study of Nathan Trotter's letters it is possible to reconstruct some of the business policies which he used in conducting his affairs. A severe shortage of money had developed as a result of the panic in 1837. Trotter wrote to his Baltimore correspondent, Isaac McKim, on 26 April of that year. "The whole commercial world is being convulsed to its very centre." Yet he remarked: "We have always endeavoured to circumscribe our business," consequently "we have no notes out." With his letter he forwarded payment of the amount he owed McKim.

Nothing is clearer throughout Trotter's business career than his prudence, caution, and moderation. "We wish to confine ourselves to a snug safe business within our own management," was just as true of the Nathan Trotter of 1849 as of the young Nathan who wrote those words in 1819. To son Edward he at one time stated what was well-known to both of them: "Thee knows I am very cautious in my operations." His cautiousness reveals itself in his accounts. From 1819 on, the firm and Nathan Trotter in his personal accounts wrote off generous amounts for possible losses, put ample sums in the contingent fund, and scaled down the value of inventories and securities.

Trotter in letters to Anson Phelps spoke of himself as one of the "little craft" and made the obvious reference:

> Little crafts must keep the shore,
> While larger Barques may venture more.

Phelps, it went without saying, was one of the larger barques.

Caution was voiced frequently in Trotter's letters during the high prosperity of 1836, just before the crash. "We must move very moderately in metals while they keep so high," or "We think all metals have reached the Top and we must move cautiously while the tendency is downward." Again, in 1846, he did not wish to purchase pig tin in quantities when the price was "wavering," and so bought only as he needed the article.

As part of his cautious practices he gave little discretionary power to others. On a number of occasions he admitted [3] that he had given his English agents too little leeway in the prices they might pay for merchandise, as in this letter to Newton Lyon & Company, 7 December 1837: "If we had left our order more discretionary with you it would have been more to our interest but always wishing to act cautiously induced a limitation."

In the letter to Isaac McKim quoted above, Trotter had said that he had no notes outstanding. Indeed, after the early 1820's he never had any notes outstanding.[4] His suppliers sometimes tried to sell him goods on credit, but he could not be persuaded to give a note. Phelps Dodge & Company wrote him on 8 April 1837, shortly before they suspended payment for a time:

> As our money matters baffle all calculation we must look a little to our friends near Nicholas Biddle, and can assure them that any thing like a liberal offer for 500 to 1000 Boxes Tin plate would be accepted, or for any thing else we now hold in this distracted city. If our good friend Trotter could for once break over that good rule of not writing his name, and let us have a note for the small balance we will engage to sell it at a premium.

But Nathan Trotter held firmly to his policy. In later years he was to make the largest part of his fortune by discounting the notes of others.

In procurement Trotter's policies seem to have been: obtain quality goods from the cheapest and most certain source of supply and once you have found that source continue the connection. Quality, price, and an assured source were all of vital importance.

In sales: treat your customers honestly and they will continue to do business with you. Be reasonable: don't expect them to pay you more than others ask. But at the same price you can count on them to give you a preference. These were rules that set the standard for his day-to-day operations.

Credit and payment policies were, in brief: to the men you expect will pay their debts, grant in normal times the usual credit. In hard times restrict credit and make a special effort to secure personal notes from those who owe accounts payable. As for your payments: pay cash and take the discount. In times of stress, particularly, he was concerned about making prompt payment. His English correspondents, Bainbridges & Brown, on 27 November 1826, commented:

The punctual manner in which you have provided for our engagements on your account gives occasion for again returning our thanks—such consideration is at all times desirable in transactions of this nature but especially necessary in these pinching times.

One of the abiding characteristics of Nathan Trotter was his emphasis on secrecy about business matters. To his son he gave the advice: "Always keep thy business pretty much to thy self." Seldom did he send an order to a New York broker or commission merchant but he added the request that nothing be said about the sale or price or commented that he did not wish it said he had made an offer to purchase.

Trotter made calculations based on the general market situation and conditions likely to affect him, such as the amount of goods expected to be produced or brought to market, tariff and price changes, and credit risks. The firm acquired a knowledge of matters affecting their particular business: when goods were best sold; quality, quantity, and sizes of the commodities needed by their customers; from whom to buy; cheapest means of engaging freight for various commodities; and, as a result of careful calculation, the cheapest means of procuring goods.

The calculating function was developed in Trotter to an unusually high degree. As the percentage of profits to sales declined, 1817–1821, he became greatly concerned about the cheapest mode of getting his goods. Beginning in 1822 he calculated the cost of every foreign invoice. Here, at the foot of the invoice at first and, after 1837, in separate calculation books, he established exactly the cost of each pound of copper, each box of tin plate. He considered not only the cost at the current rate of exchange, but what the interest and insurance charges would be. Whether to import, as he preferred, or to buy of Phelps & Peck was as he said strictly a matter of calculation, a matter of dollars and cents.

Shrewdness was also one of Nathan Trotter's characteristics—his methods of bargaining for freight rates being one piece of evidence—but he did not like being called shrewd. One of his correspondents, Rodenbough Stewart & Company, drove a hard bargain, too. In 1843 that firm wrote Nathan Trotter, with reference to his order of wire for the following year: "As to the advance in price, it is scarcely necessary to remind those so acute as yourselves of the advance present as well as prospective in the value of Iron of such quality as we require."

Trotter resented the reference, as his reply indicates: "Had we even *less* than a moiety of the 'acuteness' that pertains to our frd Rodenbough & which he imputes to us we should have been able no doubt to have agreed with yourselves for a supply of wire on much better terms than we are now able to do by our measured ability."

Throughout Trotter's business career he was accustomed to live up to every contract. If there were differences he suggested arbitration. This was, of course, customary Quaker practice. "When members of the Society disagreed they rarely went to law. Disputes were adjusted by Boards of Arbitration." [5] In disagreements with non-Quakers, the Friend proposed arbitration before using legal measures. When a matter was at issue, Nathan Trotter proposed that the question be referred to "disinterested persons, mutually chosen, to say what would be right in the case & to whose decision each party submit." He wanted "nothing but what was perfectly right & mercantile." On numerous occasions he stated that he wanted to act "mercantilely." He believed that trade rested on confidence and honorable dealings. These were the very foundations of business.

During much of its history the Trotter firm carried on its business with the help of few employees. For many years Nathan had only a clerk and an apprentice with him in the office. These employees wrote and copied letters, kept accounts, went about from store to tavern seeking wagoners and arranging for the transportation of goods. The clerk sometimes traveled to New York to buy goods and to Lancaster, Harrisburg, and Pittsburgh on collecting trips.

Some seasons were not busy: then there was time to add a few flourishes to the capital letters in the copies of the invoices or time to collect an assortment of goods to adventure to the West Indies.

Nathan Trotter's sons, from the time they were ten or eleven years old, used to come down to the countinghouse and copy letters in the big leather-bound letterbooks. Nathan's writing was a nervous, running hand,[6] not easy to read, and his sons often had difficulty interpreting what he had written. Their father always went over the copy and occasionally commented on the mistakes: "A sheep," he once wrote in the margin, when *wether* had been written for *whether.*

The first apprentice had come to work when the partnership of William, Joseph, and Nathan Trotter had been formed in 1809. Eliphaz Daisy Cheyney—Daisy in the records—was to stay for fourteen years: seven as an apprentice and seven as a salaried clerk. Among the early sums spent for Daisy was $20 paid his "Aunt N. Cheyney to procure him some winter cloath &c." In 1812 B. H. Rand, professor of penmanship on South Sixth Street,[7] was paid $10 for giving Daisy writing lessons.

Daisy continued with the Trotter firm through the depression period 1817–1822. When Nathan granted a considerable amount of credit to Pennsylvania handicraftsmen and country storekeepers and then, because of adverse business conditions, had difficulty in collecting, he sent Daisy on many hard trips over the mountains to Pittsburgh in an effort to collect money from the delinquents.

The second assistant added to the payroll of the firm was Daniel Trotter Haines, son of Nathan's older sister, Elizabeth. Daniel came as an apprentice in 1815, the year in which Daisy's apprenticeship ended and at a time when Nathan and Joseph Trotter were getting their new firm established. Daniel became a salaried clerk in 1821, receiving $300 that year and an annual salary of $500 the rest of the time he remained with the firm.

As employees of the firm, Daisy and Daniel divided the work. Daniel kept the porterage accounts, wrote and copied some of the letters, and helped keep the general accounts. When it was necessary to divide the traveling, Daisy was sent on collecting trips and Daniel to New York to purchase goods. Daniel was a practical young man. "I have succeeded in getting all from the Elizabeth except the 2 cases," he wrote from New York, "they I fear I shall have some difficulty with as they are stowed close—I will however wet the fingers of the stevedore which is the only resort I have as Capt Marshall says he must have them today." [8]

Daisy spoke of himself as a person in poor health. He had had at some time, perhaps while in the employ of the Trotter firm, smallpox and malarial fever. It was because of ill health, I believe, that he left the Trotter firm early in 1822. "I am very anxious to be doing something," he wrote in July of that year, "I dont altogether like to give up the idea of going to sea if I thought I could make out any how at all as a sailer. I would try a voyage before settling myself to any-thing being of opinion that more benefit to my health would proceed from it than from anything else I could do."

Nevertheless, Daisy did not go to sea. Instead he went, in the spring of 1823, to the little town of Lampeter in Lancaster county where his brother Moses lived. There he began storekeeping: steel and nails with which he was familiar, and thimbles, lead pencils, and drugs made up his stock of goods. His health got worse and on 15 April 1825 Moses Cheyney wrote that his brother Daisy had died on the 8th: "His store is a lonely place to me."

The countinghouse down by the Delaware could not have been a very healthy place for clerks, for on 14 July 1826 Daniel also left because of illness. Perhaps Daisy's death made Daniel more concerned about his own health. At any rate he sought a treatment common in those days and sailed for the next few years as supercargo on ships to South America. After his 1827–1828 voyage his uncle Nathan reported: "Danl Haines has returned and is well." But in the fall of 1829 Nathan Trotter bade his nephew goodbye on still another voyage with the wish that his health might again be benefited, after which, except for a few paper-discounting transactions in the early 1830's, the young man dropped out of the Trotter correspondence, leaving us to wonder whether despite his efforts Daniel was unsuccessful in recovering his strength.

Between the year 1826, when Daniel left, and 1828, when John W. Dixon came, Nathan Trotter & Company employed a couple of clerks whose stay was short. Dixon's employment with the Trotter firm lasted, however, until the close of 1836. Dixon was probably either an apprentice or a part-time employee during his first three years with the firm since Profit & Loss was debited for his services with only $50 in 1828, $60 in 1829, and $75 in 1830. Thereafter expense on merchandise was debited with his annual salary which was $150 in 1831 and 1832, $400 in 1833, and $500 thereafter.

The year after Dixon came to the firm, Richard R. Conarroe became an employee. Conarroe stayed from 1829 until well into the year 1835. As I have mentioned earlier, Conarroe is spoken of as a partner, but the accounts do not bear out the statement.

These two young assistants, Dixon and Conarroe, entered into a partnership with each other about 1835 or 1836, borrowed money from Nathan Trotter, and then failed during the difficult times in 1839, owing their former employer $3,000. In 1847 Richard Conarroe again became an employee of the Trotter firm.

Nathan Trotter's oldest son, Edward, and Joseph Trotter's son, Samuel Hough Trotter, were employed by the firm in 1834. Samuel received $400 a year but Edward was paid nothing as he was evidently considered an apprentice learning the business. He was soon given some responsibility and made his first buying trip to New York in December, 1834, shortly after his twentieth birthday. Joseph's son Samuel left the business in 1835, probably at the time Nathan's second son George began working at the store. During the late 1830's Nathan Trotter managed the firm with one and sometimes two of his sons plus the help of a porter.

Then, in 1840, a bookkeeper, Robert McCune, was hired and stayed with the firm until 1845. His books are models of neatness and he seems to have been an accurate accountant. Nathan Trotter apparently had great faith in McCune's carefulness with figures as this letter would seem to indicate: [9]

> Our Mr. McCune upon noticing the diffe. as to the time when the Bills Avge. due- went again to work and seems quite sure he is correct & gives an abstract (annexed) of the dates of all the Ince. & Says he has re- and re-examined it—& we depend upon his Statements which are Seldom in error—please try it again—

The second year McCune was with the firm he received a salary of $750—the highest paid up to 1849. Since Nathan Trotter was by that time devoting much of his time to moneylending, Robert was perhaps hired to relieve the Trotter boys of the drudgery of keeping accounts.

In 1847 Conarroe relatives appeared again on the records as salaried clerks. As already stated, Richard Conarroe returned in that year and at the same time his son, John L. Conarroe, began what was to be a long association with the Trotter firm.[10] Nathan Trotter's two youngest sons were also by then old enough to help in the business. Charles W. first received a salary in 1848 and William Henry in 1849.

So much for clerks and apprentices. There was need for porterage in such a business and in 1821, the year in which Daniel Haines finished his apprenticeship, the firm first hired a "porter in the store." Thereafter one was employed constantly. A porter's wages ranged between $220 and $390 a year. Outside draymen or porterage firms were hired throughout the entire period 1803–1849. For about half of the period, or from 1825 until 1849, the porterage firm of Deasha & Marlin and its successors did the Trotter's porterage business.

The Trotter store at 47 North Front was strategically located. Being situated between Market and Arch, it stood in one of the most active business centers. The counting room was apparently at the back on the Water Street side where, from his chair at the desk, Nathan could see immediately opposite his window the ships tied up at Perot's wharves. South along the Delaware River were Clifford's, Girard's, and Imlay's wharves before one came to the foot of Market Street. In the other direction just to the north was one of the landmarks of Philadelphia, the Old Ferry Slip.[11]

Under the counting room was a cellar opening on Water Street. Since it was too damp for most of the goods which the Trotter firm handled, Nathan rented it to merchants whose goods were less susceptible to moisture.

During the 1830's Nathan moved his store across the street to 36 North Front Street. The new location had once been the dwelling house of the shipping merchant Thomas Cope [12] and subsequently had become the place of business of the merchants Samuel Archer and Stacy Bispham. The man the Trotters bought it from was the well-known merchant George Thomas. On this property Nathan Trotter & Company built the store which appears as the right-hand building in the illustration opposite page 174. This is the building in which the firm is still doing business as Nathan Trotter & Company. In 1838 and 1839 Nathan purchased the two stores situated at the left in the picture—numbers 32 and 34 on North Front Street.

The store at 36 North Front Street had (and still has) a receiving room on the Front Street side. Here were scales—"our beam is considered first rate," Nathan boasted—wire gauges, racks for displaying copper, cupboards for old account books and letters, a safe reaching from floor to ceiling, and some merchandise. Back of the receiving room was Nathan's counting room with its windows looking out on a courtyard. The court was enclosed by stables and warehouses as pictured in the etching by Howard Cook opposite page 142. In addition to the warehouses back of the store, Trotter had a larger fireproof warehouse in Chancery Lane.

The physical equipment of Nathan's store was scanty. Large and heavy account books and letterbooks in which Nathan and his clerks and apprentices wrote with quill pens were essentials. Sand used over a century ago for blotting still falls from the account books as they are lifted from the shelves. Desks—some of them high on which the account books rested—boxes for filing invoices and correspondence, and probably a few shelves made up the furnishings of the room. Prices current and the daily paper lay at hand. By the 1830's the firm had acquired a letter press. This may have made work easier for the clerk but it made it ever so much more difficult for the researcher who attempts to decipher the faint copy.

The Philadelphia of 1815 in which Nathan Trotter began trading was a metropolis with certain essential business auxiliaries. The daily paper informed Nathan when the letter bags for London mail would be taken from the Merchants Exchange, thus enabling him to know when to transmit orders to merchants beyond the sea. There were ships and porters to move his imported merchandise for a fee. Kite's *Directory* for 1814 lists about fifty stagecoach lines, some of them offering daily service, and a number of stage, ferry, packet, and even local steamship lines. There were regular wagon and sloop services also. Over the roads and rivers to the hinterland and to New York, Trenton, Wilmington, and Baltimore moved these services in spring, summer, and fall; not so regularly in winter.

When the new firm was established in 1815, Philadelphia was still the financial center of the United States and continued to be until the 1830's. There were a number of banks in the city from which the merchant might choose. Nathan Trotter did his business with the Bank of Pennsylvania where Joseph Trotter worked and he also used the Bank of Northern Liberties at 73 Vine which was still nearer his place of business.

Insurance companies to bear the risk of shipments and to take fire risks were more numerous in Philadelphia even than banks. Some of the companies had been established in the previous century. The oldest, a fire insurance company, had been incorporated in 1754 under the title of The Philadelphia Contributionship. Both the Insurance Company of North America and the Insurance Company of Pennsylvania had been incorporated in 1794.

Trotter regularly insured adventures, goods stored in Philadelphia, goods imported from foreign ports other than England, and some shipments from New York. From 1815 until 1818 the London commission merchant was directed to "Let all be under insurance." Then, since insurance came to add much to the cost of imports and the charge for the policy was considered "monstrous," a letter might read: "If you ship in the Electra only insure three fourths of nett amt." From 1821 on, the commission merchant was requested to insure in the future only on Trotter's specific order. Thereafter he used Philadelphia insurance companies. The English correspondent gave Trotter advice about the amount of goods being shipped and the vessel on which they were coming. Trotter then sent a note, such as this, to the Philadelphia Insurance Company, dated 27 March 1822:

Please insure One Thousand dollars on goods at and from Liverpool to Philada. on board the Ship Lancaster Capt Burkhart—Premium One and an half per cent—In case the above amount of goods should not be on board—the premium on the amot above what is actually shipped to us, to be returned to us as customary

By the middle of the 1830's Trotter did not always insure his English imports and from about 1841 on, almost never. The explanation was that sheet iron and tin plate were protected by insurance only "if the vessel has come in collision at sea with another vessel or becomes stranded, and the damage amounts to 20 p ct." From any other cause no recovery for damage could be had "so that in fact a total loss is all that can be guarded against."

Nathan Trotter protected himself as much as he could by having his correspondents ship on nothing but the best ships, "particularly those that dont take salt in bulk." And he was "extremely anxious not to have it come on our Coast during the period say 15 dec to 15 Feb   it is very hazardous on account of having N E Storms send the ice in our Bay & river which prevents vessells getting up."

In 1816, shortly after starting his business, Nathan Trotter, the specialist in metals, had some trade cards printed which read: [13]

COPPER
TIN PLATES, IRON WIRE, STEEL &c.

Braziers Copper, in sheets, of all sizes and weights.
    Do.   in raised and flat bottoms,   do.
Sheathing Copper, 16 to 30 oz. Copper Rivets,
assorted, Bar Copper, Copper Tea Kettles,
Brass Battery Kettles, Brass Wire, Spelter
and Spelter Solder, Block Tin, Tin
Wire, No. 1 to 22, Card Wire, Sheet
Iron, genuine T. Crowley Millington
Steel, No. 3, English Blistered Ⓛ
and Cast Steel, &c. &c.
A constant supply of the above articles
for sale, on reasonable terms, by

NATHAN TROTTER
No. 47, North Front Street, Philadelphia

These goods which Nathan Trotter advertised were standardized metalware, semimanufactured English imports used by handicraftsmen in America. Quality was, therefore, of the utmost importance. The quality of the materials had to be good, if for no other reason than because the handicraftsmen who worked with the materials were usually, in those days of limited markets, known personally to the customers who used the final product. On one occasion an order of tin plate sold by the Trotter firm was pronounced unfit, and the smith who had bought it wrote: "In using such tin fore customers ware, it would injure my credit." An Easton dealer requested that the Trotters be sure to send good quality brass kettles since, as he put it, "they are all to remain in Easton."

The Trotter firm dealt chiefly in metals in sheets, metals shaped into patterns, rolls of wire, and, as the years passed, larger quantities of pigs and ingots. The three most important types of metal handled by the Trotters will be considered in the order in which they ranked, chronologically, in the firm's business: first steel, then copper, and later tin.

When Nathan's trade card was printed, the Trotter firm already had a reputation for carrying the best steel. Such was genuine Ⓛ Blistered steel, formed from wrought iron by a process producing blisters on the surface—sometimes called London hoop Ⓛ by the smiths—which was to be well blistered from end to end and clear of flaws. It was a thoroughly converted steel and the bars exhibited a coarse grain when broken and had a bright silver appearance, termed by the smiths "high."[14]

T. Crowley Millington's steel—No. 3 in faggots or half faggots (bundles of 120 or 60 pounds) and cast—was handled. In March, of 1816, an English correspondent had written: "Specify the purposes for which the article /N T cast steel/ is intended as in that case the sizes will be drawn proper for them and the temper shall be prepared accordingly of which there are three sorts no. 1 mild no. 2 middling no. 3 high conversion—every bar in future shall be marked."[15] The cast steel came in various sizes: ⅝ inch squares were ordered for axes; 2 inches wide and ½ inch thick for screws; and bars 1¼ to 1½ inches thick and 7 inches wide (weighing 20 to 28 pounds) for mill saws. Cast steel for axes had to be clear of flaws. "Let them be even drawn as possible," wrote Nathan, "as some are fuller at one end than the other . . . we desire this to have a very fine grain."

Coach spring steel and shear steel (which bore the usual stamp of two shears) were other steels which the Trotter firm imported.

Before the War of 1812 steel had been the most important metal handled by the Trotter firm. By the 1840's it had dropped out of the inventory entirely. The change was brought about partly because of the decline in quality of the output of the English manufacturer and partly because the American commission merchants came to sell steel in small lots directly to the consumer, in that way bypassing wholesalers like Trotter.

Trotter's 1816 trade card began with COPPER and it was as a copper merchant that some customers addressed Trotter for years. He, himself, wrote in 1826: "We think we stand most conspicuous in this city in selling copper." [16] To be a copper dealer required a large amount of capital invested in inventory if the dealer pretended to keep any degree of assortment.

Braziers copper was one type Trotter dealt in. It had to be "smooth even rolled tough good Copper" and of a light color. Trotter did not like to carry copper of a slate-colored appearance. He often remonstrated with his English suppliers when their copper was dull in color since he felt it injured his sales. "It's like a woman with a dark meagre complexion," so he wrote, "who altho possest of as many virtues will not pass off like one of a captivating appearance." [17]

Copper came in various forms: sheets, raised bottoms (often called "breasts"), and flat bottoms. These were ordered in a great variety of weights and sizes. Consider but one item—copper sheets. Nathan Trotter wrote a customer in 1831 that the standard sizes of braziers sheets were:

$$18 \times 72 \text{ weighing } 14\#^*$$
$$17 \times 68 \qquad\qquad 12$$
$$16 \times 64$$
$$16 \times 67 \qquad\qquad 11$$
$$30 \times 60 \text{ any weight}$$
$$14 \times 48\text{—}14 \text{ to } 30 \text{ oz. per sq foot}$$

* # is used for pound in the Trotter records.

Since a dealer was also expected to keep flat bottoms 10 to 30 inches in diameter and raised bottoms from 19 to 23 inches, it was little wonder that Nathan Trotter said he could have other sizes "made exactly but it would be impossible to keep on hand what would suit any copper smith."

For many years a considerable amount of the braziers copper sold by the Trotters was for the sides of stills. Here is a typical order for the copper needed for a 50-gallon still:

sides 26 × 52—17 lbs. 82 in. long
Breast 26 to 27 in. 7 lbs. flats
Bottom 22 in. raised or 28 flat 9 to 10 lbs.

Sheathing in the days of fast-sailing copper-bottomed ships was also necessary merchandise for a copper merchant. Copper sheets 30 × 60 inches weighing 16 to 32 ounces were sold for sheathing. Of course copper nails were sold along with the sheets. Here is the bill for copper for the "New Brig built by Jehu Eyre Jun":

			C	qr	#*			
1	case	20 oz. copper	10..1..11					
1		22 oz.	10..1.. 5					
1		24 oz.	10..0..20					
1		"	10..0.. 8					
			40..3..16	oz. or 4580#	28¢	1282.40
		copper nails		300#	30¢	90.00
			porterage paid			1.50
						$1373.90

* C stands for cwt. or hundredweight (112 lbs. in England and generally 100 lbs. in the United States after 1824); qr.—the fourth part of a cwt. is 28 lbs. in Trotter's accounts.

Roofing copper, although the same 30 × 60 size as the copper used to "sheath" a vessel, usually was much lighter, perhaps 9 or 10 pounds. In addition it was important that copper for roofing have straight edges.

In the 1830's and 1840's demand for copper changed. There was little call for raised and flat bottoms. Demand was chiefly for sheathing, strips for locomotive pipes, and small amounts of sheets for the use of transportation and industrial companies.

One order for locomotive strips called for 545 sheets 7 feet 1 inch long and 5 inches wide of the thickness of a 50# sheet 30 × 60. These were ordered with the request that they be cut true and of the same thickness throughout. The Industrial Revolution was demanding precision of the manufacturer.

Tin plate was the third metal to become important in the firm's inventory and remained so until the 1890's. It paid less profit (if the dealers were to be believed) and was the topic of more correspondence than any other article handled by the Trotters. Tin plate was a thin sheet of iron coated with tin. "There are," to quote a letter of Nathan Trotter's in 1827, "225 sheets in a box near 10 in. × 14 in. each sheet—the 1 C or common tin weight about 115# the 1 X about 145#

½ X means 2 Boxes 1 C & 1 of 1 X—and come thus assorted at 12½ dollars pr box." [18]

The quality of tin plate varied, especially in the period when some manufacturers were experimenting with iron. The tin plate of puddled iron was brittle and was considered an inferior article. It could be sold by the English manufacturer cheaper than that made with charcoal iron and would answer for some purposes, but not for roofing since the double grooving for that purpose required tough quality tin plate which would not crack.

There was also heavier tin plate, indicated by 1 XX, 1 XXX, etc., and Waster, a tin plate not of first quality which was ordered in small amounts for bake pans and horns.

It was essential that the sheets of tin plate used for roofing be cut square. The sides and end of each sheet had to be at right angles so that they would present a straight edge when sheets were joined. Pontypool brand was preferred by many because of its excellence in this respect while "Margam & many other brands for want of being true in the sheet required trimming," which caused a loss of time and some expense.

Terneplate was a thin sheet of iron coated with a mixture of tin and lead. It came to be used extensively for roofing and was cut 14 × 20 inches, which meant that fewer seams were required than for the 10 × 12 inch tin-plate size.

In addition to the three products for which he was best known, Trotter handled several other sheet metals: iron, zinc, and brass.

Sheet iron, to the uninitiated, is sheet iron, but not to the Trotters, who dealt in American, English, and Russian—each used for a different purpose. Sheet iron of American and English manufacture came in sheets of about 22 to 24 inches wide, 4 to 4½ feet long, and of a thickness designated in the earlier period as single, double, and—the thinnest—treble rolled. Later the thickness was indicated by wire gauge. Sheet iron of American manufacture was not always as standardized as some articles dealt in. There were complaints that Marshall's no. 27 was thinner than Wood's. Trotter ordered of Joseph Roman & Son, commenting on the fact that their iron was said to be "thinner & more correct to the gauge" than that of other manufacturers.

The aristocrat of sheet irons seems to have been Russian. Adjectives were expended on the gloss of this smooth "highly planished" iron prepared with a beautiful polish. The sheets were 28 × 56 or 60 inches and the light sizes, the sizes desired in the Philadelphia market, were 10 to 12 pounds to a sheet, "Russian weight." [19]

It would appear that Philadelphia's metal market was more particular than that of New York. Nathan Trotter declined an assortment of Russian sheet iron offered by a New York dealer, saying that his market would not accept iron of such quality at the price named. "The practice prevails here," wrote Trotter "of letting each consumer or worker take the sizes that suit them and they all require ¾th not heavier than 10 or 11# and for such not paying higher by the bundle than 11¾ & 12c on time."

Sheet zinc, or as it was called galvanized iron, was a sheet of iron coated with spelter. It came in sizes of about 25 inches by 7 feet. [20] The weight per square foot varied. Sheet brass, to conclude this list of standardized semimanufactured sheet metals, came in a variety of sizes and weights also. There were orders of sheets 8, 10, and 12 inches wide and 2 and 3 feet long; nos. 22, 23, 24, in rolls 8 and 8½ inches wide; sheets 24 × 48 inches; and strips 4½ inches wide for plating. Sheet brass had to be tough, correct in numbers, and of a handsome color to suit Trotter's taste.

Not dealing in hardware generally, as Nathan Trotter said, he only occasionally wanted a few articles to assort his sales of tin plates, sheet iron, etc. The hardware in the inventory was usually only 2 or 3 per cent of the total; but the variety constantly increased. The hardware inventory of 1815 was high—5.4 per cent. (See Appendix 4 for inventories of 1815, 1825, and 1850.) It consisted of anvils and bright and black vises. Five years later a 1.7 per cent hardware inventory included rivets, scale beams, scythes, shovels, and braziers hammers. The new items in the 1830 inventory were sad irons, bake pans, kettle ears, knobs, teakettle spouts, and candlestick springs.

The 1845 inventory of hardware included a fairly long list. Over 500 of the $1,229.28 inventory invested in hardware was in rivets. The rest included these items:

cast iron stove feet	black lead pots	kettle ears
brass stove balls and ornaments	candlestick springs	round plyers
	lamp screws	iron weights
japanned and brass knobs	bed screws	painted and bright beams
	handles for dustpans,	
tinned copper hose burrs	saucepans, and coal sifters	jack chain
cast iron mandrels		iron bake pans

Brass battery kettles were always in stock during the period of both William and Nathan Trotter's management. Early orders called for larger sizes. One specified "2 nests battery Kettles contg. 100 Kettles each—from 1 gal to 5 gallons" and a nest of 50 or 60 kettles from 1 to 20 gallons "made light with very little taper." An 1832 order called for 100 kettles of 1 pint, 100 of 1½ pints, and 100 of a quart as well as varying numbers from 9 to 20 inches across the top to be "made as light as possible, but sound and clear of brased places."

Many of the craftsmen who purchased tin plate, copper, brass, and sheet iron wanted wire also. Consequently many kinds of wire were handled: copper, iron, annealed iron, hard and bright brass, wire for cards, woven brass wire for milk strainers, and wire for umbrella stretchers. Inventories included iron wire in sizes 1 to 22, wire for cards in sizes 24 to 32, and brass in sizes 20 to 32. Iron wire had to be "tough, handsome smooth even drawn," and usually put up in separate stones of 10½# each.

Men who were starting up ("new beginners," as they called themselves) in the tin- and coppersmithing business often ordered machines and tools from Trotter. Stakes, hollow punches, swedges, hammers, and shears were among the tools ordered. An order for machines included the following items:

Folding machines	$ 22
Grooving do	18
Large turning do	13
Small do	13
Wiring do	15
Large burring do	12
Small do	12
Setting down do	15
Extra rollers for burring machines	5
	$125

Beading machines, for both round and OG (ogee) beads, were ordered by stovemakers as well as by tinsmiths.

To the request for coppersmith's tools, Trotter always replied that there were no regular sets for sale. He kept some that were used by both coppersmiths and tinsmiths, such as shears and planishing hammers; but he advised those who wished to enter the business to obtain their other equipment "from those who are declining the business or purchase them wherever they can find them, or have patterns made to suit themselves and have them cast as they vary in size and shape . . . a set will cost about from 150 to 200$."

Although Nathan Trotter specialized in metals, he made a few attempts to continue to deal in felting for papermakers' use. He sold on commission the manufacture of Samuel and Jonathan Rogers of Stanton, near Newport, Delaware, whose product the Trotters had sold before 1815. The quality was unsatisfactory and Nathan Trotter then sent a trial order to an English manufacturer. The English felting, although excellent in quality, was twice as expensive as the American for which reason the attempt to deal once again in felting was given up.

As industry developed, railroads and factories afforded a growing market for pig metals. Consequently the Trotter firm came to deal more in block tin, spelter, pig lead, and—to use the inventory designations—cake, tile, and ingot copper. Borax, antimony, mica, bismuth, spelter, solder, and Babbit metal also made up a small part of the inventory.

The firm's customers demanded a good quality of pig tin. The English manufacturer's agent, not a completely unbiased authority it is true, stated in a letter of 1822 that "The Tin from England is of a more uniform quality than from any other country being assayed by Government after it is refined." Trotter in the late 1820's stated that some English tin bearing the stamp of "a sheep with a flag" and some of Grenfell's stamp were good. Spanish tin—a designation for South American—answered well for brass castings, but Nathan Trotter bought little of it.

By the 1840's Philadelphia users were confining themselves to what they called India tin, which included tin from the Straits and Banca. The Straits tin came from Singapore and included Rajah brand,[21] some of it at least of round pigs, and some branded Revely Company Penang. The Government Banca was "mostly to be depended on for quality" since it came "under the notice of the Dutch Government in some way." The pigs "generally had the letter B cast in under the tub and were called Government Tin."

English ingot copper, Cuban copper (smelted in Baltimore), and Lake Superior copper were all sold at various times by Nathan Trotter & Company. Copper cakes weighing as much as 50 pounds and ingots of about 14 pounds each, and for this reason convenient for the brass founders, were imported from England. The Baltimore smelters made pigs averaging 150 pounds each and also notched ingots which Trotter's customers preferred.

Spelter, "the ordinary ingot zinc of commerce," came in cakes 4 inches wide and 8 inches long. They weighed 12 to 14 pounds. In 1823 Trotter said he preferred the English; in the 1840's he dealt in Silesian spelter purchased of a Belgian firm.

French antimony purchased by the keg was handled; English lead was imported; and Missouri lead was purchased in New York and Philadelphia.

Occasionally there was correspondence about a new article. In 1843 Nathan Trotter asked Samuel May & Company, of Boston, for information about mica, saying it was used in doors of coal stoves and he understood it was procured of Ruggles in Boston. May & Company informed him that mica was a sheet talc and added: "by some call'd /improperly we believe/ sheet isinglass." Later Ruggles' clerk wrote: "Mr. Ruggles is now up to the mountin with men to work to blow it [mica] out   It comes out of hard flinty rocks   quarts & Felds par   such as dentist use to make teeth with." Mica was ordered to be clear and handsome, not broken at the corners and of 5, 5½, 6, and 7 inch squares.

These were the goods bought and sold by a Philadelphia merchant in the period when the United States was changing from the handicraft to factory stage of production. Semimanufactured goods required by the smiths made up the bulk of the goods handled by the Trotters. At first practically all the goods were imported from England. Then, as product after product came to be manufactured in the United States, domestic goods supplemented or completely replaced imports. Also as we have seen, raw materials needed by the new industries bulked increasingly large in the Trotters' inventory. The Trotter firm reflects in goods, sources of supply, customers, and investments the developing stages of the Industrial Revolution.

CHAPTER V

Merchandise Procurement

F R O M their countinghouse on the banks of the Delaware, the Trotter firm during the years between 1803 and 1849 sent orders to places both close by and distant: Baltimore at home and Bristol in England, as well as St. Petersburg in Russia, to mention only a few. As conditions changed, the sources of their articles of trade varied, and with new sources came different patterns of procurement. Underlying all can be seen the influence of the Industrial Revolution.

In the early years between 1803 and 1822, that is during the years when William was head of the Trotter firm and for a few years after Nathan took over the management of the business, most of the goods handled by the firm were manufactured in England and were procured for the Trotters by commission merchants residing in London. For instance, all the firm's imported leather products were bought in this fashion, for London was an important tanning center. Most semifinished metal products were also procured through London merchants, although some were bought through agents in Birmingham and Sheffield. The purchase of woolens was the only important exception to the rule: no woolens were bought through London; the merchants from whom the Trotters obtained this commodity were located in Leeds and Halifax.

The London commission merchants with whom the Trotters did business were in effect their representatives abroad. They made certain on-the-spot decisions which the Trotters could not make from a distance. Nevertheless it was the practice of the Trotters to limit the range of these decisions as much as they could. They wished to exercise their own judgments where possible and often they left so little discretion to their agents that the latter were prevented from taking action when opportunities arose quite unforeseen. When sending an order to England the Trotters included precise *specifications* of the commodities to be procured; they stipulated the *quantities* to be purchased and stated the maximum *prices* to be paid. Thus, their orders left little latitude for the agent beyond executing the order and supervising the stowage on a vessel bound for the United States.

The English merchants objected to this limiting practice: partly, of course, because it sometimes deprived them of a commission on business which might have been transacted and also because it prevented them from being of service to their distant customer. The price of finished leather, for instance, was subject to sharp fluctuations and often exceeded the Trotters' maximum limits. The raw leather which was tanned in London came from continental Europe, and political conditions there made supply uncertain. In 1803 the London representative could not fill an order sent by William Trotter because the price of morocco leather advanced far beyond the set limits, chiefly in consequence of a decree prohibiting the exportation of skins from Italy. During the Napoleonic Wars, leather was the article most frequently missing from the Trotters' importations.

The English commission merchants typically did not carry stocks of goods on hand. To fill the Trotters' orders, they bought tin plate on the open market. For leather goods, wire, brass kettles, sheet iron, and copper, they contracted with manufacturers (put the order in hand, as the merchants would say) to have the goods made according to exact specifications.

The Trotters always took special care to send their orders well in advance of their need. In the case of steel, they wrote letters to their English agents in the fall of the year so that the agents might have the entire winter in which to place the order, allow time for fabrication, collect the completed goods in their warehouses, and be ready for shipment at the earliest possible date in the spring. A typical fall order for steel would read: "I shall want a supply of T. Crowley Millington Steel next Spring which please have in hand and ship me by an early sailing staunch American ship under full insurance." Orders for woolens were sometimes placed even earlier than orders for steel. Frequently woolens needed the following spring would be ordered in August.

When spring came and ships began to sail the ocean again, the English commission merchants arranged for space on the earliest departing vessels. They then moved the goods from warehouses to the docks and arranged to have them insured for passage. Once the goods were loaded, the merchants had no further responsibility. But their cares did not cease. It would be months before they would receive payment. Meanwhile they might have to pay the manufacturer promptly, and in the event of export duties they might have to make still further cash payments. On one occasion a cloth merchant wrote the Trotters that manufacturers were beginning to demand "prompt payment" where formerly the practice had been to pay once a year. In addition, this Trotter correspondent stated: "We have 4p Cent to pay down at the Custom house for Duty before we can ship any Goods which on large Shipments amounts to a heavy Sum." [1]

For their efforts and for the risks they ran in extending long-term credits, the English merchants received a commission. They figured this commission on the price of the goods charged by the manufacturer (or other supplier) plus such charges as export duties, warehousing expense, drayage, and ocean insurance. The price for ocean insurance was usually set at ½ of 1 per cent of the manufacturer's price. The standard rate of commission charged by London merchants was 2½ per cent of total costs, but the merchants of Sheffield and Birmingham charged 5 per cent, although usually they did not include ocean insurance in the base figure on which they calculated their commission.

The Trotters did most of their London business with two firms in that city, Bainbridges & Brown [2] and Pieschell & Brogden [3]—both, incidentally, were former Sansom suppliers. Pieschell & Brogden were known particularly for their business connections with Russia but they did a general trade with other parts of the world as well. Bainbridges & Brown also carried on a general commission business but they were known as a firm that traded particularly with the United States and the British colonies. Bainbridges & Brown provided an especially important connection for the Trotter firm inasmuch as they had dealt with T. Crowley, Millington & Company for many years and had come to be almost exclusive agents for T. Crowley Millington steel. As such they often were promised the first steel up from the works in the spring.

T. Crowley Millington steel was reputedly the best produced in England.

The Crowley Millington firm dated from some time late in the seventeenth century.[4] The founder of the firm had been Ambrose Crowley, a London ironmonger who had come to be widely known as the "greatest manufacturer of ironware in Europe." On his death Crowley owned extensive "buildings, shops, houses, warehouses, mills, forges," that were widely located in "the Counties and Bishoprick of Durham and Worcestershire and the County of Kent." These iron-fabricating properties were bequeathed by Ambrose, on his death in 1713, to his only son, John (1689–1728). After John Crowley's death, the business was carried on by his widow, Theodosia Crowley, who admitted to partnership a man named Isaac Millington.

In Trotter's time, T. Crowley, Millington & Company manufactured everything from nails to anchors "and other articles of the most massive kind." They owned their own coastal vessels in which they shipped their products from their up-country steel mill, probably located in Durham, to London where they had two large warehouses.[5] The demand for T. Crowley Millington steel was so heavy that the company neither advertised nor employed salesmen, and the price they charged was "enormous as compared with the ordinary manufacturers of steel." However, Trotter was willing to pay the price because "the name, long established character and good quality" of the product made it worth the higher rate. Even in its earliest years the Trotter firm had made a reputation in the Philadelphia area as a dealer in the best steel.

Since Nathan wished to distinguish himself for the excellence of his goods, he also insisted that his London agents buy what he considered the best braziers copper. Nathan thought that there were many good manufacturers of copper sheathing, but he regarded no braziers copper as equal in quality to that of James Shears & Sons, of Surrey.

It was not uncommon for English commission houses to maintain agents in American cities even though these agents might compete directly with such customers as Nathan Trotter. In Birmingham the firm from which Nathan Trotter bought his semimanufactured metals was Capper, Perkins & Whitehouse.[6] This firm was large enough to have representatives in the United States. The junior partner, James Whitehouse, was in charge of the branch in New York, and in Philadelphia the agent was Joshua Edwards. The Quaker firm of Oates & Colley, of Sheffield, England, had a Philadelphia agent named George

Williams though it also sold sheet iron to the American market through the Trotters.

In Yorkshire, the wool county, merchants with whom the Trotters did business were not simply middlemen but were processors as well; that is to say, the Trotters bought woolens in Halifax or Leeds from men who performed the function of finishing the goods they sold.[7] Unlike the commission merchants of London, Birmingham, or Sheffield from whom the Trotter firm purchased, these men actually owned the products they traded in and acted on their own account rather than for others. They therefore sold at a given price without adding a commission charge. In Halifax the firm from which the Trotters bought woolens was William & John Walker; in Leeds the firm was Cookson & Waddington.[8]

The dependence of the Trotters on English merchant-agents extended from 1803 through 1821. In the midst of that period occurred the War of 1812. This war was to bring certain fundamental and far-reaching changes to Anglo-American trade, but curiously enough, these changes were not immediately perceived. Certain of the changes occurred during, and indeed in some cases were brought on by, the war itself and so were regarded as being war-connected and therefore likely to disappear once the war had ended.

Chief among these changes was the development of manufacturing in the United States. Not the war alone but the years of restrictive trade legislation which immediately preceded it had separated American importers from their English suppliers and had forced these importers to encourage domestic suppliers to turn out the semifinished goods which previously had come from England.

An example of how restrictive the embargo legislation actually was may be found in the Trotter experience. No mention of the threatened interruption in trade appears in the Trotter correspondence until 23 October 1807, when an order was sent to England to be filled only under special circumstances: "In case our public differences are accommodated & goods can be safely shipped." The embargo went into effect 22 December 1807. In the following year the Trotters received only two shipments from England: some steel and wire from Bainbridges & Brown and some sheet iron from Oates & Colley.

Trade revived again in the fall of 1809 but by 1810 new restrictions were threatened and the Trotters were again forced to warn that orders were to be honored only in case the hindrances were removed. When the Orders-in-Council *were* repealed, on 17 June 1812, the commission merchants in London immediately set about filling the Trotter orders which they had on hand: Pieschell & Schreiber to about the amount of money the Trotters had advanced to them; Bainbridges & Brown far beyond that amount. The vessel *Brilliant* was duly loaded with a large shipment of leather, copper, and wire and arrived in Philadelphia on 3 October 1812—almost four months after war had been declared. By that time the goods aboard were in high demand and brought handsome prices. Thus does war work, even for Quakers.

Except for these occasional shipments from England, the business of the Trotter firm during the period of international difficulties was restricted to the handling of such materials as could be brought from domestic producers: chiefly American-manufactured steel, sheet iron, leathers, and felting. Nathan Trotter did not take easily to dealing in domestic materials, however, for their quality and uniformity were often inferior. As has been mentioned, the business of the Trotter firm fell to a low level as the war progressed.

Following the War of 1812, Nathan quickly returned to the old way of doing business. But in certain cases he discovered that his customers would no longer pay the prices he was forced to charge for imported products as a result of recently imposed tariff duties. In leather, in felting, and in woolens, domestic producers had gone sufficiently far toward improving the quality and decreasing the cost of their products so that English imports of these materials could not command a premium price. Conceivably Trotter could have continued to purchase American-manufactured goods as he had done during the war, but in other lines the importing business still yielded higher profits than domestic goods afforded. Trotter therefore dropped the less profitable lines, and, with woolens, felting, and leathers thus eliminated, became, after 1815, a specialized dealer in metals.

For a few years after 1815, Trotter seemingly tried to ignore the great changes in production and distribution which were going on about him. He persisted in doing business with the commission merchants of London even though these respected and substantial men of affairs were gradually being bypassed in the flow of goods from England's factories to its ever-growing markets. As production mounted, the passive selling methods of the commission merchant were proving ineffectual and new methods were being found to speed the output along to customers.

Chart V

NATHAN TROTTER & COMPANY

Annual Value of Goods Purchased and Stocks on Hand, 1815–1849

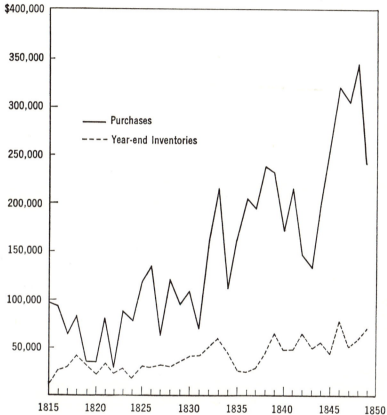

Although Trotter was slow to adjust to these broad economic movements, after 1822 it was impossible for him any longer to ignore the trend. That year marks a turning point in his business in two major respects. First he shifted the location and channels from and through which he bought his English goods: from London to Liverpool [9] and from commission merchants to sellers' agents and even directly to the manufacturer. In the same year he began to purchase some of his copper domestically, thereby bowing to the tariff in a way he had refused to do when confronted at an earlier date with a similar situation in woolen and leather goods.

Trotter adopted these changes fundamentally, because, as the expansion of industry brought about the production of increasing quantities of goods, new distributing patterns had to be found. The marketing system had to operate with new rapidity, efficiency, and directness. If the old-style merchants were not interested in pushing sales, the manufacturers were, and as the volume of Trotter's purchases expanded (see Chart V), it became increasingly worth while for the manufacturer to sell directly to the Philadelphia importers.

One of the immediate pressures operating toward a shift from London was the failure of T. Crowley Millington steel to maintain its former high quality. During 1819 and 1820 complaints poured in from Trotter's customers that Millington steel was proving inferior. No smith could make a sound axe of it. These complaints were passed on to Bainbridges & Brown and by them to the Millingtons, who declared that they had never sent Trotter a defective article. The truth finally emerged, however. As a result of changes made at the steel mill some of the output was admittedly inferior.[10] Trotter felt that his reputation as a wholesaler of the best steel had been somewhat damaged and determined to seek another source.

It was evident that the metal trade could be carried on with greater economy through Liverpool. Freight rates to Philadelphia were lower than from London; packing boxes could be obtained more cheaply; and most importantly the cost of transacting business there was lower. London merchants were still charging 2½ per cent commission; but in Liverpool, selling agents employed by copper and tin manufacturers in the hope of pushing the sale of their products, charged the customer no commission whatsoever.[11] They were reimbursed, instead, on a commission basis by the manufacturer himself. In a sense this was a price-shading device. Apparently manufacturers believed that it was worth their while to take a slightly lower price if by so doing they could count on an agent who, being tied to them directly, would aggressively promote their products.

The old era was passing, the period when the commission merchant carried the burden of financing the Anglo-American trade. Under the old system the merchant had granted nine months' credit and had allowed a discount for earlier payments. This did not mean that he always received payment within the prescribed period; frequently he did not, and in such cases he charged interest on the uncollected balance. It was a leisurely system devised to operate in leisurely times.

After Trotter had shifted from London to Liverpool, he was forced to accept shorter and shorter credit periods. The agents in Liverpool were doubtless firms with much less capital than the established London merchants and were not in a position to extend long credits. Typical terms of credit granted by the Liverpool agents were "3 & 3 Mos. or 1/—p box discount for bill drawn at 3 mos," or for large monthly amounts "5 & 1 mo." These terms meant apparently that Trotter was permitted six months in which to pay but, if at the close of three (or five) months he had not paid, he had to send a bill of exchange payable at the close of the credit period.

On one occasion when Nathan Trotter suggested that the Liverpool agents adopt the discount and interest policy of the London commission merchant, the agents flatly refused because, they said, they would be forced in that case to make a cash advance of the amount to the manufacturer on the date of the invoice.

The immediate inducement to change from London suppliers in 1822 was doubtless the establishment of a line of sailing vessels operating regularly between Liverpool and Philadelphia. Previously the best Philadelphia shipping connections had been with London. A number of vessels had been operated by Philadelphia men on the run to London, and Trotter had preferred to have his goods sent on these ships above all others. "I decidedly give our Philadelphia ships the preference to the New England vesels," he wrote to Bainbridges & Brown on 18 November 1815. At the end of the war two new vessels, the *Electra* and the *Factor*, had been added to the London run. These ships in 1812 were still the regular spring-and-fall sailing vessels as was also another new vessel, the *Tontine*, put on the London run in 1818.

Seemingly Trotter was well satisfied with the service these ships gave. They were fast and speed was important, especially when the cargo was tin plate which was easily injured by excessive dampness. Furthermore, it was always a great advantage to have goods by the first ship so as to profit from the top price, and some of the old-time Philadelphia shipmasters took pride in making the earliest crossing of each season.

Nevertheless, the new Liverpool monthly packet lines made the old London runs seem antiquated and inefficient. The first line of packets operating between Liverpool and Philadelphia was established in 1821 by Thomas P. Cope, a Philadelphia merchant. The line is referred to in the Trotter papers as Brown & Company's line or the "regular packets." William & John Brown & Company were the Liverpool agents, and both Cope and Alexander Brown & Sons of Baltimore owned ships in the line.[12] Within three years two additional lines were competing for the Philadelphia business: the Welsh line, established in 1822, and the Walker line in 1824.[13]

The new packets operated on a regular schedule, sailing from each port on a certain day each month. By so doing they eliminated much of the business risk that had been attendant on doing business in the old way. The spring and fall sailings of the earlier period had meant a time span of four, six, or eight months between order and receipt of goods. The price limits set by Nathan in December might be too high for a profitable sale in April or May. Various sizes of copper ordered in April might not be salable six months later, while the amount might prove far too large in a period of declining business.

In a letter written to Bainbridges & Brown on 11 December 1815, Nathan Trotter sets forth the difficulties of planning his purchases many months in advance:

British goods of almost all kinds . . . have depressed in price consider-ably. I have considered it therefore most prudent to be rather more limited in my Spring importations. Should this countermanding letter not reach in time to reduce all then please let it have its operation on such articles that I want omitted, that are not obtained by you for me. I am very sorry to trouble you with so many additions and Subtractions but it is very difficult to tell Six months ahead what will suit to import.

With the establishment of the Cope Liverpool line, Nathan could receive shipments about ten months of the year and could rid himself of the rigidities inherent in "Orders for Spring" and "Orders for Fall." He could carry a smaller inventory and reduce the risk of loss by price fluctuations. He could more quickly adjust to changes in demand for special sizes and weights. He could more accurately judge the quantity of goods likely to be ordered by his customers and could have enough on hand to meet demand without having to carry extensive inventories. Perhaps most importantly, payments to his English suppliers could be spread over nearly the entire year instead of grouping themselves into two peaks of outlay on a seasonal basis.

Summarizing the earlier procurement methods as we leave the 1803–1821 period, we see that the relationship of the Trotters with their sources of supply was simple. Their goods came chiefly from England and were purchased for them by three or four commission merchants and by two cloth-finishing merchants. The commission merchants assembled the comparatively small amounts of goods ordered by the Trotters and by other freight-renting importers, thus performing a marketing function which Trotter at his distance and with his scale of operations could not have performed for himself.

Looking ahead to the years from 1822 to 1849, we shall find the story of Nathan Trotter's purchasing pattern becoming more complex to present. As the quantity of a particular import increased, Trotter gradually bypassed the middleman and went directly to the manufacturer. Consequently dozens of Trotter-manufacturer relationships developed in the purchase of English goods. In addition, tariffs led Trotter to form associations with a number of American manufacturers. Only in the purchase of commodities in small amounts, bargain lots of tin plates, and pig metals did he continue to use the old-style commission merchant to any great extent. At the same time he employed specialized business auxiliaries: namely, the forwarding agent and the paying agent who took over part of the functions which the commission merchant had once performed for him.

It is impossible to give a still picture of Nathan Trotter's purchasing methods in 1822–1849. He dealt in a variety of goods obtained from multiple sources and used many channels of trade at once—English and American purchasing agents, manufacturers, manufacturers' selling agents, wholesaling importers—whichever source yielded the most favorable price. Trotter himself never thought of his purchases as having any particular pattern or design. He was always looking for opportunities to make a profit, and, since opportunities were always shifting, his business was constantly shifting also. There was some trial and error, but in the end calculations in dollars and cents determined the choice of supplier. Certain generalizations may be made, but once made they must always be qualified, for few generalizations apply to Trotter's business over more than a brief period of time.

Tin plate was, throughout Nathan Trotter's business career, a product of English manufacture. Indeed from the late 1830's on it was the article that bulked largest among Trotter's imported goods. There were many English manufacturers, especially in Wales and Staffordshire. When Trotter had transferred his tin-plate orders to Liverpool in 1822, he had shifted to the tin manufacturers' selling agents. Competition with Anson Phelps of New York caused him to order directly from the manufacturer, as an even more economical means of getting the article.

Phelps was the dominant figure in the American tin-plate market after about 1822 (and for the rest of Nathan's mercantile life). His name was synonymous with tin plate, Trotter had once said. Phelps had a contract with the Pontypool manufacturers of tin plate by which, so it was reported, he got cheaper freight rates in exchange for agreeing to have shipped to him each month a specified number of tons on the packets. To every one in the trade it was a mystery how Phelps could sell at the prices he did and still make a profit.[14] From the references to Anson Phelps' practices in the Trotter papers, it appears that he aimed at large sales and was content with a small profit per sale. Apparently he also bought tin plate of all qualities and sold boxes of both the good and the poorer quality in the same lot. The Phelps firm had agents in many cities and Anson personally marketed his goods aggressively. He sold to handicraftsmen or retailers of tin plate at about the price he sold to Trotter, a wholesaler. At least that was Trotter's constant complaint. But in spite of the vigorous competition of the Anson Phelps enterprise, the Trotter firm became known chiefly as a dealer in tin plate.

Trotter's first practical opportunity to buy directly from a tin manufacturer came unsolicited, when in 1824 he received a letter from the firm of Richard Blakemore & Company which operated the Melin Griffith Works, near Cardiff in Wales. In this letter Blakemore informed Trotter that his establishments at Cardiff and at Pentyrch were "among the most extensive and oldest establishments in Great Britain." Apparently Blakemore had been experiencing the same shift in marketing methods that Trotter had felt, for he wrote: "Friends thro' whose medium our manufacture has been accustomed to be introduced into consumption have been deter'd from making their ordinary Exports." Blakemore, therefore, had wished to sell directly to the wholesaler in America and to accomplish this end he was willing to offer the same terms he offered to wholesalers in England: namely, a 5 per cent discount for all orders of 300 boxes or more.

Blakemore's letter led to direct purchases by Nathan Trotter during the years from 1826 to 1829. Thereafter, however, the Trotter-Blakemore connection was discontinued, in part because a price war had broken out between Anson Phelps and a competitor in New York, making it cheaper for Trotter to buy tin from his fellow importers in the New York market. Equally important was the difficulty experienced in getting Blakemore's tin plate from Wales to Liverpool in time for the sailing of the regular Philadelphia packets. Whenever connections were missed storage charges had to be met.

It therefore remained for the young Trotters, Edward and Joseph, Jr., while on their trip abroad in 1835–1836, to effect a connection with British tin-plate manufacturers which was to be enduring. One of the new connections was with John and Edmund Walker, of Gospel Oak Works, in Staffordshire.[15] The second was with Robert Smith & Company, of the Margam Works in Taibach, Glamorganshire, Wales. The Margam Works were soon sold to Motley, Fussell & Company and by them to the great firm of Wm. Llewellyn & Sons, the largest manufacturers of tin plate in England. After 1843, therefore, most of Trotter's tin plate came either from the Walkers of Gospel Oak Works or from the Margam Works of the Llewellyns.

The tin plate and terneplate produced by the firm of John and Edmund Walker met with special favor among Trotter's customers, for it was "cut true so as to form square corners." The Walkers' plate was therefore especially advantageous in the piecing together of tin roofs, for it was easily fitted and produced little or no scrap. The Walkers themselves wrote: [16]

Since we commenced the manufacture of "Walkers" brand, our object has been to produce a tinplate superior and more regular than any in the market, & by all accounts we have succeeded, but it cannot be done without extra cost, and, unless we can obtain a proportionate price, we might as well manufacture an inferior article, which is in great demand, & with infinitely less trouble, is almost, or quite as profitable—

However we prefer having a reputation for turning out the best work, & we shall try to deserve it as long as we can get a moderate profit.

Nathan Trotter wished to be the exclusive dealer of Walkers' tin plate in the United States and requested that the boxes be marked "Walkers   NT & Co." With this marking request the Walkers complied, but they were reluctant to give Trotter an exclusive dealership, though they did give reassurances such as this: "We continue to refuse any orders we think may possibly interfere with you & we believe it is 3 years or more since a box of our tin has entered the States except thro' your hands." At least twice Anson Phelps endeavored to import Walkers' plate but without success.[17]

The Walkers' supply of tin plate was limited, however. In 1845 they manufactured only about 200 boxes weekly. They could not, therefore, fill all of Trotter's orders, or as fast as he sometimes wished. By the

1840's tin plate had become the largest item of importation by the Trotter firm.

Trotter tried to induce the Walkers to sell to him on a fixed-price basis, but the latter were reluctant to enter into any such agreement in view of the limited capacity of their works and the number of months required to fill an order of any size. On one occasion, when Trotter feared that prices might soon be rising, he proposed a fixed price contract and was told by the Walkers that they preferred to charge him the going rate at the date of shipment from their works.

On at least one occasion, however, the Walkers yielded to Trotter's request and contracted to ship 2,000 boxes at 32 shillings a box. As luck would have it, the arrangement turned out badly for Trotter. A letter from the Walkers dated 11 May 1849 reads:

> . . . you will now hardly thank us for fixing your 2000 Boxes at 32/ as proposed in yours of April 2nd, and we do think you had better have left the price to us at the time of shipment.
> We do not speculate either in sales or purchases, our wish being to do a steady business [interlineated: which is however almost impossible in these days] we shall therefore charge you 32/ IC as long as we may fairly do so, and if the price receeds further, but we do not think it likely, we shall give you the benefit of such fall at the time of shipment.

Trotter's other principal supplier of tin, the Llewellyns, also avoided fixed price contracts. They wrote: [18]

> If you will trust us to put the lowest value of the time on all we send you —you may rely on our doing rightly at all times—of course you can [interlineated: & it will be best] to put a limit beyond which it will not be safe for you to import, to which we will adhere strictly.

Despite their reluctance the Llewellyns had less to fear from fixed-price arrangements than the Walkers. As the largest combination of tin-plate and terneplate manufacturers in England, they had greater flexibility in meeting their shipping schedules, though even they were seriously embarrassed when a drought in 1844 cut water power and caused them to fall behind in filling their orders. "This unparalleled dry weather, from which the country is suffering very severely," they wrote, "has now lasted 10 weeks, has dried up every stream, & thrown us entirely upon our steam power." Even in the 1840's England's manufacturing plants had not converted so completely to steam power as to be unaffected by droughts.

The Llewellyns were also in a position to influence the movement in tin-plate prices. Though they may not have been strong enough to take the lead in advancing prices, they took credit, on at least two occasions, for preventing their competitors from moving prices upward. On 8 March 1849 they wrote to Trotter: "The manufers at a meeting at Bristol on Wednesday were inclined to increase prices, but they kept to the above upon our refusing to join in the movement."

Table 4

Nathan Trotter & Company
Tin-Plate Importations from England in 1846

| | Number of Boxes by Source | | |
Date received in Philadelphia	Walkers	Llewellyns	Jevons
2 February	260		
6 February	212		
9 March	60		
25 March	415		
30 March		1,000	
22 April	500		
3 June		1,187	
? June		1,000	
19 June	1,047	1,500	
30 June	324		
29 August	450		
17 September	644	1,800	300
1 October			300
26 October	500	1,000	
13 November	328		500
Total shipments for 1846	4,740	7,487	1,100

And on 5 February of the following year they wrote: "The makers of Tin Plates will meet on Thursday the 7th, & we *fear* they will attempt to raise Tin Plate still higher. In the hopes of frustrating that intention we have [interlineated: as the largest Manufacturers] issued Circulars fixing our wholesale prices as above stated. To run up prices will be but to serve and assist the purpose of speculators, and to injure all who are legitimately engaged in the trade here and abroad." Despite their strong position, the Llewellyns stood firm against any suggestion from Trotter that they contract for future delivery at a given price.

It may be of interest to list the quantities imported during 1846, as a sample year, together with the dates on which shipments were received in Philadelphia (see Table 4). It will be noted that shipments from the Llewellyns far exceeded those from other firms.

As Trotter moved toward buying his goods directly from the English manufacturer, such as the Walkers and the Llewellyns, he came to operate on shorter credit terms and more regularly paid cash and took the discount. In 1821 Trotter had already come to regard as vital to his business the discounts which might in some cases be obtained by sending a remittance to accompany an order. As he wrote: ". . . on that depends in a great measure our profits." [19] In 1822, when he first began purchasing directly from a manufacturer, the firm of Naylor & Sanderson offered him four months' credit or a discount of 5 per cent

Table 5

Nathan Trotter & Company
Interest on Foreign Account and Gross Profit Figures, 1840–1849

Year	Interest on foreign accounts [a]	Gross profits [b]
1840	$2,886.25	$24,578.95
1841		26,363.27
1842	4,473.80	10,000.00
1843	3,289.18	23,537.01
1844		25,777.97
1845	8,712.08	32,817.60
1846	5,844.24	31,820.44
1847		42,061.66
1848	10,065.36	34,398.50
1849	7,727.54	45,707.00

[a] Obtainable for these years only. The "Interest on foreign accounts" figures represent the cash discount.
[b] Computed by subtracting the invoice cost of foreign and domestic goods (before cash discount) from total sales for the year. See also Appendix 5.

for cash with the order. Twenty years later, in purchasing such items as tin plate, Trotter almost always took advantage of the cash discount, although by that time the amount of the discount frequently declined to 3 per cent. In effect his growing capital was enabling him to buy for cash and at the same time extend his personal credit to his American customers; thus Trotter was helping to replace the English capitalist in financing American trade.

Trotter kept a separate record of the amount of money which he saved by his ability to buy English goods for cash. This he called Interest on Foreign Accounts. As Table 5 indicates, savings which Trotter made by paying cash for his foreign goods added significantly to his profits for the year.

Although tin plate bulked large in the Trotters' business and was to remain an important article of their trade for several generations, it is not so representative of the changing nature of their business as were certain other metals, such as copper. Tin plate remained for decades an imported article; indeed it was one of the few metals which

Nathan Trotter and his descendants regularly obtained from abroad. Most other metals came to be obtained from American sources. In the years before the Civil War, America's great wealth in mineral resources was beginning to be exploited, and domestic manufacturers of semimanufactured metals were beginning to spring up. After the War of 1812 these manufacturers, of one product after another, obtained for their own benefit a protective tariff. Apparently the protection operated greatly to their advantage. It may be true, as has sometimes been alleged, that American industries in most instances started without the assistance of a tariff. But if the Trotter records are any indication of what was taking place, these rising tariffs must have greatly assisted the domestic producer to overcome foreign competition. Time after time, as new tariffs were imposed, Trotter shifted from his foreign sources of supply and gave his business instead to local manufacturers.

Trotter's purchase of copper provides a good example of how these shifts occurred. Some copper products, such as sheathing, were not protected by the tariff and these Trotter continued to obtain in England. But other products, especially braziers copper, he came to buy domestically.

The tariff on braziers copper was levied by the Act of 1816. Trotter complained of the heavy duty, but at first he made no attempt to purchase any but the imported article, perhaps because, so he wrote his customers, he did not think that there could be a "certain dependance for a regular supply on the domestic product." Although he was able to effect economies in freight and in methods of packing and to save commissions, he complained in 1822 that his profit on copper did not amount to 5 per cent. Finally he was forced to admit that "superior" braziers copper was manufactured in the United States and could be sold "in detail"—to consumers, usually in small lots—at about his cost of importation. American braziers copper had generally superseded the English. Nathan then turned to Baltimore for much of his supply, particularly of braziers pattern sheets and later strips for locomotive pipes. Sheathing, which was often duty free, and bottoms, usually unobtainable from the American manufacturers,[20] were still imported.

In the English copper industry for some reason there seems to have occurred more competition among the manufacturers than among the dealers. Copper was produced in England in the 1820's by a number of well-established firms. James Shears & Sons was, as noted, a producer of high-quality sheathing and other fine copper products, as were also the Harfords. Others were John Freeman & Company, Vivian & Sons, Newton Lyon & Company, and Williams & Grenfell.

In the years following the War of 1812 the Grenfell house was rumored to have tried to "rule the Trade," [21] and the price of English copper fell so low that Trotter found he could import even braziers copper despite the American tariff. But, he wrote, should the higher rate return, English copper "would not answer, owing to the American make, which is in very good repute, and is selling, other than sheathing as low as we can import it—as we have to contend with a heavy duty. . . ." [22]

When Trotter shifted his buying from London to Liverpool, he purchased sheathing made by Vivian & Sons and by Newton Lyon & Company. The Vivian & Sons copper was sold to Trotter through the manufacturer's agent, Mather Parkes & Company.[23] The Newton Lyon & Company copper was at first sold by George B. Brown on a commission basis. Brown was a relative of Thomas Brown of Bainbridges & Brown and had made the shift from London to Liverpool, though he had remained a commission merchant and had not become a manufacturer's agent. It was not long, therefore, before Trotter had also bypassed him and was purchasing copper from the manufacturers, Newton Lyon & Company, directly.[24]

The connection between Trotter and the Newton Lyon firm remained close for the duration of Trotter's activities as a copper importer, and, when his son Edward and his nephew Joseph Trotter were in England, they were instructed by Nathan to call on the Newton Lyon firm. Edward wrote his father about the reception he and his cousin had received: [25]

> Mr. Lyon has devoted his entire time to us going with us to visit the different curiosities of this place and paying us every other attention he could think of—we dined with him in company with a large party of gentlemen and Ladies and after the cloth was removed Mr. Lyon in a neat speech expressive of the great satisfaction he had experienced in doing business with thee proposed us a toast the health of his friend Mr. Nathan Trotter to which I responded as well as I knew how.

When Trotter turned to domestically produced copper, Baltimore was a center of pig copper importation in this country, and a number of firms there were engaged in the business of rolling copper. The copper company of John McKim, Jr.—whose partner had been Levi Hollingsworth up to the time of Hollingsworth's death [26]—supplied Trotter with braziers copper, particularly pattern sheets, from 1822 until 1828. Then, when the McKims often did not fill his orders either because of lack of pig or because of previous orders, Nathan shifted for two years to E. T. Ellicott of the Avalon Company, for whom he sold on commission.[27] When Ellicott turned from rolling copper to roll-

Table 6

Nathan Trotter & Company
Annual Purchases of Copper from American and English Firms, 1829–1833

Year	American	English
1829	$ 5,015.58	$ 983.72
1830	19,828.27	4,642.42
1831	27,775.58	10,262.03
1832	31,166.51	23,280.59
1833	37,595.49	15,024.86

ing iron because of lack of copper and scant profits, Trotter purchased from another McKim, Isaac, who for ten years was almost his exclusive American source of supply, and then from Isaac's successors, William and Hazlett McKim. Between 1846 and 1849, when William and Hazlett gave up the copper business, Trotter purchased from the New Yorkers, Hendricks Brothers, whose Soho plant in Belleville, New Jersey, was one of the oldest in the country, or from Phelps Dodge & Company, who had a copper mill in Connecticut.

Isaac McKim, merchant, shipowner, member of Congress, and flour-mill owner, had turned his steam power from flour to copper in 1828 shortly before Ellicott gave up the copper business.[28] There was little difference in the quality of copper manufactured by these Baltimore firms; Ellicott wrote, 17 June 1828: "It is manufactured on the same plan—of the same material, and frequently by the same workmen, who are passing from one establishment to the other. Isaac McKim's workmen mostly learn the business with us." It was easy to get goods sent on from Baltimore and, except when he lacked a supply of pig, Isaac McKim could fill large orders promptly. The quality was good and the price satisfactory. "I have always put the price of my copper rather lower to your House than any other," Isaac McKim declared at one time.

The story of Trotter's procurement of brass products is not unlike that of copper. The effect of a tariff came somewhat later, but its results were the same. For certain articles, especially those of high quality, Trotter continued to depend on English sources, but otherwise his purchases shifted to the United States.

In England Trotter obtained his sheet brass, brass wire, rivets, and kettle ears, from a Birmingham commission house which maintained a representative in Philadelphia. This English firm of Belles & Harrold and later that firm's Harrold successors, charged, for assembling various goods a commission of 2½, 5, and 10 per cent, depending on the goods purchased.

The tariff of 1824 increased the duty on brass from 20 to 25 per cent and caused Trotter to look more intensively for American suppliers, though he continued to make some purchases from Harrolds. Even before the tariff was increased, Trotter remarked that his orders for English brass wire were limited, chiefly to heavy sizes, as a result of the extensive manufactures in the United States.[29]

The Naugatuck Valley of Connecticut was at that time becoming an important brass manufacturing center. By 1834, when Trotter's stock of English sheet brass was greatly reduced, since "the recent heavy duty on it added to the substitution of American Brass at lower rates has rendered importations unprofitable,"[30] he turned to the Waterbury, Connecticut, firm of Holmes, Hotchkiss & Company and later to their successor Brown & Elton for sheet brass and brass wire.

Iron wire was protected in the Tariff Act of 1816 and of 1824 by a duty of 5 cents a pound on sizes through Number 18 and 9 cents on sizes over that number; yet during the 1820's Trotter continued to import most of his wire. In a letter of 1829 he commented that wire of very good quality was made in the United States at about 20 per cent under importing cost. He then began a search for a domestic wire he considered good. From a manufacturer's agent, A. Norrie & Company of New York, he turned to the manufacturers, G. Small & Sons of York, Pennsylvania. To his annoyance, the production problems of this firm appeared greater than the amount of wire they produced. Trotter still had not found a satisfactory domestic source when he wrote Wm. Harrold & Sons in 1834: ". . . the American article has so supplied the place of the imported & is protected by such an enormous duty of 5 & 9 Cents pr # that we have fear'd to import any as it appeared certain loss to do so." An order for English wire was accompanied by the comment: "We really don't expect to make it much object [to purchase English as well as American wire] but some of our customers ask for English wire and we must have a supply of both." [31]

Finally in 1837, by which time Trotter declared that nine-tenths of the wire used in Philadelphia was American, he found a satisfactory source of supply in Rodenbough Stewart & Company of Easton, Pennsylvania. Nathan Trotter occasionally differed with them about terms; he and Rodenbough each considered the other shrewd in business transactions. But as to quality, Trotter seems to have agreed with this description in the Franklin Institute's pamphlet on exhibits of 1842: Rodenbough Stewart & Company's samples were "very superior articles . . . [which] reflect the highest credit upon the makers, especially the *finest* wire. Both samples are round, well polished in the drawing, of uniform thickness, and extremely pliable and tough."

English brass battery kettles had been manufactured for decades by the old firm of Harfords Brass & Battery Company of Bristol. Their product was good but their methods antiquated, according to American reports. Nathan's son, Edward Trotter, wrote his father in January, 1836: "Harfords were made for the last century not for this with an establishment which looks [as] if it were big enough to Swallow Bristol. An order for a few Cwt of Brass Kettles takes them till June to execute."

In the 1840's, Trotter began purchasing American-made battery kettles. The Wolcottville Brass Company in Connecticut, by the time Trotter began dealing with it, had lived through the experimental period, so the historian of the brass companies of the Naugatuck Valley reports, and were reaping huge profits.[32] In his correspondence with them in 1844 and 1845, Trotter complained because they did not fill his orders promptly and wrote that they, as well as other manufacturers, were squeezing the wholesaler. To L. W. Coe, Secretary of the Wolcottville Brass Company, he wrote, 12 July 1844:

We are the friends of a judicious protective Tariff as operating for the general benefit of the Country; but our individual interests are Sadly invaded upon by its operation. we cant all be Manufacturers. Some *Must* buy and Sell & many such have been in the habit for many years importing their goods, and that mode is to a great extent Superceded by Fabrics made at home—now as to this change *we* have no kind of objection, if we could be supplied by the makers on terms both equitable & liberal—and that wd in Some measure reconcile the deprivation we have had to submit to—But we have found our Sales of certain articles much abridged and profits cut off by the Manufacturs Supplying *Consumers,* even with small comparative quantities, so near what we must pay that all inducements are abstracted and our sales confined to such as the Makers dont know, or they dont know the Makers. . . .

And later to the same firm, when they failed to fill his orders, he complained: [33]

The season for selling Brass Kettles is rapidly passing away   Customers have been promised that we should have them. . . . The excluding of the foreign article by a heavy duty would have been reconcilable to those who had depended on importations provided they could have been supplied at home on terms affording them some little profit   but to be deprived of the article in our Sales by so heavy charge on imports and non Supply at home presents a feature in regard to the Tariff rather onerous.

Sheet iron was at first obtained from English commission merchants and then from such sheet-iron and tin-plate manufacturers as Blakemore and the Walkers. Russian sheet iron, usually of Yacovleff's make, was purchased from Boston or New York importers or brokers and occasionally from houses in St. Petersburg, usually on London credits. J. D. Lewis and Thomas Wright & Company were two such firms. Some purchases were made of William Ropes & Company of St. Petersburg and 36 India Wharf, Boston, Massachusetts.

Duties had been placed on sheet iron, but there were few complaints about it in the Trotter correspondence. In 1844, following a drought which curtailed American production by water power, Nathan Trotter declared he had never been so put out about sheet iron. He had been depending on a supply from certain mills in the United States and ordered but little from England because of the heavy duties and costs. Consequently he found himself with neither English nor American.

Abraham Sharpless (1748–1835), owner of the Pennsylvania Slitting Mill in Thornbury, Pennsylvania, from whom Trotter obtained sheet iron in the 1820's and 1830's, was another of the men who ranked with Anson Phelps and Isaac McKim in the Trotter correspondence. He was described by Nathan Trotter as a grand old patriarch. Incidentally he made sheet iron of such good quality Trotter could find a market for it with Phelps Dodge & Company. After the death of Sharpless, Trotter procured sheet iron from two nearby firms: A. J. & T. Roman (later Joseph Roman & Son) of the Octoraro Mills, Port Deposit, Maryland, and C. & J. Marshall & Company of Marshallton near Newport, Delaware.

The purchase of steel did not conform to the general shifting nature of Trotter's procurements. Indeed Trotter never bought steel from American producers except in the period of embargo and the War of 1812. It will be recalled that after the War of 1812 he had been disappointed in the imports of T. Crowley Millington steel and had decided to change to new sources of supply. He turned directly to the English manufacturer, Naylor & Sanderson, of Sheffield (and after the dissolution of that partnership in 1829 to the firm of Sanderson Brothers & Company). This firm, in 1823, effected a vertical integration with several other steel firms so that it was able to advertise that its steel was "commenced & entirely finished" under its own inspection. By 1830, however, Trotter was selling Sandersons' steel only on commission, which meant that he had given up stocking it himself, and by 1840 he had practically discontinued the sale of English steel.

Tinners' tools and machines were purchased only in the United States. J. & E. North, J. & W. Buckley, and Wilcox & Roys made tinners' tools. Their output was small at first. The sickness or death of a workman so a firm wrote, "puts us back a good deal." Cold weather at times made it impossible to grind and finish. These manufacturers later expanded their plants and there was considerable competition between them, especially from 1837 to 1842. In January of 1842 Trotter received a statement of the "prices established and agreed to" by these manufacturers, but before the year was out two of the three firms offered to reduce their prices.

Tinners' machines were purchased of Peck Smith & Company, Plant Neal & Company, and S. Stow & Company—all of Southington, Connecticut. There was keen competition between these firms, also. "We would like our prices kept confidential and we will do, as well if not a little better than any other manufacturer," runs one letter of 1847. Little wonder that eventually, from this Connecticut competition, emerged the firm of Peck, Stow, & Wilcox.

Various other firms supplied the Trotters. The New Englanders, Farris Edes & Company of Plymouth, Massachusetts, furnished the type of rivets which suited Trotter and his customers. The Cornells of New York, with a factory for the manufacture of sheet lead at Port Chester filled his orders for that product; while zinc—another sheet metal—was obtained from the New York agents, Peter Remsen & Company and their successors, and finally from the manufacturer himself.

Eventually Trotter became an agent for the Belgian manufacturers of zinc, The Vieille Montagne Society.

To explain how pig metals were obtained throughout this period is difficult. The methods varied so greatly that up to 1849 not so much of a general pattern appeared as in the semimanufactured metal market.

A few generalizations can, however, be made. New York was the most important domestic market. Boston and Salem from time to time were sources of pig tin and Baltimore of imported and American pig and ingot copper. But most of the time for most of the metals, New York predominated.

Pig metals were obtained in New York from the regular old-time importing firms and, increasingly, from brokers who wrote short informational letters full of "goods afloat," "cash," "goods to arrive," and bargains offered "if unsold when I hear from you."

The pig-metal marketing system did not function as smoothly as the system for semimanufactured goods.[34] There were times, of course, when the market was bare of both types of goods. But the flow of raw metals seemed, from the Trotter correspondence at least, more irregular. There is mention of Indians retarding the Missouri lead supply, late arrival of ships delaying receipts of pig copper, and speculation preventing the broker from purchasing pig tin.

In making payment for his goods, Trotter encountered remarkably little difficulty whether the goods came from home or abroad. This is in marked contrast to the experience described as of the middle of the eighteenth century by Baxter in his study of *The House of Hancock*. Because it was possible in his time to buy bills of exchange, Trotter was not forced to carry on a roundabout trade to pay for his English imports. Much of Trotter's facility in effecting easy payment can be attributed to the close family connection with the Bank of Pennsylvania. The only occasion when he found payments difficult were in times of depression and in those periods everyone had the same experience. Except in such unusual times as the depression of 1837–1842 bills of exchange were readily available.

In the 1803–1815 period, the bills which the Trotters purchased were chiefly bills drawn by well-known Philadelphians on their English correspondents. Among these sellers were John Warder & Son, Elliston & John Perot, John C. DaCosta, and William Montgomery & Son. Doubtless these men obtained their bills in exchange for the grain and other commodities which they exported and services—such as shipping—which they rendered the English payers of the bills.

Bills from Britain's colonies began to be purchased about 1826 and continued to be a source of foreign payment for decades. Although it is not clear how all these bills came into the Philadelphia market, their initial purchase may well have been associated with the fact that in 1826 England forbade the British colonies to trade with the United States.[35] The bills originated in Bermuda, Halifax, St. John, and various West Indian islands. They were drawn often on Her Majesty's Treasury, the Commercial Bank of London, the Union Bank of London, and such big Lombard Street private banking houses as Mastermann & Company, Glyn, Hallifax, Mills & Company, and Smith, Payne, & Smith. Twelve out of Trotter's 19 purchases of bills of exchange in 1830 were on Halifax, St. John, and Bermuda.

By the 1830's and early 1840's cotton bills from southern states were purchased by the Trotter firm in large amounts. Of the 56 bills which they purchased in 1840, 43 were from the South: 30 were dated Lynchburg, the others were from Richmond, New Orleans, Clarkesville in Tennessee, and Charleston in South Carolina. In the 1820's a number of the old cotton houses had failed and possibly this had resulted in a change to Philadelphia for the marketing of cotton bills.

Throughout the period from 1803 to 1849 the 60-day bill predominated: 50 out of the 56 purchased in 1840 were for that term; and most bills were payable in London even though drawn on a house in Liverpool, Manchester, or Glasgow.

Often Trotter, particularly in the early years, purchased bills in a casual fashion. He might receive from Joshua Emlen, the Philadelphia merchant, a note stating "I want to sell £400 Stg on Bainbridges & Brown. Do you want it at the current rate which I believe is about 8 pr ct?" Or perhaps he met his friend Hahn at the Merchants Exchange and obtained some bills from him there.

Beginning about the year 1830 the Bank of Pennsylvania became an important source of the Trotter firm's bills: in 1840, 31 out of a total of 56 were purchased of that Bank. Many of the southern bills were obtained from that source. These bills had been endorsed first by bank officials of southern banks and secondly by an official of the Philadelphia bank from which they were purchased.

A great many of the West Indian bills were obtained from two Front Street biscuit bakers and represent doubtless the proceeds from

Philadelphians' sales to the British colonials. Purchases of bills of exchange from the Philadelphia private bankers, a development which in the second half of the nineteenth century came to predominate in the Trotter firm's methods, were gradually appearing by 1840. In 1849 about one-fifth of the total number of bills purchased by the Trotters was drawn by Browns & Bowen on Brown, Shipley & Company.

Table 7

Monthly Rates of Exchange on England from the Trotter Accounts and from the New York Market, 1824 and 1826

	Jan.	*Feb.*	*Mar.*	*Apr.*	*May*	*June*	*July*	*Aug.*	*Sept.*	*Oct.*	*Nov.*	*Dec.*
1824												
Trotter bills [a]	7¾	7¾	—	8¾	—	9	9	—	9¼	—	9½	9½
New York bills [b]	7½	7¾	8¼	9	8¾	9	9	8½	9¼	10	9¼	9½
1826												
Trotter bills [a]	8	8	7¾	7	9½	9½	10	10	10	12	11⅛	11
New York bills [b]	8½	8½	8	7⅛	10	9¼	10¼	10	11	12¾	11½	11

[a] First purchase of the month.

[b] Purchased in time for the first packet for England of each month (*The Banker's Magazine,* II, 532).

It is perhaps significant that the Philadelphia money market apparently lacked exchange in guilders and florins since bills for these currencies were almost always purchased from a Baltimore or New York house. But bills on England were normally available in the Philadelphia market. The daybook records usually that bills which Trotter purchased on a certain day might be remitted to England that same day or at least within a week.

The prices which Trotter paid for bills, at least as the two sample years in Table 7 would indicate, matched New York prices fairly closely.

In the early years, when considerable time elapsed between the receipt of goods and remittance of bills, it was difficult for the firm to estimate the final cost of goods and the profits on them. Premiums on bills of exchange might range between 4 and 10 per cent, and since bills were, of course, an item regularly included in the cost, it was only after Trotter had purchased his exchange that he could finally estimate what his imports cost him.

In times of severe depression Trotter's payments abroad and at home became difficult. By June of 1837 it was at least expensive, if not impossible, to get good bills on England. If a satisfactory bill came into the market it was instantly seized and it was only by accident that Trotter was able to obtain one, even at a premium of 18 per cent.

On one occasion in 1837 Nathan Trotter sent to his correspondents Jevons Sons & Company as payment a Certificate of Loan of the Lehigh Coal & Navigation Company, amounting to $15,000, with directions that it be converted into funds "not more detrimental than bills at 10% premium." The transaction almost caused a break in the long-standing friendship between the two houses. Jevons, in the course of an acknowledgment, concluded that the sooner Trotter replaced the Loan Certificate "with something marketable the better." Not until the middle of September was Nathan Trotter able to secure a bill with which to replace the Loan Certificates. He described his difficulties to Jevons in these words: [36]

. . . there has hardly been a day for a fortnight past but what we have been in search of something to remit you—but where there are fifty buyers to one seller it is almost impossible to get hold of a bill offered for sale, as its seldom on hand an hour—to have the funds provided to pay, having the greatest anxiety to do so, and yet find so much difficulty in effecting it thro the medium of Bills gives us much concern and unpleasant feelings . . . the writer spent two hours this mong and succeeded after much running in getting a Bill for 1000 £ at 21% prem: and which you have herewith and he much desires by the packet of 20th to send more. . . .

The debt was finally settled by bills at 17 and 20 per cent, at an expense, so Trotter wrote, "equal to our profit on 12 or 1500 Boxes Tin."

Nathan Trotter's credit had always been, as he said, a matter of pride and "deep feeling" with him. Correspondents at home and abroad spoke of the satisfaction they always had in his punctuality. Even in the trying times of the depression of 1837, one English correspondent wrote: "We cannot conclude without expressing our thanks to you for the handsome manner in which you have continued your remittances to us in such difficult times."

On occasions Trotter opened letters of credit with English firms in order to pay for English, Russian, and Oriental imports or to provide for Edward Trotter's needs on his European tour in 1836. Timothy Wiggin supplied some credit at that time and Edward recorded a most unfavorable impression of this London banker whose firm's crash shortly shook the financial world.[37] "Every one to whom we have had letters," he declared, "have shown us every attention except

Mr. Wiggin. He is one of those cold blooded mortals who if they can gain a sixpence out of you, you may find out what is to be seen and heard as you best can."

One letter of credit transaction proved most unsatisfactory to Nathan Trotter in 1837.[38] This was in connection with the bankers, Morrison, Cryder & Company. John Cryder had been a fellow passenger of the young Trotters on their voyage to England and he seems to have taken an interest in them. "At the particular request of Mr. Cryder," they attended a ball at the "Collisseum" in London, and shortly afterwards Cryder wrote Nathan Trotter that he would be happy to render him any "Banking or monied assistance . . . without however wishing to interfere" with any arrangements Trotter might already have.

Trotter arranged with Cryder for a credit, purchased goods from a firm with whom he had not previously dealt, and requested the firm to draw on Morrison, Cryder & Company for payment. Then came the depression. Morrison, Cryder & Company first wrote Trotter that "owing to the critical state of the times they would come under no more engagements"; next they wrote to the Trotter's new English correspondents to go ahead and draw funds; and finally they changed their minds again and refused to accept the draft. All this was "perfectly unaccountable" to Trotter, particularly so, he wrote, "as we owed them nothing but had a balance in our favour."

Nathan Trotter then arranged to settle with his new suppliers for his goods in another manner, vigorously and indignantly asserting:

. . . we are determined to give M Cr & Co nor any other House the opportunity of dishonoring drafts negociated by our orders   they invited our business or we would not have opened an a/ct with them and therefore if our credit will not entitle & obtain for us a direct account with the makers we will not pay a third party & be liable to such usage.

Domestic payments were often made by checks on one of the two banks with which Nathan Trotter had accounts—the Bank of Pennsylvania and the Bank of Northern Liberties—or by bank drafts. Occasionally Trotter gave a correspondent permission to collect by a sight draft, "value at sight," in his phraseology; but he would not give notes. "We come under no acceptances" was his unchanging response to merchants who did not know his practice. Apparently he felt that if he paid a note it might well be discounted by his supplier and might therefore circulate among other merchants; this he did not want to happen possibly because he did not want the slightest suspicion to arise that he could not pay cash. Since some manufacturers were willing to give four to six months' credit and Isaac McKim of Baltimore was willing to extend as much as eight months, Trotter profited by prompt payment—the longer the accepted credit period, the greater the discount.

The depression of 1837–1842 created difficulties in domestic payments, just as it had in payments to foreign suppliers. On 10 May 1837, the banks of New York suspended specie payments and on the following day the banks in other cities in the North did likewise. Not until the latter half of 1838 did banks generally resume specie payments, and even then some of them, including the banks of Philadelphia, were forced to suspend again. Since Philadelphia banks did not resume effectively until March, 1842, the 1839–1842 period presented difficulties in making payments to New York. The high premiums on New York funds rankled with Nathan Trotter, particularly since exchange on New York cost him $301.40 between 14 April and 20 November 1840 and amounted to $712.39 in 1841.

To J. E. Smith, an American residing in England, he unburdened his feelings on 15 November 1839 when exchange in Philadelphia on New York drafts was 15 per cent:

> Why? because their banks professedly pay specie—but with the feeling—which is carried out in her community that none shall be required of them—her local situation you know creates balances against her sister Cities, who we presume have mainly supplied her exports of specie, and if they have suspended without emptying their vaults it is no argument that they are not virtually as sound as the NyK folks—but the disparity is only productive of vexation—and even should this maintaining of specie payments be considered by them as a *germ* from which is to emanate a general resumption, and however desirable such results is—yet we fear her traders will have to experience a good deal of suffering before such event is brought about.

Various expedients were resorted to in making payments to other cities. On one occasion when Trotter's Philadelphia bank could not draw on Boston banks, he paid R. C. Mackay and J. T. Coolidge for pig tin purchased of them in Boston in this fashion. Stokes, Gilbert & Company of New York, to whom Nathan Trotter had sold 500 pigs of the tin purchased, were asked to procure a New York bank sight draft on Boston, drawn in favor of Nathan Trotter & Company. They secured one for $11,266. This, plus some drafts on Boston which Trotter "accommodated" two neighbors by taking, made the payment in Boston. Since Stokes, Gilbert & Company owed Trotter only $7,100.28, they were reimbursed for the difference—$4,165.72—by "valuing" on Trotter at sight.

On the whole it may be said by way of a summary that Trotter's principal business function was wholesaling. The service which he rendered was to buy goods in large quantities and to keep them on hand for the small user. The profit which Trotter made came somewhat from buying in bulk at a discount and selling in small quantities at what the market would bear, but more frequently from the higher price he was able to charge because he was willing to grant long credits.

In performing his wholesaling function, Trotter also served as a specialist on the subject of quality; he knew more about the goods he handled than the small user could possibly know, and he had the ability to stand between the user and the manufacturer when matters of quality were involved. The manufacturer knew that Trotter would not accept goods which were below standard; and the user knew that any goods carried by Trotter could be relied on as being high-grade.

Another service which Trotter performed as a wholesaler was to have on hand a varied selection of sizes and shapes of metals from which a handicraftsman might choose. In so doing he saved the craftsman from carrying a large inventory. He also saved him time and reduced waste in fabrication by providing sheet metal that was accurately shaped and of good quality.

Through his insistent pressure on the manufacturer and through his efforts to find new producers when the old source of supply failed, Nathan Trotter was able to keep a steady flow of goods going to the consumer. This was a function which the small handicraftsman could not have performed by himself.

The marketing organization of which Nathan Trotter was a part was changing greatly in the period 1815–1849. Since he was a wholesaler, Nathan reflected frequently and feelingly the pressures which bore down on the wholesaling function. During this period some competition came from the manufacturer. On one occasion Trotter warned his manufacturing supplier not to put his label on packages and thus inform customers where Trotter procured his goods. In that case Trotter would become merely "the medium of informing" his customers where they, too, could secure the article.[39] The American manufacturer, in some periods, sold to the consumer at about the amount he charged Trotter. The manufacturer also marketed his product through commission merchants whose price was so low that Trotter, as a competitor, could not profit much in his sale of the same merchandise. There were times when Nathan Trotter complained about the competition of English consignments in his market.[40]

During this period Trotter, too, was participating in the elimination of units in the marketing system. He sold to some former handicraft customers of his inland merchant customers when the improved transportation facilities made it easy for inland handicraftsmen to buy directly of Philadelphia wholesalers. One deterrent to both the manufacturer and Trotter was the credit risk involved in selling to the small and distant customer.[41]

Trotter's customers were for the most part handicraftsmen, and Trotter confined himself almost wholly to dealing in the softer metals which these customers used in hand fabrication of their products. As the art of metal manufacture developed and harder metals came into prominence, Trotter did not alter the nature of his business.

In order to keep his customers supplied with a broad line of goods, however, Trotter made one of the exceptions to general policy of which his story is so full. He consented on occasion to do business on a commission basis.[42]

In general Trotter did not do a commission business. He was a merchant, and in its technical sense a merchant is a man who deals in products which he himself owns. A commission agent deals in goods to which the supplier retains title. In the later years of Trotter's life, that is to say the 1830's and 1840's, the general merchant was disappearing. The commission agent was becoming common, for commission selling required less capital. Nevertheless the old style merchant continued to occupy a position of prestige, for to do business he had to have a substantial capital, even though the volume of the business he did was no greater than the volume done by upstart commission agents.

Trotter did not like doing business on commission, and he went so far as to conceal the fact that he did not own all the goods in which he dealt. Moreover, he did not find commission selling very profitable. Between 1835 and 1848 there were only three years in which he made more than $1,000 from his commission business.[43] Nevertheless, his customers virtually forced him to participate in this profitless business; had he not done so, many a customer would have gone elsewhere.

It is a little sad to read the Trotter correspondence toward the close of Nathan's life. The old days of the general merchant were clearly gone—the days when a merchant could enter in his books: importing cost, add 120 per cent. Nevertheless Trotter continued to think of himself as a general merchant, running his own risks, making a profit that was more dependent on thoughtful planning than on the hustle and bustle that had come to characterize business as it was practiced in his later years. He preferred the days when the initiative for a sale came from the customer and when customers came to him knowing that from him they could be sure of getting quality products. The new system was characterized by a constant drive and pressure from the manufacturer. The manufacturer took the initiative in urging a sale, and if the wholesaler was not willing to push the product the manufacturer bypassed him to the customer or found another wholesale outlet.

Trotter was sometimes offended by the lack of respect shown to him, a merchant, by the supplying manufacturers. One source of supply, the McKims of Baltimore, long-time personal friends of Trotter, sometimes poked a little fun at him for his insistence on the sacred right of the merchant.

Whether he stated the reasons fully or not, Nathan Trotter did deserve some preferential treatment as a merchant. First of all his credit was A-1. The manufacturer did not have to worry about payment from the Trotter firm. In fact the McKims, with adequate capital of their own, often wished that Trotter would not be so eager to take the cash discount, since they had no immediate need for the money and were glad to have it in such safe hands and earning some interest.

Trotter was also a desirable outlet for a manufacturer's goods. He bought in large quantities and contracted for goods well in advance, giving the manufacturer an opportunity to plan production. He took some of the inventory risk off the manufacturer's shoulders, and he was absolutely reliable in his business dealings. He also had an intimate knowledge of markets, and the size of his purchases served as an indicator of general demand.

He would not, however, serve as a reservoir of inventories to help ease the effects of lessening demand on the manufacturer. He would order to the extent of keeping on hand a stock of goods in which he was expected to deal, but he would not go further. If the manufacturer expected the wholesaler to take an active hand in promoting the sales of his product, he was destined to be disappointed in Nathan Trotter's methods of doing business. Trotter helped the manufacturer market his goods up to a conservative amount. Beyond that he would not push.

CHAPTER VI

Sales, Trends, Customers, and Market Areas

THE America in which the Trotters began to do business was a country in the early stages of the Industrial Revolution. It was still importing some manufactured goods from England but it was securing an increasing number of its essential needs from its own handicraftsmen. Tench Coxe, writing on the economic conditions of the new country noted in 1792: "We have exceedingly diminished our importation of coarse linen and woolen goods, cordage, copper utensils, tin utensils, malt liquors. . . . We either make these articles from native productions . . . or we manufacture them of foreign raw materials. . . ." [1]

As the preceding chapter has shown, the rapid development of the American economy affected Trotter's methods of procurement both abroad and at home; Trotter might have preferred to remain an importer of what Tench Coxe called "foreign raw materials," but he was forced by circumstances to deal increasingly in articles made "from native productions." This chapter shows that the rising industrialization of America also brought a shift in the marketing of Trotter's merchandise.

Chart VI indicates that between the years 1815 and 1849 the general trend of the Trotter firm's business was upward. If anything, the trend is understated. The chart is based on dollar sales and con-

Chart VI

NATHAN TROTTER & COMPANY

Annual Value of Sales and Ratio of Gross Profits to Sales, 1815–1849

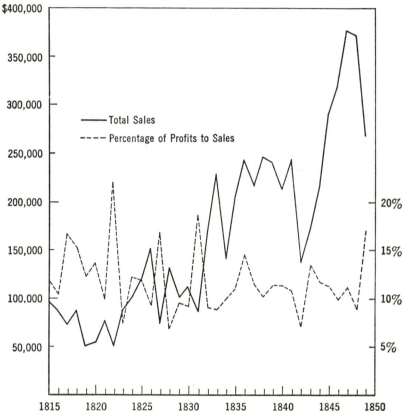

sequently does not show the physical volume of the goods Trotter dealt with. We know, of course, that during most of that period the price of goods in general, and of metals in particular, was declining (see Chart VII). It may be, therefore, that the rise in volume was even greater than the rise in value would indicate.

Within this general upward trend a number of cycles may be seen. Usually Trotter's business activity followed rather closely the business cycle of the nation, but sometimes there were marked deviations, notably in the depression years 1837–1841, when Trotter's sales continued at a high level. Depressions were frequent—approximately one every decade—and sometimes long-lasting. Depressions are hard

Chart VII

NATHAN TROTTER & COMPANY

Indexes of Total Sales and Wholesale Prices of Nonferrous Metals in Philadelphia, 1815–1849

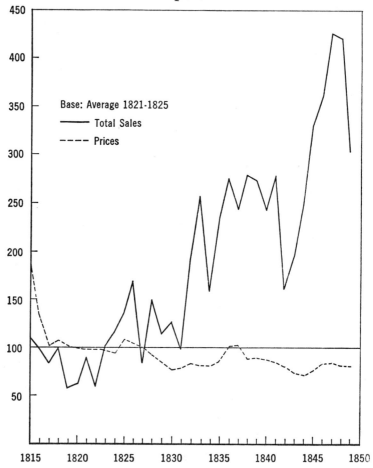

enough for any businessman, but for Trotter they were doubly difficult because they recurrently forced him to adopt new methods to catch up with the fast-moving times. We can almost feel the accumulating pressure as tightening business conditions compelled Trotter to forsake, often reluctantly, his former ties and connections in favor of new alliances that gave promise of restoring his markets and regenerating his profits.

The years from 1803 to 1815 marked the first upsweep of sales for the Trotters. It was a period which exactly coincided with the Napoleonic Wars when, throughout most of the world, goods were in short supply, prices were inflated, and business was relatively easy to get. Those were the years when the Trotters dealt in a variety of imported goods, including wares from the Orient.

In that period the firm's principal customers were keepers of small retail stores, mostly in Philadelphia, itself, but also in the surrounding countryside. A few customers, it is true, even then were handicraftsmen, men who bought raw materials of the Trotters and fashioned from them goods of a finished nature: papermakers who bought felting for use in the papermaking process; tailors who bought bolts of woolen cloth; and leatherworkers who bought semifinished leather goods (the Trotters' leather business was with the carriage trade—both literally and figuratively—for they sold red roans to carriage makers with which to line the insides of carriages and they sold many-colored kidskins to specialized craftsmen who made ladies' fine shoes). But the most numerous by far of the Trotters' customers in the years 1803–1815 were the storekeepers. They numbered 173 of the total of 282 customers who can be identified for those years.

Some of these storekeepers, especially the women among them (usually widows), ran stores which specialized in Oriental imports—cotton and silk cloth, sewing silk, and silk shawls. But others carried a wide line of merchandise, including metal goods. These latter remained Trotter customers for long periods—well after Trotter turned to specialization in metals. Beginning in this early period Ferris & Gilpin of Wilmington, Keim & Drinkle of Reading, George Mayer and Christopher Hager of Lancaster, and John Hoke of Lincolnton, North Carolina, were customers for one, two, and sometimes three decades.

The Keims had established a general hardware store in Reading as early as 1755.[2] The founder, Nicholas, dealt also in grain and his place of business, at the "Weiser Store Stand" or "Old White Store" on Penn Street near Fifth, continued to be the location of the business of his successors. The firm had a fairly extensive market which included customers in Union, Northumberland, Columbia, Center, Lycoming, and Mifflin counties.[3] The Keims were typical of the storekeeping group of their day and spoke of going into partnership with a Reading coppersmith or of getting the coppersmith to work for them;

they bought tin plate for the tinner, Johnny Babb; and they asked Trotter to sell for them in New York 45 to 100 rifle barrels which were "warranted good." "In case one should break, burst & &," they wrote, "we will take it back again & give another in place—." They also requested Trotter to sell for them bar iron and flaxseed. These inland storekeepers operating in a money-short economy, like Thomas Hancock and other Colonial merchants in a similar economy, were forced to diversify. They asked Trotter to engage in a two-way exchange and he was able to co-operate, in part, because he could easily dispose of his goods from the inland to specialized dealers who were appearing in the Philadelphia market.

Another typical storekeeper was John Hoke, merchant and manufacturer in the German section of North Carolina, at Lincolnton. Hoke relied on Trotter principally for copper which he had made up into stills by the local coppersmith. He also got Nathan Trotter to supply him with various specialty items even when the items were not carried by the Trotter firm. Some of Hoke's orders indicate the composition of his market and of his own manufacturing interests. One such order was for "12 doz Hidleburg Catacism English Translation taken from the German"; and "1 dz calf Skins for top Roler Covering in a Cotton Factory." Hoke wrote, "We have formerly got them from Pautuckett Rodeisland, but hope they can be had as well at Philadelphia."

From 1815 to 1822 Trotter encountered a period of decreasing sales. Naturally the close of the war period was followed by adjustments. Markets, previously monopolized by American manufactures, were suddenly flooded with British goods. The banking and credit situation deteriorated. In a letter to his English correspondents, 7 August 1819, Nathan Trotter described in these words the circumstances which led to the deplorable state in which American business then found itself:

. . . sales have been and continue extremely slow indeed, & confidence so lessened that really there is but little satisfaction in doing busyness—the numerous Banking institutions that had crept into existance in all parts of our Union had emitted such a flood of circulating medium /paper money/ as give fictitious value to all kinds of property & afforded by aid of loans from them such facility of doing busyness without the aid of real capital as has proved of ruinous consequences in very many instances, for when some of the most prominent of these institutions began to draw in their business in order to bring the circulating medium nearer its specie value those of minor capitals had to adopt the same course, & this general retrograde march having been persevered in for a considerable time past has drawn out of circulation say one third to half the circulating medium, & the notes of many of those

Banks particularly in the interior which had issued a large amount in proportion to their means & not redeeming them with specie when presented are reduced to a considerable discount—These circumstances added to the low price & little demand for country produce, occasion extensive difficulty & delay in collecting debts particularly from the country and a number of houses, who have extended considerable credit there have had to suspend their payments solely on a/c of not being able to make collections. . . .

Until things are restored to a level of more security we mean to be very particular indeed whom we credit, of course our sales will be less—in fact Copper &c are quite a drug now.

Difficulties were experienced by all merchants and handicraftsmen doing business under such adverse circumstances. But Trotter was faced, in addition to these general difficulties, with another problem, that of increasing his sales at a time when he had just become a specialized dealer in metals.

Specialization came about in his business at this particular time as the result of his desire to remain an importer. He had been accustomed to the importing business ever since he had entered his brother's countinghouse on Front Street in 1803. Then too, as already noted, margins on American manufactures of felting, woolens, and leathers were small—not to be compared with the importer's profit.

By dealing exclusively in metals and giving up leather, woolens, felting, and Oriental imports, he lost most of his storekeeping customers and all his shoemakers, coach and carriage makers, tailors, paper manufacturers, and keepers of small shops, since they bought domestically. Therefore, he had to look for new markets. These he found largely among the handicraftsmen in Philadelphia but increasingly in the urban centers of the hinterland.

The handicraftsmen, as a group, belong to all periods rather than to any one in Trotter's business life. As frontiers moved economically, new localities needed and found craftsmen suited to their wants. This type of customer, ever moving but never changing in character, demanded quality in goods and credit in terms.

Among the handicraftsmen whom Trotter supplied in the years before this group became his most important customers, a substantial number were "master-workmen and journeymen from abroad," to use the description given by Tench Coxe.[4] Typical of the times is a statement in Poulson's *Daily Advertiser* of 31 June 1803 which announced the arrival in Philadelphia of Swiss and German Redemptioners, among whom were shoemakers, tailors, bookbinders, and papermakers—all potential Trotter customers. Surely the French Revolution accounts for the numerous references made in Trotter daybooks to such craftsmen as a "Frenchman suspender maker" and "Dermerlier —a Frenchman shoemaker."

The foreign craftsmen, mentioned in Poulson's paper in 1803, had attracted unto themselves apprentices of native stock and soon spread their imported skills across the countryside. It took little capital for them to set up business, for at first they used practically no machinery and perhaps only a few tools, some of which doubtless they brought from Europe. The following order, sent by a merchant for his nephew, "anew beginner . . . a sober, Industrious young man," gives us an inkling of the capital required by one who was "aboute to commence the Tinning" business, and certainly the outlay for this stock of goods must have been modest enough: [5]

1 stone no 8 wire	1 Hundred Heavy American Sheet Iron
½ do each no 13, 15 & 17	2 Hundred Light Do Do Do
1 paper stove pipe rivets	2 Sheets Light Russian Do
1 do Tin rivets small	1 Do Light Tined Copper
3 Boxes Tin ¼X	10 lb Solder

Craftsmen like this young tinner had two methods by which they kept at a minimum their capital invested in inventory. In the first place they were hand-to-mouth buyers; they kept an inventory of as few materials as possible and relied on the Trotters to stock their further needs. A study of one customer's transactions for the year 1835 shows that he made purchases in every month of the year with a total for the year of $6,082. During the month of May, as a sample month, he sent orders to Trotter on 15 different dates. The smallest purchase amounted to 35 cents and the largest to $555.93.

A second method by which craftsmen stretched their capital investment was to buy on long credit. Often they did not pay Trotter till after they themselves had received payment for the goods they had made with Trotter's merchandise. Trotter consequently performed a double service: he provided goods for manufacture and furnished part of the craftsman's capital (either through credit or through stocking a heavy inventory).

Most of the Trotters' customers did "bespoke" work; that is, work ordered to the specifications of the consumer. A typical letter to Trotter ran: "I stand in great need of tin plate as I have a good deal of work bespoke." The Trotters might receive orders for copper sheets size

30 × 60 from a coppersmith who had "teakettles engaged to the store-keepers." Sometimes the Trotters' customers were ultimate users; sometimes they were storekeepers who wished to stock an item for sale to the craftsmen.

A few craftsmen made goods for inventory. Occasionally one of them wrote to Nathan Trotter that he was "making up work on hand" in the summer; and for about three months in the fall the tinsmiths and blacksmiths typically devoted most of their time to making sheet iron stovepipes and stoves. Sometimes the craftsmen who produced goods for inventory engaged also in the retailing business by operating, in conjunction with their shop, a store in which they sold brass kettles, boxes of tin plate, bake pans, etc. It was also a part of their business to do repair work; indeed a fair share of their income may have come from that activity. Some of them did a little farming on the side. According to a report of an English traveler in Montgomery County, Pennsylvania, in the early 1800's, the blacksmiths, wheelwrights, tailors, etc., shut up their shops to assist the farmers in harvesting.[6]

Without doubt the most useful of the handicraftsmen to a people clearing a continent of its trees, building homes, cultivating lands, and harvesting crops was the blacksmith. The ledger of a late eighteenth-century Pennsylvania blacksmith, Joshua Baldwin, illustrates the diversity of a blacksmith's activities.[7] He sold sickles, cooper's adzes, heel-making knives, straw knives, drawing knives, shopping knives, saw sets, hunting saddles and bridles. He cut sickles and handles for others as well as for his own trade; he ground sickles, razors, sheep shears, small shears, and scythes; he steeled a broad axe and the end of mill picks; he sharpened mill picks and plough irons; and he mended a sidesaddle, a pillion, a chair, and a skillet. A versatile fellow was the smith. The purchases by any one blacksmith of blistered and cast steel, refined borax, salt petre, and scythes were never very large at one time. But orders came in from each one regularly two or three times a year and, since Pennsylvania had over twenty-five hundred black-smith shops in 1810 with a production valued at $1,572,627,[8] the black-smiths' trade was of considerable consequence to the Trotter firm.

However, it was the coppersmiths who were the firm's most important group of customers from 1815 until the 1830's. An advertisement placed by a Trotter customer of Lancaster in his home-town paper, gives us an idea of the work in which a combined tinsmith and coppersmith engaged: [9]

Henry Reigart, coppersmith & tin-plate worker, respectfully acquaints his friends and the public, that he carries on his business in all its various branches, in the house of Susanna Edwards, south Queen-street, Lancaster, where he manufactures, and has for sale, a general assortment of *stills, washing kettles, colouring, planking, fullers, fish and tea kettles, boilers, sauspans* &c. &c. also Anderson's (much approved) Patent Condensing Tub. The above articles will be so[l]d on the most reasonable terms, by which he hopes to merit and receive the encouragement of a generous public; a reasonable allowance will be made to persons purchasing ware by the quantity. The highest price will be given for old pewter.

The only activities commonly engaged in by coppersmiths which are not mentioned in this advertisement were occasional roofing jobs, ship sheathing, construction of boilers for steam engines (after about 1820), and (somewhat later still) fabrication of locomotive pipes.

Since distillation of whiskey from grain and brandy from apples or peaches provided a cash product with which farmers could purchase needed supplies, most farmers owned a still house and "a pair of stills." The market for copper for stills declined by the 1830's, probably because distilling was becoming a large-scale industry.[10]

The tinsmiths to whom the Trotter firm sold were of two types: the village tinsmiths, usually with German names; and a few large-scale producers located principally in Trenton and in Wilmington.

Typical of the village tinsmiths with whom the Trotters did business was John Fry, of Germantown. This craftsman's daybook for the years 1795–1798 is preserved in the Manuscript Collection of the Historical Society of Pennsylvania. It contains an amazing list of handicraft products: saucepans, tin cups, "scimmers," lamps, bowls, sugar boxes, "segar" boxes, kettles, teakettle lids, lanterns, nutmeg graters, oil pots, half pint and pint measures, pint cups, funnels, coffee pots, sausage stuffers, milk strainers, pans, tea canisters, "cullenders," candlesticks, pot lids, water pots, pepper boxes, knitting needle cases, candle molds, lamp funnels, a cooler (for distilling, probably), a pair of scales, flour boxes, cheese toasters, patty pans, egg slicers, tinder boxes, something called a tin kitchen, scoops, dredging-boxes, and tin pipe.

In addition to making this great variety of articles, tinsmith Fry repaired goods (the usual pots and pans, and also a shower bath), tinned pans and kettles, and cut and put in panes of glass. In the fall he sold goods which probably made up stock for a storekeeper: three lanterns, six lamps, six bowls, two dozen oil pots, and two dozen tin cups.

Tinsmiths also made and put up water spouts, and those located near the textile mills began working in the mills as early as 1811. Then the correspondence began to mention orders of tin plate for spools, cams, bobbins, and cylinders for factory use.

All the large-scale producers of tinware who purchased from the Trotter firm were originally from Connecticut. Tradition has it that the craft of tinsmithing was introduced into this country in 1740 by William and Edward Pattison, Scottish tinsmiths who came to Berlin, Connecticut, by way of Ireland.[11] Probably the Pattison tradition arose from the fact that they, and the people whom they trained, became large-scale producers employing many apprentices and many peddlers with carts to market the ware.

Among the Trotter firm's customers were the Wilmington tinsmiths, the Beckleys who came from Beckley's Quarter in Berlin, Connecticut, and Daniel Belden, a Trenton tinsmith who was also from Connecticut, as was Blakesley Barnes, a pewterer and tinsmith in Philadelphia. The Beckleys and Belden did considerable business with William Trotter from 1804 until 1810. During the winter months they employed a number of workmen, some and perhaps all of whom came from Connecticut. Some of the Trotters' later customers—Stoughton & Belden of Salem, New Jersey, and L. & F. Stoughton of Milton, Pennsylvania, also came from Connecticut.

At first most of these larger tinsmiths marketed their wares through peddlers. In the fall of 1804 Belden had six peddlers out on the road and expected six or seven to come down from Connecticut that winter. In late 1807 the Beckleys had six peddlers "agoing" and expected three more in a week.[12]

These, then, were the smiths, old-time handicraftsmen, and one of the constant groups of customers whose purchases helped to replace the volume of Trotter's business that had once been done with storekeepers. Between 1815 and 1822 it was their business on which Trotter chiefly depended.

On one occasion Trotter pushed hard to obtain new customers among this handicraft group, especially along a main route to Ohio and Kentucky. In 1817 he sent his clerk Daisy Cheyney on a combination collection and selling tour. After visiting Pittsburgh and a series of Ohio and Kentucky towns, Daisy wrote a market survey. Nathan Trotter had hoped that this tour would result in "the selling of double the quantity [of goods] next year." [13] Daisy's forecast, however, was not so rosy. His statement of "the standing of our customers & of others who possibly may visit the store to purchase" concludes with the words:

> The consumption of the article of Copper is very considerable, throughout Ohio & Kentucky but most of the consumers have already formed connexions which they are satisfied with either in this City or Baltimore & do not wish to change without something of an inducement is offered, which I had not in my power to make nor which I presumed would be satisfactory to you if made, you are acquainted with what this is an extension of credit & reduction of price—they were all willing to patronize an establishment at Pburg, for obvious reasons, they would in a very short time be in possession of their orders, they need not run themselves so much in debt & the same cr as they get east of the mountains would be at least 2 months more from Pittsburgh—

The tour did result in the acquisition of more business; sales went up in 1818. But some of the newly acquired customers were bad credit risks and the attempt to push individual sales beyond the normal demands of a handicraftsman was unsatisfactory.

There were physical difficulties in reaching customers in the hinterland, not only in the winter months but even in July, as this letter from Daisy written from Pittsburgh on the third of that month in 1817 indicates:

> You are (I presume) by this time anxious to hear what progress I have made, but were you to only travel over such roads as I have once you could easily make an apology for my silence, previous to writing you anything in the business line I will give you some account of my journey "and then you will be the better Judge." I did not leave Philada. untill ½ past 5 o'clock, and had as pleasant a ride as the wet weather & hard jolts of the stage would admit of   about 5 PM arrived at Lancaster but owing to the rain could not do anything there   arrived at Elizabethtown abt 9 O'clock where we lodged, here I found a bed very comfortable having slept but 2½ hours the night before   here I had abt 5½ hours sleep, started from here at 4 and at 8 was at Harrisburg . . . at Middletown began our troubles . . . . The roads at MTown began to get bad owing to the rain the preceeding day & we had them bad with but little intermission all the rest of the rout . . . . Left Carlisle abt ½ past 1—passed through Shippensburg & got Chamburg [Chambersburg] abt 9 Oclock here where had a good nights rest as the stage did not start untill 8 O'clock   from Cburg to the Cove Mountain the road very bad . . . over the Cove mountain their is an excellent turnpike   frequently on one side of us would be a precipice the deep of which would turn ones head to look down it, and almost constant prospect of the country for miles . . . on the summit of the Mountain we must have had at least 50 miles in view— about 4O'clock arrived at McCburg   found a dull place, did not leave here

untill 4 the next morning (Sunday)   soon after starting a very heavy rain commenced, the road was bad enough before—the rain made them frightfull, we this day crossed the sidling hill, a very appropriate name for it, for we sometimes travelled so sidling as to have the wheels on one side 8 or 10 Inches above ground—got to Bedford abt dusk, the handsomest town on the road. . . . left here abt ¼ past 3—roads very bad, here we had an accession of passengers, the stage was full enough for comfort before, they did not

Chart VIII

MAP OF TROTTER MARKET IN PENNSYLVANIA, 1803–1815

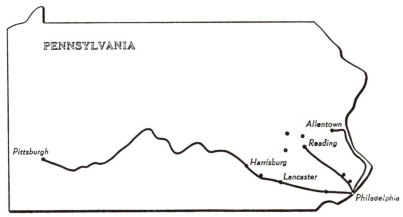

Heavy lines indicate turnpikes. Each dot represents a town in which customers purchased $200 of goods from the Trotters in any one year during 1803–1815.

think proper to get in the stage until they had ridden 14 miles on horse-back   they then sent 2 horses back to Bedford & the gentleman made me an offer of his . . . to ride to Somerset, which I accepted with pleasure, glad enough to get away from the jolting of the stage—I soon left the stage far enough behind it only going abt 2 miles an hour, roads so bad it could do no faster but I could pick my road with horse, rode all the way over the Alleghany or "great" back bone of America by Myself and arrived at Somerset abt 5 hours before the stage did, left here abt 4—our road now beat all I had ever seen, you Can form no conception of it—we this day crossed the Laurel & Chestnut ridges. It almost made my blood run cold to think of them—

The roads which Daisy described were overland routes which connected Philadelphia by wagon service with the four general inland areas in which the Trotter firm had customers.[14] As the first of the accompanying series of state maps shows, these were (1) Easton-Allentown, (2) Reading, (3) Lancaster-Harrisburg, and (4) Pittsburgh. In the spring of the year, it might be added, Easton-Allentown customers could also receive goods by boats which left the Vine Street wharf.

Transportation over the Pennsylvania turnpikes was carried on in a number of ways. Sometimes an inland farmer or merchant sent his own wagon to Philadelphia for goods, but ordinarily Trotter's customers engaged freight with one of the regular commercial wagon lines. It would appear, from the Trotter records, that Philadelphia was seldom if ever the commercial wagoner's headquarters. These useful business auxiliaries originated their trips in interior centers and transported goods to the Philadelphia area where they picked up a return cargo. Often before leaving for Philadelphia they went about to the stores of their various local customers to learn if anyone wished to have goods picked up and brought back from the city. Frequently they acted as the agents by which local merchants sent money to the city in payment for goods.[15]

In Philadelphia the wagoners made their temporary headquarters a tavern or a store and any Philadelphia merchant who wished to send goods inland would call at these recognized locations to arrange for shipping space. Wagoners from Reading often put up at the Spread Eagle Tavern on Third Street; Lancaster wagoners might be found at the Black Horse Tavern in Market Street or at the "Sign of the Buck in Market St. just up at the Academy of Fine Arts." Frequently teamsters from Lancaster or Harrisburg started from Gratz's store on market Street. John Jordan & Company, "wholesale grocers and dealers in East India saltpetre," was the headquarters for drivers from the region of the Moravian settlements—Bethlehem and Nazareth—and from Allentown.[16]

The wagoner on the regular lines, to quote from Thomas Searight's *The Old Pike*,[17]

> was on the road constantly . . . and had no other pursuit than hauling goods and merchandise on the road. . . . The regular drove his team about fifteen miles a day on the average. . . . Line teams were those controlled by an association or company. Many of the regular wagoners became members of these companies and put in their teams. The main object of the combination was to transport goods more rapidly than by the ordinary method. Line teams were stationed along the road, at distances of about fifteen miles, and horses were exchanged after the manner of stage lines.

The Conestoga wagon was used. This was a covered wagon which was originally manufactured in Conestoga, Pennsylvania, so constructed that it could be pulled easily over uneven roads and the load would not slip on inclines. They were drawn by Conestoga horses—"a superior class of draft horses, a mixture of various breeds, which attained a great degree of efficiency" for the purpose of drawing "waggons, heavily laden with produce, to Philadelphia." [18]

Over the Pennsylvania turnpikes by such means of transportation much of the produce of the United States was moved. The stir of autumn traffic is described in this letter to Trotter from a Reading customer: [19]

it beets all I ever seen in regard to Teams mooving along with flour Wheat &c &c   our Town is at present quite brisk in regard to Trade   there ware this week from 40 to 60 Waggons in every day to deposit all the produce here   the[y] Crack their whips as the[y] go along the Streets   you can not hear your own word if two Speaks to gether.

The Trotter firm's market area beyond the state of Pennsylvania in the period before 1822 included New York, New Jersey, Delaware, and Maryland. Much of this territory was reached by coastwise sloop service. There were regular sloop connections with Trenton and Burlington, New Jersey, and Wilmington, Delaware, so long as the Delaware River was open. Captain Ashmore's boat, which left the Arch Street wharf not far from Trotter's store, was much used by Trenton customers, although goods wanted in a hurry might be ordered by "first boat that comes" or the "first packet." In the winter, goods were sent to Trenton by stage if they were not too bulky. From 1814 on goods were occasionally ordered to be sent by steamboat. The steamboat, *Phoenix,* built by John Stevens, was making regular trips between Bloomsbury and Philadelphia as early as 1809. Although other steamboats were also in service shortly after, sloops were ordinarily used—probably because of the cheaper rate—by the Trotter firm's customers until well into the 1820's.

In the early years of the nineteenth century there were at least two regular sailing sloop services with Wilmington: Captain Bush's and Captain Milnor's. Captain Samuel Bush, son of a West India trader, established regular weekly service between Wilmington and Philadelphia in 1774 with the sloops *Ann* and *Nancy.*[20] He continued this weekly service, later in partnership with his sons, until about 1804, when the *Mary Ann* was built and the service became semiweekly. Captain Bush's service was popular with the Trotter firm's customers who accompanied orders with such requests as "send goods by Bush or first boat / tho' we always give Bush a preference if there/." Captain Milnor, "famous for carrying sail," also ran a line of sloops between

Wilmington and Philadelphia. As was true of the Trenton trade, steamboats were not patronized extensively by Trotter's Wilmington customers until the late 1820's.

Beyond this market which was but a slight extension of the Philadelphia area were more distant customers. Those in the Ohio Valley states—Ohio and Kentucky—received goods by wagon and, from Pittsburgh, by boat. Virginia and South Carolina market areas were reached by coastwise ships.

Let us again turn our attention to the graph of total sales in Chart VI. From the turning point in 1822 the sales figure eventually reached a high in 1826. An important factor was the favorable climate which prevailed for business in general into the year 1825: trade and manufacturing flourished. Increased trade, and the prospect of still more, encouraged shipbuilding. Consequently Trotter received numerous orders from shipowners for sheathing copper. He was able to share in the increased business at the time partly because, as we have seen, he had adopted a more economical means of purchasing his goods in 1822. This must surely have put him in a favorable competitive position in his selling market.

The volume of sales stopped mounting at the high of 1826 and from there declined to 1831. There seems to be no simple explanation of the downward trend in these years. Occasionally Trotter lacked an adequate supply of goods and naturally the lack was reflected in decreased sales. The period was one of falling prices and tariff changes—conditions which Nathan Trotter found unsettling and which doubtless exaggerated his naturally cautious practices. Complaints ran through his correspondence indicating that he was not selling his products as cheaply as his competitors. He, himself, felt pressures from the competition of New York and Baltimore copper, English consignments of copper and cheap tin plate resulting from a price war. In the midst of his decline in sales—in 1828—Trotter's percentage of profits to sales reached the lowest point in the firm's experience between 1803 and 1849. Fortunately during the phase of the cycle from 1822 until 1831 new markets were being tapped which eventually would lift sales to a higher level.

One type of customer which Nathan Trotter acquired was the specialist in metals. These specialists appeared in increasing numbers in the Philadelphia directories of the period. For example, the Trotter Ledger of 1827–1831 included such specialists as brass founders, a brass and bell founder, lamp and chandelier manufacturers, manufacturers of grates and fenders, a screw manufacturer, an engine manufacturer, a hose manufacturer, roofers, plumbers, and stovemakers. Specialized craftsmen and rising manufacturers enabled the specialized metal dealer—Trotter for example—to increase his sales.

Stovemakers came to be an important group of these handicraft specialists, as well as purchasers of a considerable amount of the goods which Trotter sold. During the early part of the nineteenth century, as mentioned earlier, the making of stoves and stovepipe was a late summer and early fall occupation of the tinsmith and blacksmith. After the use of anthracite coal for heating became common in the 1820's, the number of specialized stovemakers and grate and fender makers increased rapidly. These groups were a market for American, Russian, and English sheet iron, stove knobs, rivets, stove ornaments, brass for fenders, and hoop iron for stove-door hinges. The Russian sheet iron, and later an American substitute which Trotter considered "very handsome good iron of a smooth glossy surface" which did not "scale in the working," was used to make stoves for burning anthracite coal. The fire was "contained in a castiron cylinder within the stove."

There is no evidence that these new customers, the specialists, purchased from Nathan Trotter as a result of any drive on his part to secure new business. It appears, rather, that normal growth of the metropolitan centers fostered specialization. Some specialists doubtless had been Trotter's customers as unspecialized handicraftsmen and, as specialists, continued to purchase from him, merely requiring more of a particular product and less variety in their purchases.

The development of canals in the period brought Trotter customers from a wider area in the late 1820's and the 1830's. As the map in Chart IX indicates, three areas of the state in particular offered an extended market by canals.

In the Easton area the Lehigh Coal & Navigation Company opened a canal about 1829 which made this area a more important Trotter market, and the Delaware Division of the canal from Easton down to Bristol opened still other markets.[21]

In the Reading area the Schuylkill Navigation, officially opened in 1825,[22] extended the firm's market north to Orwigsburg. When Danville and Milton customers used this route, they wagoned their goods north from Mount Carbon.[23] The Reading and Harrisburg districts both were extended by the Union Canal, completed in 1827.[24] This canal ran from the Schuylkill, just below Reading, to the Susquehanna at Middletown and brought the Trotter firm new customers at Berneville and Lebanon—towns along its banks. When there were interruptions to canal transportation, customers along the canal route were forced to go to the Lancaster market for their supplies.[25]

Chart IX

MAP OF TROTTER MARKET IN PENNSYLVANIA, 1827–1831

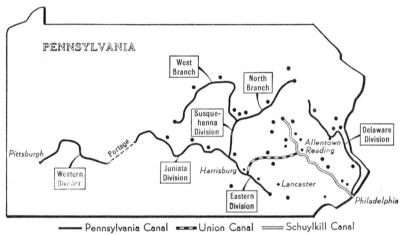

Heavy lines indicate canals. Each dot represents a town in which customers purchased $200 of goods from Nathan Trotter & Company in any one year during 1827–1831. The larger dots indicate new markets since 1815.

Farther west a third area was tapped when the Pennsylvania Canal system along the Susquehanna and its branches was opened. This system was a composite route connecting Philadelphia with Pittsburgh: there was a railroad from Philadelphia to the Susquehanna at Columbia; [26] a canal up the Susquehanna [27] and Juniata [28] rivers to Hollidaysburg; a portage railroad from Hollidaysburg over the mountains to Johnstown; [29] and a canal from Johnstown to Pittsburgh [30] completed the system. Carlisle, Lewistown, and Huntington were new Trotter markets along this route.

Various extensions of this system likewise expanded the market. Danville and Wilkesbarre were reached by the Susquehanna Division, the Susquehanna River, and the North Branch Division; [31] Williamsport and Bellefonte by the West Branch Division [32] of the Susquehanna

Canal. The opening of the North Branch Division was announced in a newspaper item dated 1 June 1831: [33]

Arrived this morning, at Bolton's wharf on the Schuylkill, canal boat Wyoming, with flour, coal and lumber, from Wilkes Barre, Luzerne county, Pa. being the first arrival here from that place. Great praise is due the enterprising owner, Captain Derrick Bird for his very successful undertaking. Thus we witness the vast riches of our state brought to market by means of our canals.

Trade flowed both ways, of course, and interior markets were also brought to such seaboard merchants as Nathan Trotter by means of these same canals.

Although regular shipments along the canal routes were often interrupted by breaks, and the canals were closed on account of ice during the winter months, canals were the most important factor in the extension of the Trotter firm's market area in the late 1820's and in the 1830's.

For its publicly financed canal and portage system, the state of Pennsylvania incurred a debt of over thirty million dollars. Although not financially profitable, the system, if Nathan Trotter's experience is typical, brought to Philadelphia merchants customers from many new towns along its banks.

An examination of the market area outside Pennsylvania in this 1827–1831 period shows that there was little change from the earlier years. The chief development in methods of transportation to these places, as reflected in the Trotter papers, was the shipment of goods to the lower Ohio and the Mississippi Valley states by way of New Orleans rather than through Pittsburgh. From New Orleans, goods were transported up the Mississippi and Ohio rivers by steamboat.

From 1832 until 1841 the sales trend was upward. A definite drop in sales in 1834 corresponded to the general pattern of business at the time. But the graph of sales (Chart VI) in 1838, 1839, and 1841 displays an unexpected feature. Instead of falling, after the depression of 1837, sales continued high. In 1836, 1837, and 1838, Trotter secured former customers of Phelps Dodge & Company when, as he said, the Phelps Dodge "Monopoly of the Trade was interrupted and other venders come more into notice." Trotter was one of those who "came more into notice" with some of the New York firm's former customers. These customers continued to buy tin plate from Trotter as long as his prices did not exceed the New York figure.[34] He was enabled to stay near the New York price since, at this very time, as we have seen in the previous chapter, he was beginning to go directly to the English manufacturer for tin plate and could pass along the savings to his customers in the form of lower prices.

Some of the increased business came from roofers and architects. Building, particularly institutional building, was active in this period. Much earlier than 1831, of course, the Trotters had sold supplies for buildings: nails and materials for water spouts and window shutters, for example. Then came a demand for tin plate and terneplate, comparatively inexpensive materials for roofing. Trotter's purchases of these materials increased from only 2,000 boxes a year in 1822, when tin plate was used chiefly for utensils, to 13,327 boxes in 1846, by which time it was in wide use for roofing. An English manufacturer, in that year exclaimed: "We do not see what you do with all the tinplate you Americans import."

Specialized roofers also brought the Trotter firm some of its business in copper, as is evident from this excerpt from Trotter's letter to the manufacturer E. T. Ellicott, 31 March 1829: "The principal worker for light copper for roofs informs us there will probably be a good deal wanted this Spring. We shall therefore wish to be prepared with a supply. . . . The worker will always do his best to get the buyers to take ours and has a good deal of influence."

The upswing of Trotter's sales in the 1830's coincided with a boom in institutional building and a resulting sale of copper—the costlier roofing material. Philadelphia, at that time, boasted of architects whose work was outstanding. One was John Haviland who "specialized in prison architecture." [35] For two of the buildings which he designed, Trotter supplied the copper. The Eastern Penitentiary in Philadelphia was one, better known for its system of solitary confinement of prisoners [36] than as a market for the Trotter firm, but to Nathan Trotter it represented a copper sale. The State Penitentiary in Trenton, New Jersey, was the second. [37]

William Strickland, another well-known architect, [38] designed what Nathan Trotter called the New Almshouse—better known as the Blockley Almshouse. The copper sold for this building amounted to over $28,000.

Thomas U. Walter, the "architect of the main building of Girard College and of the wings and dome of the national capital at Washington," [39] on two occasions requested Trotter to put in a bid for furnishing copper for institutions which he was building. Trotter's bids were accepted and his copper roofed the Wills Hospital for the Diseases of the Eye and Limbs and the New County Prison in the District of Moyamensing.

New churches—the Central Presbyterian, "a large and imposing edifice" at the corner of 8th and Cherry [40]—and the New Jersey State Lunatic Asylum [41] were supplied with his copper. Even halls of learning helped swell his sales when copper was ordered for Bristol College in New Jersey and for gutters for "prinston Colage," to quote the smith who wrote the order.[42]

The years 1842 and 1843 were clearly years of depression for the Trotters, as for the country in general. Money was scarce, failures frequent; confidence was prostrate; little or no business was being done; and Trotter never knew business more depressed, he declared. In a sense he himself helped create his decrease in sales. Since he was "more anxious to save debts owing than make sales on time," he was inclined to restrict himself to cash sales.

An upward trend, starting in 1843, reached in 1847–1848 the highest point it touched in Nathan Trotter's mercantile career. In large part the sales volume resulted from purchases by manufacturers. Industrial expansion was well under way and Trotter's business reflected the increased demand, particularly for raw materials, of the factories and railroads.

Manufacturers were not new among the firm's customers. One group of them had been the papermakers in the early part of the century— such important papermakers of their day as Joseph Bicking, John Fulton, Thomas Levis, and Mark Wilcox were among the Trotters' customers. Also in the first two decades of the century the tinsmith customers, as I have noted, turned from the production of their usual ware to the making of "machinery" needed for the textile mills: cams from heavy (XX) tin plate, bobbins, and spools. Coppersmith customers, in the 1820's and 1830's particularly, were making boilers from copper boiler plates cut by the manufacturer according to the pattern sent him by Trotter.

By the 1840's manufacturers whose wide hinterland markets enabled them to become large-scale producers helped to account for Trotter's increasing sales. One particularly well-known manufacturer was C. Cornelius, a producer of lamps, chandeliers, and gas fixtures who bought substantial quantities of brass and pig metals from Trotter.

At the Franklin Institute exhibition in 1847, Cornelius & Company was awarded a First Premium for the chandelier which they had made for the New York Opera House. This "magnificent" chandelier surpassed in "beauty and effect" all theretofore exhibited at the Franklin Institute.[43] The factory of Cornelius & Sons, as the firm came to be called, was described as "immense." And their product was well

Chart X

MAP OF TROTTER MARKET IN PENNSYLVANIA, 1840–1849

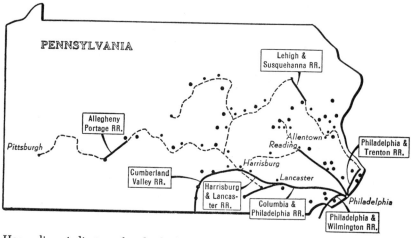

Heavy lines indicate railroads; broken lines indicate the canals which the railroads were intended to connect and supplement. Each dot represents a town in which customers purchased $200 of goods from Nathan Trotter & Company in any one year during 1840–1849. The larger dots indicate new markets since 1831.

enough known to be advertised by name: a Cincinnati dealer, Baker & VonPhul, advertised, in 1846, at their EMPORIUM OF LIGHT "a large assortment of Cornelius & Co.'s Patent Solar Lard Lamps and Chandeliers" constantly on hand.[44]

Another Philadelphia manufacturer with a national market was Lewis Debozear, who advertised that at his Brass & Bell Foundry he continued [45]

to cast to order every description of Bells, from one to ten thousand pounds weight. Corporation, Church, Steamboat, Factory, and Fire Bells, which for excellence of material, tone, workmanship, and correctness of modelling cannot be excelled in the United States.

Northern, Southern, and Western Merchants, will find it to their advantage to call at the above Foundry.

Chart XI

NATHAN TROTTER & COMPANY

Series of Three Maps Showing Areas in Which the Firm Had Customers
1803–1815, 1827–1831, 1840–1849

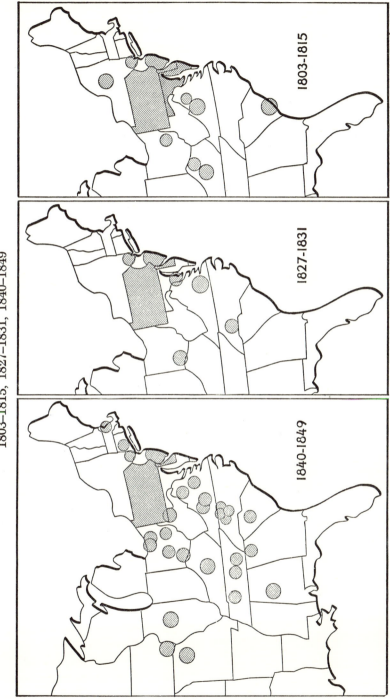

1803-1815

1827-1831

1840-1849

Stephen P. Morris & Company, manufacturers of wrought iron tubes and fittings for gas, steam, and water; [46] Peter Cooper, the well-known wire manufacturer of Trenton, purchaser of pig and scrap iron; the Gloucester Machine Company, purchaser of ingot copper and antimony—all were Trotter customers. Another equally well-known firm was the successful Lehigh Crane Iron Company, a fairly regular customer for sheet and pig metals.

The locomotive manufacturers also became important customers. This leads us to the other important cause of Trotter's increased sales: further developments in transportation. Philadelphia was, by the middle of the nineteenth century, the center of a network of railroads which were customers of the Trotters and transporters of their goods.[47] Over these lines, as the map in Chart X shows, Trotter customers received goods: to the eastward the Philadelphia & Trenton Rail Road; to the southwest the Philadelphia & Wilmington Rail Road; to the west the Columbia & Philadelphia Rail Road; and in a generally northward direction the Philadelphia & Reading Rail Road. One effect of the railroads on Trotter's market, as the map indicates, was a more thorough working of the nearby counties, a development which may have lessened Trotter's sales to merchant middlemen in such surban centers as Reading and Lancaster.

The market area outside Pennsylvania also was extended in 1840–1849 (see Chart XI). The firm by that time sold goods in most of the states east of the Mississippi. They also had customers west of the Mississippi in Iowa, Missouri, and Texas. The Pennsylvania Canal System, which made it cheaper and speedier to transport goods to Pittsburgh, facilitated trade to the west.

From the early years of the Trotters' business, the transportation market accounted for some of the Trotter firm's sales. Coach and carriage makers had purchased, in the prespecialization days, the "elegant and large roans, even colored and sound skins," in red, green, and blue to line their vehicles in a "handsome style." Steel was sold for coach springs and hoop iron for the wheels.

Shipping too was important to the Trotters' business, the demand for copper sheathing being particularly heavy in the 1820's and again in the 1840's. In 1828 Nathan Trotter had written that, although the sales of sheathing were limited, there were no large vessels then being coppered in Philadelphia except those he had supplied.[48]

The canal development in Pennsylvania had opened up new markets both geographically and industrially. The canal companies themselves bought tin plate for pipes to blow rocks under water and to cover hatches of the cars on the Portage Railroad of the Pennsylvania Canal System. Tin plate was also sold to a handicraftsman who made horns to be blown on the canal boats announcing their arrival.

By the late 1830's, strips for locomotive pipes were Trotter's principal sale in the copper line, he declared. Mica, 15 inches square, was sold for locomotive engine lanterns. The locomotive manufacturers—New Castle Manufacturing Company, the Baldwin firm, and Norris Brothers—became important customers.

The railroads also became customers, particularly for such pig metals as tin and lead, cakes of antimony, cakes of copper, and plates of spelter, as well as sheets of copper, tin plate and tinned copper, copper bolts, and spelter solder. The Camden & Amboy Rail Road Company, the New Castle & French Town Turnpike & Rail Road Company, the Columbia & Philadelphia Rail Road Company, the Philadelphia & Reading, and the Pennsylvania Railroad purchased from the Trotter firm. The importance of this new market may be gathered from the fact that the Pennsylvania Railroad once purchased 675 boxes of terneplate to cover a bridge across the Susquehanna.

During the last two years that Nathan Trotter engaged in merchandising, sales dropped: slightly in 1848 when there was a "dullness in industry and trade" in the country as a whole and considerably in 1849 when there was "widespread activity in industry." The 1849 decline possibly reflects lessened effort on the part of Nathan Trotter as he withdrew from merchandising to devote himself entirely to his discount and investment interests.

Throughout the years from 1803 to 1849 the Trotter firm's sales and market area expanded as economic conditions changed. Nathan Trotter seems to have benefited from the changes rather than to have exploited them. He kept himself, it is true, in a position to satisfy customer demands. As a well-established merchant, he supplied the goods and credits required by his market.

CHAPTER VII

Selling Methods

WHEN it came to personal selling, Nathan Trotter was alert, determined, and active; and since a great deal of his business was with Philadelphia customers, he was successful in this aspect of his merchandising. He recognized the importance of getting out and working for business. On one occasion he wrote to his son:[1] "The weather being so exceedingly damp and unpleasant I can go out but little and the[e] Knows business must be hunted up."

But though Trotter may have been an effective salesman when doing business at home, in his correspondence with customers outside Philadelphia he never used high-pressure salesmanship. There were periods when he said that it was more difficult to procure than to sell goods. When such a sellers' market prevailed, customers were forced to seek out the supplier. Much of Trotter's business was consequently conducted on the basis of orders sent to him by mail.

In the course of business Trotter received thousands of orders from customers—and preserved them one and all. There were scrawls from handicraftsmen who wanted tin plate by the first wagon; there were torn scraps of paper with daily requests for metals from Philadelphia mechanics; and such letters as this from an Ohio storekeeper who wrote to Trotter from Woodstock, Virginia:[2] "I am thus farr on my way to Market. I wish you to write me to this Place immediately and say what youll sell me copper & tin and wire &c. I like wise wish you [to] forward your acct. to Balte. at which Place I'll Discharge the same."

Some new customers were acquired when their Philadelphia source, unable to supply an order, passed it along to the Trotter firm. James Black of Easton was acquired in this way in 1815, and he and, after his death, his wife and son continued to be customers into the 1840's. Or perhaps one satisfied customer informed another: [3] "by Mr. Bardill I have Herd you have a handsome Sort of Des condre [this country] Sheet Iron, which is Blue of both Sides. Please let me have 1 Hundred of it."

Trotter was not only a seller but also a creator of valuable services. To acquire and hold his customers he placed special emphasis on rendering four types of services. He tried at all times to have an assortment of goods on hand when wanted. He carried the qualities needed by his customers. He attended to packing and shipping with the greatest of care. And he helped his customers to finance their purchases by extending credit. As to price, it seems to me that he sold at what the New York price compelled him to sell at, and that was usually a lower price than he would otherwise have accepted.

It was essential for Trotter to have a stock of goods on hand or to have a supplier who could respond promptly when there was a sudden demand. Shipowners had to have sheathing when the ship was on the screw dock waiting for it; roofers had to have tin plate or copper when the roof was ready; sheet ironworkers had to have goods in time to make up the fall stock of pipe elbows and pans. Delay was costly and trade would be given the dealer who could furnish merchandise on time.

An illustration of Trotter's prompt service to his customers by having goods readily available was his quick delivery of copper for the Alms House in 1831. He took particular pride in this achievement and gratification from the fact that it was a matter of comment in the trade. Indeed, Trotter wrote Isaac McKim, copper manufacturer of Baltimore: [4]

We quite astonished the coms [building commissioners] at the rapidity with which the copper was delivered, they had no idea of your despatching business so quick or rather that the works was of such magnitude, as to deliver the parcell so fast, in addition to your other orders—it has made some impression among the Copper men we assure you.

By August of the same year, when there was "exceeding press for Copper for certain stores" and other dealers could not fill contracts on time, Trotter had secured the business.

Trotter's reputation for promptness was especially good among his roofer customers. One of them, a man who had contracted to roof a building with copper, wrote [5] that he had run the risk of engaging to keep his men "agoing" since he had "never failed yet" aided by Trotter's prompt attention to his orders.

We have already seen some of the ways in which Trotter ensured that his customers received only the best quality of metals.[6] When he was selling tin plate on commission for Phelps, he complained: [7] "send no more P tin at present—buyers generally ask for first quality & we cant say this is." In writing customers Trotter again and again stressed the fact that he imported only the best brands. It was one of the few promotional devices he ever permitted himself to employ. Walkers' tin plate, Millington steel, and Sharpless sheet iron were known as first-quality goods. Evidently the domestic copper purchased from the McKims had a good reputation also, since Trotter wrote them on 4 February 1842 that he had sold a suit of their copper for the ship *Washington*

which made an East India Voyage shortly after, and perhaps run in a straight line 30,000 miles—She has been repairing for a month or more, & ship owners are of course noticing these things, particularly if they have a vessell in port requiring repairs—the appearance of the W[ashington]'s copper was so satisfactory that it induced the application of a purchase [of ten or twelve cases of sheathing].

Trotter concluded: "There must have been strong feelings in favour to overcome a difference of two cents p # & all the persuasion of holders of English copper."

In order to keep customers it was necessary to give satisfaction in engaging freight, settling on freight rates, and attending carefully to the stowing of goods. Throughout the period 1803–1849 some member or employee of the Trotter firm personally attended to engaging wagon space. So great was the demand for transportation at times that bargaining for rates was of secondary importance—the merchant was lucky to get the goods off. To customer Hager, Nathan Trotter wrote, 16 March 1830: "Our young man has been to every tavern in Market St. but has not met with a wagon. There were two in town but the carters could not be found—he will this evening go up and if possible dispatch it in the morning."

Although the canal era was accompanied by the establishment of many forwarding houses, which took the burden of engaging freight off the Trotter firm's shoulders, freight rates were variable and Nathan Trotter could still use his personal influence to get the lowest price, as this typical letter which he wrote a Pittsburgh customer illustrates: "We spent a good deal of time . . . in running among the Forwardg Houses from Broad St. to the Delaware to squeeze the lowest figure of Fgt & altho many asked us 60c we obtained it finally for 51c p 100 lbs which is much lower than the regular rate." [8]

Not only was the Trotter firm's services required in engaging freight and settling on as low freight rates as possible, but the nature of the goods which they sold made personal supervision still important. Tin plate, round, hoop, and sheet iron, and sheet lead were easily damaged by water. They needed to be moved in dry weather, stowed properly, and transported under cover. Nathan Trotter gave to the stowage of goods the extreme care which he gave to all branches of his business and he must have retained many satisfied customers because of this. He furthermore employed only careful shippers of his goods and even then gave them explicit directions.

This letter to James Black of Easton gives some idea of the care taken: [9]

46 Bundles of sheet iron sent this morning by De Hart and all the rest of the goods by Rosebery's boat—every possible attention was paid by us in getting them on board and stowing them to best advantage & particularly charged them to cover them well to keep off the damp and in case of rain, which they promised most strictly to attend to—the sheets of copper were spread over the Tin &c and they said they have tarpauling or oil cloths, besides their sail so that they could not get injured.

But of all the services which Nathan Trotter performed, granting credit was one of the most important and surely the most profitable. To his merchant customers in the hinterland, circumscribed in their payments by the seasonal rhythm of an agricultural community, he granted the long credits which they required. Handicraftsmen, too, found long credits essential. So important was this aspect of Trotter's business that a section of the following chapter will be given to it.

Occasionally Nathan Trotter "hunted out a little business" through correspondence. But the most he might do would be to inform a customer, perhaps one who had not given an order for some time, that certain goods had just arrived. Quality of goods might also be mentioned—indeed almost certainly would be. Attention might be called to reduced freight rates or the fact that goods could be sent at low freight through the canal by sloop to Baltimore. An overproduction of raised and flat copper bottoms might lead to a special offer of 500 to 1,000 pounds at a low cost. After a dull winter when his stock of tin plate had "accumulated to a larger extent" than was "comfortable to hold," Trotter might say he would submit to a positive loss. Late in his business career Trotter offered an inducement which the New Yorkers had offered their customers decades earlier—low prices for tin plates delivered from the ship.

On one occasion a letter from a firm named Halderman & Cotrell inquiring about the price of tin plate and intended for a rival merchant, Mr. Taylor, was delivered to Trotter by mistake. Trotter, after noting the letter's contents, directed the bearer to Taylor's store and then sat down to write Halderman & Cotrell a note which in tone combines the eighteenth and nineteenth centuries. "Whilst we would not for a moment influence your place of purchase it may not be indecorous to say we have just recd some tin plate of the best brands," Trotter began. Then, since Taylor was "sustained by a New York house whose monopolizing views would engross all sales from 1 box to 1000"—obviously Phelps Dodge & Company—Trotter offered the best brands at a figure "lower than it can possibly be afforded," at a price not to be mentioned to others.[10]

As was typical in the first half of the nineteenth century, various members and employees of the Trotter firm, while on collection trips, also endeavored to secure new customers and make sales to some former ones. Daisy Cheyney's trip to Ohio and Kentucky, already mentioned, taught the firm that it was a mistake to encourage handicraftsmen to buy. They purchased goods as wanted—"the use of copper cannot be forced, it's like medicine and used only when wanted"—and a handicraftsman who purchased more than his immediate need was a bad credit risk. If there was any sales promotion, it was to country storekeepers and merchants, men with enough capital to carry an inventory with safety.

Occasionally the Trotter firm used their customers as selling agents. These agents, residing in the larger centers such as Reading and Lancaster (1816–1828), and Pittsburgh (1816 through the 1840's) and Baltimore (the late 1830's and the 1840's) sold on a stated commission. One Pittsburgh customer, on 21 July 1837, shortly after the suspension of Phelps Dodge & Company, suggested what was probably the customary commission arrangement at the time: [11]

the way that my neighbour park does with Phelps & Co. in gineral is he sells for them for 50 cts per box the[y] paying the Exchange and all costs of drayage & Fraight   if you would be agreed to do so with me and keep me constently suplyed with a Stocke of Plate wire & Block tin I think I could sell nearly as much as park can do   our tinners do not like him much although him & myself is on the Bist terms of friendship.

The most active selling of the Trotter firm came after they began making annual contracts to buy tin plate and wire. Then they exerted themselves more to get rid of stocks of goods. The contract with the wire manufacturer led Trotter in the spring of 1848 to urge that the merchants F. Lawson & Brothers of Cincinnati contract in advance to take 500 bundles of Trotter's iron wire. "We would propose," stated Trotter, "selling the quantity to you at 43 p cent disct nett cash say deliverable 125 bdles a month in May, June, July, & Aug as near as we can   you to define the different sizes wanted, to enable us to have it prepared." [12] This was a selling device which Anson Phelps had successfully used years earlier.

Sheet iron was sold on commission for the American manufacturer. This seemed to be the usual procedure and Trotter expected to be the sole outlet in the Philadelphia market. This was a great advantage in the years when he sold Sharpless sheet iron. The arrangement with the sheet-iron manufacturer was made fairly early in the year since, as Trotter wrote in February, "Now is the time when we should be looking among purchasers a little." [13] The following year he wrote the manufacturer even earlier about engaging a supply, saying "Some customers or consumers are now as usual about making their arrangements for sheet iron and we must be early to meet them, or others will supply them." [14]

In the 1830's, during the spring and fall, while the Trotter firm was selling steel on commission, they wrote prospective customers telling them what steel was on hand or offering to order a case for them, "say 10 Cwt, assorted in any way of any size of cast or shear or both."

Although the Trotters did not wish it known that they were selling on commission on many occasions during the 1820's and 1830's, in 1847 they actually wrote a customer that they had been appointed agents for the sale of sheet zinc and were able to supply the article as low as it could be sold in the United States.

The men from whom Trotter bought his goods promoted their wares scarcely more than Trotter did his. Of all the correspondence in the Trotter papers, that from the Belgian house of the Vieille-Montagne Zinc Society shows the most aggressive selling methods. This Belgian firm was ahead of its century. As soon as Trotter became their Philadelphia agent they wrote him saying that they counted on his activity and care to push the sale of their zinc. The Society's general agent in New York City—F. Millerous and in his absence Charles Aragon—kept Trotter informed about new and old uses of zinc, published testimonials from satisfied customers, and suggested new opportunities for marketing the product. When the general agent went to Washington he had interviews with the Secretary of the Navy. The younger Trotters seemed to have caught a little of the enthusiasm of the Society and solicited customers for zinc orders fairly actively.

Nathan Trotter seldom advertised and never employed a traveling salesman. Salesmen were a selling device to be used later by his sons. He once spoke slightingly of racks which a competitor had fixed up in which to display his copper and scoffingly showed his disdain for such unseemly "frills" by writing: "our f[rien]ds wont leave us while we treat them as well as we can." [15] Although Trotter came to use racks later, perhaps for convenience in sorting and not for display, sales depended chiefly on treating his customers, as he put it, as well as he could.

Occasionally Trotter permitted a little "decorous" promotion, but the exceptions were so rare that they serve only to emphasize his characteristic conservatism. He had trade cards printed in 1816, as we have seen. His name also appeared as agent for the sale of tinners' tools in the advertisement of one manufacturer, doubtless with Trotter's permission. But when a manufacturer of tin horns asked if he might advertise the firm as agent, Trotter replied—perhaps because he considered tin horns a petty business—that the manufacturer could use the address, 32 North Front Street, but not the name Nathan Trotter & Company. The store at 32 North Front was owned by Trotter but was not his place of business.

Within Philadelphia itself Trotter's selling methods were more forceful, and occasionally there are glimpses of Trotter engaging in a free-for-all for business and showing his delight in the battle of the market place. About the Alms House affair he wrote: "We had no idea that the opposition would have set so hard against us   it was a struggle you may depend and we left no stone unturned to succeed in getting it—for having entered into it we were determined that strong efforts should not be wanting on our part." [16]

The most exciting struggle for business came in 1833 when an extension to the Alms House was being built.[17] Trotter got the contract, though he remarked that he had all the odds against him. The chairman of the Building Committee, Mr. Bunker, was agent for a rival manufacturer, J. McKim, Jr., & Sons of Baltimore, and the architect was thought to favor the copper of Crocker's of Taunton. "You will admit it will require care in our movements in regard to the alms House Copper," Trotter wrote Isaac McKim. "Mr. Bunker . . . will we think be our heaviest opponent. We will keep you apprised as far as we can and abide by your advice." On Trotter's urging, Isaac McKim made a price concession, enabling Trotter to hand in a proposal of 23 $9\%_{100}$ cents per pound. Since this was less than other bids "of equal qty" he got the contract. As it turned out the odds had not all been against him after all; in a letter of 14 May he wrote that he had some friends among the commissioners.

On one occasion he spoke of some manufacturer's agent in Philadelphia trying to get the sale of a suit of copper for a vessel, "but we having spoken abt it a month ago were furnished a chance on the arrival of the vessel—it requires considerable exertion to secure a sale." Again he wrote: "It is only by being alert and having our orders quickly attended to that we can hold on to many customers who are much solicited to go elsewhere." [18]

Quality, price, services in shipping, credit—these were the main factors in selling goods. But on one occasion, when soliciting an order from the Pennsylvania Railroad, Nathan Trotter thought it would do no harm to mention also the ownership of stock. On 16 January 1849 he wrote J. Edgar Thomson, chief engineer of the railroad:

> We were informed a few days since by a customer of ours Mr Wm H Griffin of Wilmington that you proposed covering the Bridge across the Susquehanna with roofing Tin. Holding considerable stock in the road and having an excellent article on hand we should be pleased to supply the company and trust we can do so on as favorable terms as it can be purchased elsewhere

The quality and terms proved satisfactory and Trotter secured an order for over seven thousand dollars worth of terneplate.

CHAPTER VIII

Credit and Collections

IN the early years of his business career Nathan Trotter usually let the commission merchants of England finance his operations. By purchasing on long credits he was able in turn to advance long credits to his customers. This practice continued until competitive pressures forced him to finance his trade himself—to make payment either at the time of purchase or fairly soon thereafter in order to obtain a favorable price in England. At the same time, however, competitive pressures at the selling level forced Trotter to continue the practice of granting his customers in America extensive credit privileges. In short, Trotter was taking over from the English commission merchants a part of the burden of financing industrial development and westward growth of the United States.

Long credits were necessary in a rapidly developing economy and a merchant had to be ready to grant them if he wished to obtain and hold customers. The agricultural nature of the American economy had much to do with these long periods of credit. Farmers did not receive payment for their produce until it had been harvested and meanwhile the goods which they bought from merchants or handicraftsmen had to be charged. This also meant a seasonality in the flow of payments to Trotter. Some country storekeepers, such as Keim & Drinkle of Reading, made a regular practice of paying off their accounts each spring and fall, and Trotter, if he was to hold their business, had to meet their needs.

Although Trotter frequently sold goods on six months' credit, he was reluctant to admit to that practice as a general policy. A letter dated in 1818 illustrates his efforts to make it appear as the exception: "Four months is our general credit tho' to particular customers we don't mind its extension say 2 mo. longer." Beginning in the 1820's, however, he adopted the practice of sending out semiannual statements to customers. He explained the new policy in these words: "The plan we have adopted here . . . is to consider due the 30 June & 31 Dec the amount of all goods had the preceding 6 mos. and whatever monies they pay on a/c in the intermediate periods to allow them interest for." [1]

Country storekeepers usually required a longer credit from Trotter than Philadelphia merchants, but in the case of handicraftsmen Trotter found himself forced to extend long credits even to those located in the city. There is no specific information in the Trotter papers to explain this practice. Some Philadelphia craftsmen bought from Trotter over a period of many years and continued to settle their accounts at the close of each six months' period. It seems unlikely that shortage of capital could be the only explanation; some of Trotter's Philadelphia customers must have derived a respectable income from their craftsman's trade. It may be that these men of moderate means and moderate ambitions had fallen into a custom of the trade and did not see an advantage in pushing business for its last cent of profit by striving to secure cash discounts.

As was customary, Trotter sold goods on a multiple price basis: the cash price and the credit price, with many shadings on either side. The basic price for purposes of computation was the credit price. When Trotter quoted a price of $500 he meant that $500 was due at the end of a credit term, four months for example. If the customer paid before the end of the credit period, Trotter treated the payment as though it were a cash advance and therefore he granted what amounted to an interest credit. If he received cash on delivery, he allowed the full interest credit in the form of a cash discount; the net payment was in that case the cash price. If payment was delayed beyond the credit period, he charged interest at the going rate—often 3 to 5 per cent.

By 1832 Trotter had succeeded in reducing his "usual average credit" to three months, but he was still making sales on longer terms. Only on tin-plate sales was the credit period typically shorter. Frequently he insisted on 60 days' credit for tin plate since, as he said, the article paid so little profit.

Sometimes Trotter granted credit on open account; sometimes he asked customers to give him their personal (or partnership) notes as evidence of indebtedness. For the years 1819, 1820, 1821, and 1822, the clerk who compiled the balance sheets listed the two types of indebtedness separately and in addition indicated whether the outstanding indebtedness was owed by city (i.e., Philadelphia) or by country customers. It is clear from these figures (see Table 8) that country customers were not in the habit of giving notes for goods purchased. Even in 1819 when times were hard and Nathan Trotter was especially eager to obtain notes as evidences of debt, the country notes amounted to less than $3,000 out of total receivables of nearly $32,000.

Table 8

Nathan Trotter & Company
Business Receivables on 31 December 1819–1822

| | Accounts Receivable | | | Notes Receivable | | |
Year	City	Country	Total	City	Country	Total
1819	$ 5,778.92	$10,999.20	$16,778.12	$12,314.33	$2,850.49	$15,164.82
1820	6,733.71	10,941.95	17,675.66	11,298.67	2,000.18	13,298.85
1821	13,111.85	9,983.07	23,094.92	14,867.65	1,648.28	16,515.93
1822	14,971.42	9,145.45	24,116.87	10,849.91	2,291.18	13,141.09

Inland customers were constitutionally opposed to signing notes. They felt they had so little control over the flow of currency that they should not be obliged to commit themselves legally to payment within a given time period. A young Lancaster handicraftsman submitted an order for tin plate, but on one condition: "provided you can send them as heretofore without my giving you my note for the amount as I can deal at other places in that way and am determined not to give my note."

There were a number of reasons why Nathan Trotter stressed the importance of notes. They were useful to him in collecting a debt since he could deposit them in a Philadelphia bank or even in the customer's local bank and the bankers would attend to collecting them when due.[2] Moreover they were a clear evidence of debt about which there could be no misunderstanding or quibbling. They were also a method of avoiding difficulty over legal limitations on collections. To keep his claim valid, Trotter on one occasion wrote to a customer whose payment had been overdue for several years and asked for a new note so that the claim would not be "vitiated by the statute of limita-

Warehouse of Nathan Trotter & Company

Philadelphia, 22nd January 1842

Sundries   Dr. to   Cash

James Woods & Son
     Paid them this day on account
     as per receipt 150 00

Merchandize
     Paid for 13 doz Sauces and Candle
     @ 21¢ per doz 2 73
             22   152 73

Sundries   Dr. to   Richd. P. Cumming

Bills Receivable
     for his Note in our favr dated
     1st inst @ 4 mos for 1900 00
     less this amt Credited Int on
     below 39 30   1860 70

Contingent Fund
     allowed him this Amt being amt
     of bills 10, 14, 18, 22 & 31 Oct 1841 for
     Bank Pos which he fraudulently
     was fraudulently obtained by his
     nephew C. C. Thomas under false
     representations 74 75
             22   1935 45

Bills Receivable   Dr. to   Interest Acct.
     For this amt included in Rich
     P. Cumming Note as per entry above 39 30
             24

Cash   Dr. to   Sundries
     To Bills Receivable
     for Albert Murray Note paid this
     day at Counting House amtg to 33 99
     To Francis Fields & Francis
     received this day on Account 200 00
     To Pancoast & Trotter
     received this W. Protts 22 88
                           256 87

A Page of Robert McCune's Accounts

tions." Inland customers frequently argued that they had no control over payments when they themselves could not collect for their goods. Trotter replied that some of his customers had found it useful to remind their own delinquent debtors that collections were imperative to enable them to meet their notes to Philadelphia suppliers.

To the extent that notes induced punctuality, Nathan Trotter must have played a part in making the American businessman prompt in settling his business commitments. "I have to be punctual to a day in taking up my notes," he pointed out, "and must depend on my customers paying me punctually to enable me to do it." [3]

The system by which notes were collected contributed as much as anything to the habit of punctuality. "You will be careful," Trotter advised a customer, "to have the money at the Bank at the time or a day or two before otherwise the note might be protested as we should not have control over it you will probably receive no notice from the Bank as they are made payable then."

It was this very punctual character of notes to which some of his customers objected. J. & J. Arter of Danville, Pennsylvania, did not wish to give notes payable in the bank because, so they wrote: [4]

[We are] not certain positively that we could meet them at the precise time and by so doing we would injure ourselves—business in our place is governed to some extent by the Rolling Mill—that is if they do not pay at the time generally expected it puts us all back very much and for these and similar reasons we do not wish to give our notes payable in bank rather than do it we would curtail our business.

A conflict between the desire for security of debts, in the form of notes, and the wish to satisfy customers stands out in this letter of 2 September 1818. The letter was written by Nathan Trotter to his clerk Daisy who was on a collection-selling trip:

Since you started we have been thinking about what we told you relative to getting notes of our difft. customers—We hope you will not press the thing except in *Some Cases* as perhaps it wd. rather have a tendency of dissatisfying them. Whenever you are satisfied of their goodness the best way is to humour their ways a little at the same time using such management as wd. be most likely to secure our interest in relation to them.

Unlike his brother, William, who doubtless knew personally all the men to whom he sold, Nathan in many cases had to entrust his goods to strangers. The selection of credit risks was therefore a serious problem. Like his contemporaries, in the years before Mercantile Agencies were established, Trotter relied on other merchants for credit information. When he inquired about a man's credit he asked to have the matter considered confidential: "Please dont say we made an enquiry but have the goodness to say by return mail whether in your opinion we may safely extend credit to——?" Apparently some writers hesitated to give advice for fear they might be considered to have some responsibility if they vouched for a man's credit. In such instances they added to a favorable comment on a man's credit, "We guarantee nothing."

Of course there were times when other merchants volunteered to take responsibility for payments by someone else. Friend Matt Ralston went surety for the payment of sheathing needed to copper Captain Walker's brig, and J. L. James, time after time, wrote such letters as this: "If Mr. Luke Read should pay off his account with you that I became responsible for you may let him have goods to the amount of Forty Dollars on the same terms as the other and consider me responsible for that Amot."

When Trotter had extended credit at the request of a third party, he frequently addressed himself to that person when payments had not been made. "We think you ought to pay me amot due from Warner," wrote Trotter to one customer, "as it was owing to your recommendation that we trusted him." And again, "We apprehend there is a liability attached to you in this matter as solely at your instance was the credit extended at all & we trust you will take care that we are not sufferers by the transactions." In many of these instances, Trotter may have been using this method to get the recommender to bring pressure to bear on the delinquent rather than requiring payment from the house which introduced the customer.

As is evident in Table 9, the amount of credit granted by Trotter fluctuated with the times. When business was prospering and collections were fairly easy, he tended to be lenient. But when depressions hit, he could be a very cautious credit manager. In 1819, in 1830, in 1833 and 1834, and again in 1839 and 1840, he drastically restricted the amount of credit he granted. In those years he was "not disposed to extend any more credit even with old customers," preferring to keep his goods rather than "create greater anxiety about debts." [5] Here we see the businessman adding to depressed conditions by refusing to do business even on the terms usually considered normal. "Until trade revives and more facility is apparent to enable our friends to remit, we shall be obliged . . . to forego executing many orders." He recognized

Table 9

Nathan Trotter & Company
Notes Receivable and Accounts Receivable as of 31 December 1815–1849

Year	Notes Receivable	Accounts Receivable
1815	$12,925.58	$20,481.89
1816	25,360.76	20,018.41
1817	34,593.92	25,240.50
1818	38,130.72	26,238.31
1819	15,164.82	16,778.12
1820	13,298.85	17,675.66
1821	16,515.93	23,829.64
1822	13,141.09	24,116.87
1823	21,700.78	b
1824	20,134.90	b
1825	47,694.94 a	b
1826	40,410.08	b
1827	67,407.37	b
1828	62,442.43	b
1829	83,158.15	36,366.98
1830	47,853.79	b
1831	69,135.89	b
1832	68,071.77	b
1833	43,630.58 a	b
1834	16,280.69	b
1835	19,726.40	b
1836	21,927.91	b
1837	21,212.73	b
1838	43,079.08	b
1839	34,027.79	b
1840	22,447.54	23,640.73
1841	29,367.34	20,523.31
1842	22,960.41	10,833.46
1843	20,812.45	12,113.21
1844	32,484.78	23,486.26
1845	37,168.61	31,572.85
1846	38,223.06	49,185.26
1847	41,234.61 a	74,510.17
1848	52,898.52	59,778.68
1849	81,000.48 a	74,027.81

a From 1825 up through the year 1833 and again 1847–1849 these figures include a considerable amount of commercial paper discounted as well as business notes received from the firm's customers.

b For these years no totals for book accounts—accounts receivable—were calculated by Trotter or his clerks.

that his sales would be less, but, he added, it was better to mourn *over* his goods than *after* them.[6]

Nathan Trotter really considered that he was doing customers no favor in granting too much credit. In 1819 he lost heavily through a Pittsburgh customer named Kepner. Concerning this debt he wrote to a third person: [7]

it is hard to bear but it shall be a lesson for us to take special care hereafter who we let have goods on a credit—K however we still believe a well meaning man but has unfortunately done too much business for his ability to manage, and by representations and promises has got a large credit from us which proves of great disadvantage to us without perhaps any benefit to himself.

Trotter summarized his credit policy in these words written in 1829 to one of his suppliers:

We feel desirous of acting with a liberal prudence in our dealings and by keeping as far as we can all our accounts within proper bounds we hope to give equal satisfaction to our friends and avoid the rock on which many has split by having their business too much extended.

Nathan Trotter was, I believe, a lenient creditor. He chose his customers with a view to their financial standing; then having granted them credit, he treated them as honorable men who could be expected to pay their just debts. When times were difficult and payments were hard to meet, he made the necessary allowances. To make certain that his good customers did not misunderstand the innovation of semi-annual bills in 1820, he took special pains to indicate that he was not doubting any ability to pay: "We send the balance in our favour that you may examine it and would like your order." But to slow-paying customers he was more abrupt, simply stating that "payment would oblige."

Trotter resorted to various devices when dealing with habitual delinquents. Sometimes he would fill new orders only when earlier ones had been paid for. Or he might charge a dollar more than the usual price for tin plate with the understanding that for payment within 30 days the extra dollar would be dropped.

Frequently he based an appeal for payment on the "honesty and integrity" of the debtor. For instance: [8]

. . . we are free to confess that our dependence has been on your honesty and integrity more than any legal compunction having confidence at the time of sale that we were extending credit to a Gentleman highly worthy of it & yet hope not to be mistaken.

Here is another version of the theme: [9]

We know times have been difficult and hence payments have been delayed but we again repeat we depend on your honour & integrity to pay us and you will hereafter find by having held fast to honesty of intention, you will be more likely to succeed in any business you may engage in.

Trotter liked to be informed of the possibility of ultimate payment, and many customers obliged. "I will be punctial to forward the amount in sixty days," wrote one; "I have got a station in the Land Department as clerk," he explained, "and Receive $550 per year—That with my Trade will Enable me to be Punctial in my Engagements."

Some of Trotter's letters to debtor customers are full of good advice. On 29 April 1819 he wrote a delinquent customer: "Prospects generally look very gloomy and confidence exceedingly impaired—" This being the case, he concluded, the customer should be extremely careful to whom he extended credit.

Even for the fairly successful and diligent customer, prompt payment was not always possible. Ability to pay was closely allied to the economy of the immediate locality. When a depression hit the countryside, local consumers often were not able to pay their debts to Trotter's customers and the latter in turn were unable to pay Trotter. John Bollinger, a handicraftsman in Hollidaysburg, described his predicament movingly in the depressed year of 1840: "as to collecting money from Iron men, or Store Keepers, its a matter out of the question, nor from the Commonwealth agents or in fact any person else." In 1842 he was still having his troubles: "I sent my brother out with accounts to amount of three hundred dollars, and he came home with a ten dollar note of the Bank of Woster, Ohio, as the result of that expedition. . . . I have Brought Suite against many, but all take the Stays [stay laws which protected debtors], and that is worse still." [10]

Some customers lived in areas that were dependent on a single cash crop or commodity. A depression in the area's specialty made currency unobtainable. The Stoughtons, who sold Trotter's wares in the canal town of Milton, wrote in 1832: "Money is hard to get this summer   their has not Been any lumber out of this Branch this spring or summer which makes money scarce hear."

When money became tight, Trotter's customers often had to accept produce in payment of debts owed to them by their own customers. They disliked to do so but often they had no alternative. It meant they had to find markets for the produce before they could meet their debts to Trotter—and in a depression this often was not easy to do. Frequently they sent exchange items—barrels of whiskey or of flour or some peach brandy—to Philadelphia to be sold and at the same time they informed Trotter that he would be paid if the sale was successful.

Sometimes the Trotter firm itself undertook to sell produce for customers to help them settle their accounts. In 1815 Trotter received Louisiana cotton, white lead, and tallow to be sold for the account of Isaac Wickersham of Pittsburgh. In the 1830's and 1840's he received, especially from his country tinsmith customers, such varied items as beeswax, tallow, rags, feathers, furs of rabbits, fox, muskrats, mink, and deer, buck horns, bristles, and quills. Fortunately for Trotter there were in Philadelphia by that time a number of specialized dealers in many of these articles and he was able to dispose of them readily. In earlier times he himself would undoubtedly have been forced to find customers for these items.

Trotter's produce transactions remind one of the old colonial merchant who, along with his foreign trade, took payment in goods. It is evident that bad times brought a partial breakdown in the exchange system and a retrogression to an earlier stage of business development.

When times were good and obligations were promptly met, Trotter received his payment supposedly in cash. But "payment in cash" was not the simple statement it would seem to be. It might mean currency, but as frequently it meant cashier's checks or drafts drawn on the customer by Trotter or drafts drawn for some reason on a third person. Even in the case of currency, the merchant had to take care to protect himself by stating explicitly that payment was to be made in "Current money of Philadelphia." Otherwise he might receive some of the unreliable currency printed by small banks in the interior.

This currency, usually in the form of bank notes, was so little trusted by Philadelphians that they frequently accepted it only at a discount. The reputation of some notes fell so low that merchants refused to accept them at any price. Doubtless much of the produce sent down to Philadelphia from towns in the interior came from storekeepers and craftsmen who preferred to accept payment from their own customers in the form of commodities rather than take their chances on bank notes of uncertain value. On occasion Trotter offered to split the discount with his customer. To one, Weitzel of Lancaster, he wrote: "if you will send me down the balance in Western notes I will pay part of the disct myself as I am much in want of money, it is abt. 10 p Cent now & I will take them from you at 5 pCt in order that the loss may be divided between us." [11]

In the late 1830's and early 1840's currency was a businessman's constant worry. He did not know from day to day what paper currency would be worth. Notes which on one day were discounted at 3 or 4 per cent might, on the following day, so Trotter declared, be discounted by as much as 10 per cent.[12] A customer remitted a batch of notes and Trotter disposed of them to best advantage. It then remained for him to render to his customer a statement showing the face value of the notes and the amount of "Current money in Philadelphia" they had brought in exchange.

Despite the care he took in selecting his credit risks, Trotter was not always able to collect. Some debtors took the benefit of insolvency laws while others went West to start business afresh.

Between 1815 and 1820 it was Daisy who bore the burden of trying to collect bad debts, and it was a difficult task in many ways. For one thing, he was asked by Trotter to do some selling while on his collection trips. Psychologically the two functions were incompatible. No wonder Daisy sometimes wished Nathan were along to make decisions. But they both seemed to accept the fact that Nathan could not have withstood the rigors of the journeys.

In later years some member of the Trotter family went out personally to arrange for the collection of debts. There are records of nearly 20 collecting trips made either by the Trotters themselves or by one of their employees. With a member of the firm on the scene it was sometimes possible to work out an arrangement whereby at least part of a bad debt could be recovered. Edward Trotter went once to see a debtor over whom there was hanging a judgment for more than he was worth. In a letter to his father, Edward explained the settlement he had made: [13]

[I] represented to him our leniency and finally found out he had between 7 and 800 old Copper which had been sold under a judgment but bought by a friend for him to enable him to purchase Stock to proceed with his business after a long Talk and hard persuasion I finally told him if he would send us that lot of old Copper we would return him his Note I consider it so much saved.

Sometimes, though not often, Nathan relied on a fellow merchant to help him collect a debt of long standing. For instance, he might ask an inland correspondent to check on a customer's current financial standing: "whether worth anything," he wrote, "or if thee thinks it advisable to prosecute learn the name of some responsible good attorney."

Nathan Trotter, the Quaker, was, as he put it, "repugnant to legal measures," although late in his business life he seems to have altered somewhat his attitude toward the use of lawyers. "We have suffered very heavy in many instances where others have got their money," he ruefully reflected. Had he pressed suit, he concluded, he might not have had to "endure the inconvenience of losses that might have been saved." In self-commiseration he wrote that he had indeed been wearing "the robe of patience" until it was threadbare. Finally he concluded that where payments were not punctual, legal measures should be resorted to at once.[14]

This bitter conclusion, however, does not reflect Trotter's attitude toward slow-paying customers so fairly as does this extract from a letter of 1843 which ran: "We know times are difficult beyond parallel. You need not be apprehensive of our resorting to legal measures. An honest man wants no law to compel him to pay & that is our estimate of you." [15] Trotter lost thousands of dollars to men who could not pay because of depressed conditions. But let a man of no principle cause him to lose $60 and Nathan Trotter almost steps forth from the page. One prosaic entry of a loss concludes with the notation that this particular customer turned out to be a rascal: "thus by this Scoundrel have we been mulched into a loss of over $500. dollars, a lesson hereafter—Look out Boys!" [16]

The figures for Trotter's credit losses may not be complete, but, so far as entries in the profit and loss statements show, the amounts charged off for bad debts, during the thirty-five years Trotter was in business as a merchant, totaled $39,567.59. Since this figure covers the entire 1815–1849 period, it amounts to a yearly average of $1,130, or less than $\frac{1}{10}$ of 1 per cent on sales. Considering the hard times which business experienced in those years, Trotter's credit management would seem to have met with remarkable success.

PART III

Trotter as a Monied Man

CHAPTER IX

A Merchant Turns to Investment

ALTHOUGH Nathan Trotter considered himself a specialized metals merchant, and although he conducted his affairs in surroundings that were typical of the metals wholesaler, the fact remains that this Philadelphian of the nineteenth century was, in the diversity of his business interests, not far removed from the unspecialized sedentary merchant of earlier times. Alongside his metals business, and often inextricably intertwined with it, Nathan conducted an investment business which took his funds into a variety of activities. In brief he was an investing capitalist as well as a merchant. The combination is found repeatedly in history, especially in the four or five centuries before 1800.

It would be incorrect to imagine that Trotter was first a merchant and then an investor, that he first acquired his capital and then invested it. In reality he was an investor almost as early as a merchant. The functions were part of a whole and to treat them, as this book does, as though they were separate is one of those unrealities we fall into when we try to split life into comprehensible parts.

In the first years of his business career, 1803 to 1815, the years when he was under the strong influence of his brother William and of the Sansoms, Nathan was already putting money to work outside his importing trade. With a business that was not yet developed fully enough to require a steady flow of funds or to need reserves against a break in continuity, Nathan, the freight-renting importer, found himself recurrently liquidating one transaction and seeking opportunities to invest in another. If upon selling a batch of goods, Trotter saw no immediate opportunity to replace his depleted inventory, he might, and frequently did, keep his capital active by investing it temporarily elsewhere. Under such conditions the activities of the investor and the merchant were not only intermingled but the one was as likely to be diversified as the other.

There was pressure on the man with capital to make it work. Whether the capital was in ships or money, even though conditions were not ideal, the urge to use it was present. McMaster portrays Stephen Girard as a man whom neither "the high price of syrup nor the low price of flour discouraged. . . . His ships must be kept busy." [1] On one occasion Girard wrote: "I have at present four of my ships in this port. As I am not in the habit to keep my vessels idle, their sight at our wharves is unpleasant to me, therefore I must do something with them." [2] Trotter commented in the course of making a discount entry at the rate of only 4 per cent a year: "too bad, but had the money idle." [3]

For every day that money was idle a potential income was sacrificed. On 12 August 1831 $4,000 of guardianship money became available for Trotter to reinvest. As a responsible custodian, seeking a safe, liquid, profitable investment, Trotter turned to commercial-paper discounting. On the very day he received this money, he purchased a lot of 22 notes, discounting them at the rate of 5½ per cent.[4]

This desire to keep money constantly employed often had caused the Trotter brothers, in the years before 1815, to participate in the business ventures of other merchants. These ventures might be purely local—the purchase of cord wood or a raft of logs—or they might be one-voyage partnerships—a venture to the West Indies or to the Orient. In either case the brothers contributed their capital as a risk-bearing equity and not as an interest-bearing loan. Stock certificates in a turnpike, a steamboat line, or a bank were another form of temporary investment. A third was commercial paper, valued for its ready liquidity, though sometimes low in yield.

After the death of Nathan's brother, William, and the reorganization of the partnership to include the other brother, Joseph, there came the decision to specialize in metals and with it a tendency for the firm's outside investments to become more specialized also. What Trotter called in his records "purchases in company"—that is, joint purchases of particular lots of goods—ceased completely. Participation in other men's ventures, though continuing, became less important. Such investments as the firm made in this period of transition were in real estate and, increasingly, in commercial-paper discounting.

By 1826 the Trotters clearly recognized that their commercial-paper investments were becoming sufficiently important in themselves to deserve more careful attention and they set about regularizing the accounts and putting them in clearer order. Nevertheless the firm continued, as before, to interweave their investments with their merchandise accounts. It was not until 1833 that the brothers began to keep their investment accounts completely apart from the mercantile records. On 31 December of that year they transferred the firm's investment accounts to a separate daybook and ledger entitled "Nathan Trotter & Co. Private."

On the first page of the new daybook Nathan Trotter set forth, in typical Trotter detail, the reasons for setting up separate books:

> The above accounts, as well as those following under same date, are thus abstracted from the General Ledger in order that they may be kept more private and that the profits arising from the general business of Merchandising as well as Interest on Stocks, Rents of Real Estate and the discount on notes, may be condensed in these Books without as heretofore so conspicuously appearing in the General Ledger which it is hereafter intended to confine to individual accts & such general accts only as ar[e] necessarily connected with them.

Possibly the brothers intended to pursue a more vigorous investment policy and felt that their increasing investments should be treated as a separate activity.

The investments transferred to the new books were valued as follows:

Securities	$ 4,445.00
Real Estate	35,443.49
	$39,888.49

The amount of commercial paper held by the firm was not transferred but was left to mature in the regular receivables account of the firm. Thereafter, however, all new discounted paper was entered in the private books. By the close of the first year the value of the discounted paper amounted to $39,291.43.

For a period of about three years the brothers built up their investment account and actively managed it. Then, with the coming of depression years, they gradually divided their holdings. It may be that, in a deflationary period when good investments were difficult to make and when some losses were inevitable, the brothers concluded that it was wiser for each to manage his own investment account. On the other hand a separation of partnership holdings was not unusual when brothers were advancing in years and were planning to turn over some of their property to their children.

About August, 1837, Joseph sold to Nathan his half interest in the firm's securities for $21,753.94. Within the next two years he also sold to Nathan his joint interest in nearly all the firm's real-estate holdings. By the close of 1839 he had severed the last of his business connections with his brother.

There are several bits of evidence that the division of property between the partners was in anticipation of Nathan's gradual withdrawal from the metals trade. Indeed I am of the opinion that Nathan would have abandoned the trade entirely sometime early in the 1840's had he not wished to keep it active as a business venture "for the juniors."

Beginning about 1836 there are indications in Trotter's letters that he wished to be free of the cares of business. Here is part of a letter written to his son Edward when the latter was touring Europe: [5]

If thee could see me thee would find me in the Shafts bearing the burden and desiring to be unharnessed awhile and indulge in the green pasture for a Season   a resort which is as necessary for my health as it would be gratifying to my feelings but I see no prospect of this relaxation without the business suffering from my absence.

Edward assured his father: "I am quite anxious to return home and use my best exertions to relieve thee from the active part of the business and however poor the substitute may prove, rest assured that the *will* is good and that all exertions will be used to keep up the business." And he concluded one letter, "Hoping this will find you making 20 per cent on all you sell, thy health restored, and all the family well." [6]

Nathan Trotter talked of relief from business, but he meant, doubtless, relief from the mercantile business of Nathan Trotter & Company so that he could devote much more of his time to what he came to call "my own business," or commercial-paper discounting. By 1840 he had gained his wish. In that year the firm hired a remarkably competent bookkeeper to attend to the details of the office, and the sons of Trotter were by then giving their attention to the metals business.

With his metals trade in competent hands, Trotter took steps to limit his other business activities so that he might give increasing attention to his discounting business. As a director of the Lehigh Coal & Navigation Company he had taken his duties seriously; now rather than reduce his activities as a director to the level of the perfunctory, Trotter decided to resign. With customary detail he gave his reasons to Friend James Wilson: [7]

as the time is near at hand when a new Election will take place for Managers of the L C & N Co I now communicate to thee my desire of withdrawing my name, as a candidate, for a further term of Service, and will state the reasons that have induced this conclusion—It was with considerable hesitation that I first consented to serve/and I yielded only at the solicitation of our departed friend E.H. [Ebenezer Hazard]/because I was then apprehensive that I should not be able to give that attention which the situation would require or be competent to its dealings—and since that period I have been more and more convinced, that in accepting a trust of this kind, we come under imperative obligations, and assume duties to Stockholders which ought to be faithfully attended to, and hence I have felt a long time rather unpleasant in continuing, because my own business required my almost constant attention and precluded my rendering that service to the Company which was incumbant on me, and I now view it rather as a matter of duty, under such considerations to withdraw. . . .

Beginning in 1840 commercial-paper discounting was to employ the largest part of Trotter's capital. It had taken him thirty years as a merchant and investor to make $350,000. It would take but thirteen as a commercial-paper specialist to gain an additional $600,000.

By withdrawing more from the metals trade and concentrating increasingly on investments, Trotter was behaving in a manner typical of his time. A Boston contemporary, John Perkins Cushing (1787–1862), withdrew from the Oriental trade in 1828–1831 and put his surplus into stocks and bonds, real estate and moneylending.[8] The New Yorker, John Jacob Astor (1763–1848), withdrew from the China trade in 1828 and the fur business in 1834 and put his money extensively into Manhattan real estate.[9] The steamship millionaire, Cornelius Vanderbilt (1794–1877), put his fortune into railroads.[10] In each case these men made far larger profits in "retirement" than during their active business careers.

In one important respect Nathan Trotter differed from the pattern of these wealthier contemporaries. In comparison with these men of more capital, one fact stands out: Trotter was putting a larger amount of capital as well as a larger proportion of his wealth into commercial-paper discounting.

Since we have the investment records of Cushing and since Cushing's general investment policy was somewhat similar to Trotter's, a comparison of the two will serve to emphasize the special attention given by Trotter to paper discounting. In the decade of the 1840's, Cushing's total investment was two to three times as large as Trotter's. Both men put about the same dollar amount into real estate. Neither invested much in trade adventures. Both dealt in securities and in commercial paper. But whereas Cushing put two-thirds of his fortune into common stocks, particularly stocks of New England firms, Trotter invested only about a seventh of his in that manner. Over half of Trotter's capital found its way into the commercial-paper market whereas only about a fifth of Cushing's did. At the close of the year 1850, Cushing had $350,750 invested in notes receivable (including, apparently, a number of personal—and probably not very current—loans); at the same time Trotter's total notes receivable amounted to $599,913 (see Table 10).

Because commercial paper was so important to Trotter and because Trotter's discounting activities must have made a substantial contribution to the liquidity of the Philadelphia money market, they are the subject of a separate chapter. The present chapter deals, therefore, with Trotter's other investments, grouped for convenience under three headings: Adventures, Real Estate, and Securities.

ADVENTURES

As a young man Nathan Trotter had spent his working hours down on Front Street in an atmosphere of "ventures" and "purchases in company." Early in his career he was frequently drawn into making such investments, using either his personal capital or funds of the partnership. Yet there are indications that adventures outside his own management and purchases of a speculative nature did not really appeal to him.

The following transaction, although unimportant in itself, is enlightening. It shows Nathan in a business by himself rather than in a family relationship with his brother; it indicates that early in his life he was putting money into adventures; above all it reveals his caution.

In the year 1807 Nathan Trotter purchased from his brother William and from George Halberstadt one-seventh of a joint venture to Havana on the Schooner *Republican* for $111.28 plus insurance. In addition he paid his joint venturers $12 to insure him that the voyage would net him $100 clear of expenses. A twenty-year-old investor could scarcely have acted more cautiously.

Table 10

Personal Investments of Nathan Trotter on 1 January 1840–1854

Year	Real Estate	Stocks & Loans	Adventures	Receivables	"Stock" [a] Figure
1840	$ 99,776.64	$ 48,023.61	$8,828.40	$ 52,197.77	$350,000
1841	100,554.50	56,750.00	2,433.29	124,448.54	350,000
1842	102,961.58	57,860.00	——	172,654.88	375,000
1843	112,276.28	55,147.00	——	125,547.95	405,000
1844	121,825.78	56,597.00	——	184,989.44	430,000
1845	121,972.73	62,669.50	——	237,819.47	475,000
1846	121,000.00	77,194.63	——	242,796.54	520,000
1847	122,859.36	78,541.87	——	360,905.88	568,184
1848	122,881.06	89,328.47	——	408,646.86	640,000
1849					
1850	126,734.28	99,816.47	——	488,132.21	750,000
1851	135,954.44	101,414.01	——	599,913.50	800,000
1852 [b]	135,954.44	110,186.91	——		800,000
1853 [c]	109,506.99 [d]	150,709.76 [d]	——	529,357.43	
1854					958,540 [e]

[a] Nathan Trotter used "stock" to mean total wealth.
[b] As of 30 June 1852.
[c] As of 31 January 1853.
[d] An estimated written-down value.
[e] The total value, as of 29 December 1854, of property which had belonged to Nathan Trotter (died 11 January 1853).

The effect of burned fingers appears in this daybook entry of 30 June 1814:

Profit & Loss Dr to mdse
    For loss by speculation in pepper
    & Sugar a lesson for future guide   783.60

It may have been experiences such as this that led Nathan Trotter not to venture much in a trade with which he was not familiar.

Since the War of 1812 cut off the Oriental and West Indian trade completely, Trotter was temporarily unable to put money into ventures. But with the war over he proceeded to return to former patterns of investment, just as, in the case of importing, he had returned to former patterns of procurement. Once peace was declared he busied himself with collecting Spanish dollars in Philadelphia, Baltimore, and Burlington, New Jersey, preliminary to taking a substantial interest in the first postwar voyage of the ship *Pacific* bound for Canton. Of a total shipment of $21,000 in specie made under Trotter's management, $9,000 belonged to him, $4,500 to his brother-in-law Ephraim Haines, and $7,500 to the merchants Thomas & Kille.[11] The specie was consigned to the ship's supercargoes, William Chaloner and Matthew C. Ralston. It was Trotter's friendship for Matt Ralston that later led him to make many investments in the China trade. On the returns of the *Pacific*—nankeens, shawls, handkerchiefs, "sattins," senshaws, and tea— Trotter's profit was over $2,500.

While Nathan Trotter was managing this venture, he was also sharing in another venture managed by Thomas & Kille—this one to India on the *Kensington*.[12] The *Kensington* sailed from New York to Calcutta and on her return cargo—"taffatas," handkerchiefs, block tin, indigo, and gunny bags—there was also a profit. As in other ventures Trotter invested in commerce with India not so much because of his faith in the trade as because of his faith in a man. John W. Rulon, long-time Trotter acquaintance, supercargo, and at times resident agent in Calcutta, was the individual whom Trotter recurrently backed when he put money into ventures to India.

From the standard accounts of the Oriental trade we learn that American trade with China had, before the War of 1812, attracted the capital, usually in small amounts, of a great many firms and individual investors.[13] The Trotters, of course, had been among the small investors.

After the War of 1812, this trade came to be concentrated in the hands of about five large firms in Boston, New York, and Philadelphia. Nathan Trotter's associations with the China trade followed the general trend; in this postwar period, his investments were made principally in partnership with Philadelphia's two largest importers of Oriental goods—Samuel Archer and Jones, Oakford & Company.

Samuel Archer, at one time Trotter's tenant at 36 North Front Street, frequently invited Trotter to participate in ventures to the Orient. Here is an example of a venture which took place in 1836. It shows Trotter carefully hedging against any loss of his capital. He paid $9,420.75 for ginseng shipped on the *Chandler Price* to Canton. The purchase was made "at the instance of" Samuel Archer who, according to Trotter's daybook: [14]

agreed to buy one half the shipment at 10% profit and allowed interest on the amot until we are refunded out of proceeds of shipment & shd there be no profits on the adventure after paying Interest, Insa [insurance], &c then in that case S Archer agrees to allow & pay such other profit in addition to the price agreed upon for his half, as shall be equivalent to what money is worth in the market after the arrival of the ship home, not however less than it wd be at 6 pr Ct pr ann.

Since Samuel Archer's son, Joseph,[15] was a resident agent in Canton, the father wrote to him indicating clearly the personal factor involved in the venture:

By my recommendation Nathan Trotter has been induced to purchase and ship per Chandler Price a quantity of Ginseng consigned to Isaac Field, and the present is to request thy assistance or advice in the disposal of it, and also point out the articles for the returns most likely to pay best. . . . The adventure being made altogether by my advice I feel *particularly desirous* of a favorable result and have said to N T that I was confident thee would lend thy aid and advice both in sales and purchases of said adventure.

Joseph Archer's choice must have been good. The returns of "sattins," shawls, raw silk, and teas were sold by the merchant house of Field & Taylor for a commission of 1 per cent, and some goods were shipped to the West Indies to get them out of the Philadelphia market. Trotter made a profit of $3,190.26 on the venture even though the goods had reached the United States when the market was depressed.

Nathan Trotter seems to have felt that he could not control decisions concerning the Oriental Trade. This may well have been one of the reasons he seems not to have been happy about it. Usually his directions to the supercargoes or resident agents stipulated that they be guided in their purchases of returns by observing what Samuel Archer or the other large shippers accustomed to the trade were shipping.

Along with the rest of the merchants engaged in the Oriental trade, Trotter gave up the exportation of specie soon after 1815 and came to export bills of exchange almost entirely. Trotter's bills were on such firms as Timothy Wiggin & Company, Morrison, Cryder & Company, and Baring Brothers & Company of London; they came into his hands through a number of channels, many through the Second Bank of the United States.

Bills of exchange had many advantages over the old method of shipping specie or goods. For one thing they could be procured and shipped with less trouble. And there would be less loss if conditions in

Calcutta or Canton seemed unfavorable: "Should any circumstances of high prices, or other sufficient reasons, render it inexpedient to sell the Bills, then return them, first *cancelling them*, as we had better pay the Bank the one pr cent than submit to a greater loss," wrote Trotter to his Calcutta agent, Thomas N. Richards.[16]

The 1830's were years when the Oriental trade was becoming less profitable. Even so, Trotter shared ventures in 1838 and 1839 with Richard Oakford of Jones Oakford & Company. Oakford was a friend of such long standing that his signature was among those of the witnesses on the marriage certificate of Nathan and Susan Trotter in 1813. With him Trotter had once shared in a purchase of silks—an exceedingly disappointing investment, entered into at Oakford's solicitation, as Trotter reminded him in a note of 8 February 1830. Four ventures were shared equally by Richard Oakford and Nathan Trotter in the years 1838 and 1839.[17] Two were to Calcutta and two to Canton, some of them being in Oakford's ship *Washington* and brig *George Graham*. The investments were made in sterling bills purchased of the Bank of the United States and a letter of credit on Baring Brothers & Company. Profits were small on the returns from Calcutta—indigo, gum copal, shellac, green cow hides, Madras and Cawnpore goat skins, and handkerchiefs. Profits on the Canton ventures were scarcely any better.

The first Canton venture, begun in 1838, with returns in teas and pongees, resulted in a profit to Trotter of $1,075.03 for his half-share. His second Canton enterprise—a Baring credit sent to Wetmore & Company "at the suggestion of" Oakford on whose judgment and advice the order was predicated—was not so successful. The returns of silks and teas reached New York by the *Robert Fulton* and the *Morea*. Some of the teas were sent to London to Baring Brothers & Company to sell. Not finding a market, Baring Brothers shipped the teas back to New York. On the whole enterprise there was considerable expense: insurance and storage in New York, George Trotter's trips to that city to attend to the shipment, and a commission paid a Philadelphia firm for selling some of the goods. It is perhaps remarkable that when Nathan Trotter wrote off his one-half loss on 13 December 1842 it amounted to only $414.71. Thereafter he stayed out of the Oriental trade.

In addition to investing in the Oriental trade directly, Trotter also supplied capital indirectly. In fact, on balance, the indirect amount was the greater. He made loans to the Archers and Oakford by discounting their commercial paper, particularly during the years 1826, 1834, and 1836–1840, years which were critical in the Oriental trade. Trotter's financing of these well-established firms trading with China must have been important factors in prolonging their business existence.[18]

It is easy enough to summarize Trotter's investments in ventures to parts of the world other than the Orient. The only other areas of importance were the West Indies and South America.

Ventures to the West Indies were, in a sense, a branch of the Oriental trade. Before the War of 1812 the Trotter firm had been fairly active in this trade, but after that time I find record of only three voyages, of which two were clearly undertaken as a means of getting Oriental goods out of the glutted Philadelphia market. Trotter's shipment of nankeens to St. Thomas in 1817 represented part of the returns he had received on the first postwar voyage of the *Pacific*. A shipment of "sattins" to Cuba in 1837 was also a disposal of goods received from Canton. The third venture, a shipment of tin plate to Cuba, has the ring of a modern song title—"on the *Hannah* to Havanna."

Ventures to South America were made for special reasons and in spite of the fact that markets there had only recently opened and were very risky.[19] The 1820's were still revolutionary times in South American countries. Blockades, among other factors, made trade so uncertain that invoices frequently read "bound for Rio Janerio"—or some other port—"and a market," since it was never possible to know in advance where a free market might be found. Shipments usually consisted of tin plate, flour, and chairs; returns were frequently in hides. Profits were never large and there were some losses. This deficiency of profits and surplus of risk would make Nathan Trotter's participation in South American ventures difficult to understand except that he himself has left a partial explanation. Trotter desired, so he wrote, to assist his nephew, Daniel Haines, who in an effort to "reestablish" his health served as supercargo on a number of these voyages, and so whenever Daniel was aboard, Trotter invested at least a token amount in the goods being carried.

Between 1815 and 1839, Nathan Trotter & Company invested in a total of about 30 ventures in these various foreign markets. The dollars and cents records of these investments, though probably not complete, indicate clearly that it could not have been the profit motive that kept Trotter money flowing into these channels. In some years the gains on various ventures exceeded the losses, but the *total gains* of Nathan Trotter & Company ventures over *total losses* were only $827.17, the greatest gain being $3,503.91 recorded in 1816 and the greatest loss being $1,747.80 in 1823.

Since profit was apparently not the motive, we must seek an explanation elsewhere. It is to be found in the desire to assist a fellow merchant, a friend, or a relative. When a neighboring merchant needed funds to round out a one-venture partnership, Trotter co-operated. When Samuel Archer or John Rulon was looking for financial backing, Trotter was willing, though not always happy, to oblige. When Daniel Haines required an excuse to serve as supercargo on an ocean voyage, Trotter provided the wherewithal. But these were actions taken without economic motivation. Soon after 1840, when Trotter began to concentrate on his commercial-paper business, he forsook his investments in adventures entirely.

REAL ESTATE

At the time of his retirement from the routine of the metals trade, Nathan Trotter owned some houses, a farm, and a number of stores and shops including a group of commercial properties near the Philadelphia waterfront. In fact more than a quarter of his entire fortune at that time, or about $100,000 at a conservative value, was invested in real estate. Buildings, however, concerned him chiefly as a home for himself and his family and a place of operation for his business. Real estate was more important to him for its use than for the money income it yielded, though it did return him a fair income on his investment.

Trotter made his first real-estate purchase in 1819—a depression year—when he bought the two Front Street lots on which he built his own house.[20] There, at 170 North Front Street he lived until the year 1830, when he sold the property at a loss of $5,540.15, explaining: [21]

the inducement to sell this property at this loss, was in consequence of my having purchased a lot on 4th. near Green on which I am building a House adjoining one building by J Trotter—the situation was very objectionable owing to the unpleasant Houses & Occupants opposite & was in fact the main cause of my concluding to move & it was thought more advisable to sell than to rent.

The house which he mentioned on Fourth Street—256 North Fourth—remained his home for the rest of his life.

Not until the 1830's did the Trotter brothers acquire their own place of business. For about a quarter of a century they had sold their goods in a store belonging to William Sansom on the east or Delaware side of Front Street. Then, in 1833, the firm moved across the street to the location which, in the 1950's, they still occupy—36 North Front.

Even before purchasing their own store, the Trotter partners had invested in some income-producing properties. Their first investment of this type, a property at 420 North Front Street, was purchased at sheriff's sale in 1823. Joseph Trotter attended to the taxes, collected the rents, and settled with Nathan Trotter & Company for the balances. The rent book in which he recorded the transactions, now in the Thompson Collection at the Pennsylvania Historical Society, states that this North Front Street property had belonged to their uncle, Thomas Conarroe.

By the close of the year 1833, when the Trotter brothers transferred real estate, along with the other investment accounts, from the General to the Private Account Books, their joint real-estate holdings consisted of two dwelling houses, a Crown Street lot on which they later built a house and stable,[22] a store and warehouse on Chancery Lane,[23] and their North Front Street store.[24] After the separate investment accounts were set up, the firm purchased a brick house and lot next to a house they already owned on Coombes Alley [25] (now Cuthbert Street; see picture facing page 175).* They also erected a new building at 36 North Front and improved the back store there. This brought the firm's real-estate holdings to $46,824.65 by the close of 1835.

Then came the depression years and, as mentioned earlier, the division of real estate and other investments. Joseph took the house at 420 North Front which he had attended to since the firm bought it in 1823, and Nathan took the remainder of the property except the Crown Street house and stable where both brothers kept their horses.[26] In purchasing Joseph's half interest in 36 North Front and the Coombes Alley properties (for $18,250), Nathan's account books contain this comment: "Joseph seems anxious I shd. take this Estate which I concluded to do, altho' at an advance which I considered rather high, but

---

* Since Coombes Alley ran at right angles to Front Street, close by the Trotter store, these brick houses opened onto the firm's back yard. A porter in the firm's employ often lived in one of the houses, possibly to keep a watchful eye on the property.

as he relinquishes all income from them, not already apportioned, & concentrates the property into one ownership I concluded to take it." [27]

Nathan Trotter, whether by design or circumstance, bought real estate in times of depression. His first purchase had been made in the depression of 1819. In 1838 and 1839, in addition to buying out Joseph's half interest, he purchased two pieces of commercial real

Table 11

Real Estate Holdings of Trotter and His Firm
at Various Dates between 1820 and 1853 [a]

	Income Properties		Nonincome Properties Nathan Trotter's	Total
	N. Trotter & Co.	Nathan Trotter	Dwellings	Holdings
1820			$12,627.04	$ 12,627.04
1825	$ 3,084.81		14,179.88	17,264.69
1830	11,620.66		2,070.19	13,690.85
1835	46,824.65		8,892.55	55,717.20
1840		$81,726.46	18,244.18	99,970.64
1845		82,089.10	30,576.68	112,665.78
1850		85,667.00	40,964.69	126,631.69
1853 [b]		85,769.59 [b]	61,337.06 [b]	147,106.65 [b]

[a] These are cost figures except for 1853.

[b] In 1853, after the death of Nathan Trotter, his nephews made a list of Nathan's various properties. They wrote down the valuation as listed below. The write-down of the farm in 1853 was surprisingly little: only from $22,593.52 to $20,000.

	Cost Value	Written-down Value	Loss
Income Properties	$ 85,769.59	$ 53,000.00	$32,769.59
Dwellings	61,337.06	56,506.99	4,830.07
	$147,106.65	$109,506.99	$37,599.66

estate just south of his store at 32 and 34 North Front and took a lease on the lot at 38 North Front for $400 a year and taxes.[28] On this lot he agreed to build a store "to be left on sd premises." He also made improvements at numbers 32 and 34 costing $11,657.47. By 1840 his income-producing real estate amounted to $81,726.46. The purchase of a brick house on Frankford Road, Kensington, at sheriff's sale in 1841 concluded Nathan Trotter's investment in income-producing property.[29]

Nathan Trotter & Company occupied the first floor of the four-story brick building at 36 North Front Street. The Trotters rented to others the stores at 32, 34, and 38 and the upstairs space at 36 North Front. Many of the tenants on Front Street and at the firm's Chancery Lane warehouse were men they knew well: Samuel Archer, Grant & Stone,

Henry Farnum & Company, Gihon & Company, and Thomas & Martin, among others. The stores at 32, 34, and 36 North Front Street are shown in the picture facing page 174. In general appearance, the store remains today very much as in the picture.

Although much of the income-producing real estate was bought in depression times and therefore supposedly at low prices, the return on this form of investment was not exceptional. The early 1840's was a period of declining rents, if the Trotter's experience is characteristic of the times. In 1842 Thomas S. Field & Company, who occupied the second story at 36 North Front Street, complained of hard times and succeeded in having $50 deducted from their yearly rent of $500. Times evidently got worse, for in 1844 Nathan Trotter recorded that he accepted that year a rent of only $400 from Field & Company and that the next year he really received only $381.44 since he had to abate their rent "as they demurred."

The Trotter rent accounts were not kept as carefully as the mercantile accounts. Sometimes rental income and interest on securities were lumped. The closest estimate I can make of the percentage of rental returns on the money invested in income-producing property is as follows in these selected years: 1825, 5½ per cent; 1830, 5 per cent; 1835, 3 per cent; 1840, 6½ per cent; 1845, 4½ per cent; and 1850, 3 per cent.

Nathan Trotter put a little more than half of his real-estate investments, or $56,000, into nonincome-producing property. This may seem a large amount but it should be remembered that it included a farm valued at $20,000, his own house, and four houses for his children. Edward Trotter was married in October, 1843, and the previous month his father had purchased a lot at 10 Franklin Square on which to build a house for the newly married couple.[30] He also bought 11 Franklin Square where his second son George went to live when he got married.[31] Situated between Race and Vine and Sixth and Franklin, Franklin Square was at that time described as a "noble square" with trees and shrubbery and "a splendid fountain, with forty jets of water."[32]

In 1852 Nathan Trotter purchased property at 138 and 140 North Ninth Street.[33] For one piece of property he had in mind his only daughter Elizabeth, married to John J. Thompson on the 15th of December of that year; for the other he probably was thinking of one of his younger sons.

Nathan with his brother Joseph twice bought a farm for family reasons. In 1832 the Trotter brothers had purchased from their brother-in-law, Joseph Hough, at his request the old Hough family homestead and farm in Springfield, New Jersey. The Trotters sold that property in the depression of 1837. Two years later they bought a farm in Oxford, Philadelphia County, Pennsylvania—now in the 35th Ward of the City of Philadelphia [34] so that their niece, Elizabeth Haines Walmsley, and her husband Thomas, who had been occupying the farm for six years or more would have a home.

In 1843 Nathan purchased Joseph's half interest in this farm and thereafter concerned himself with many details of his country property.[35] The farm account in his private daybook records expenditures for such items as the building of a new tenement and a chicken house and the purchase of 12 head of cattle. Since Trotter does not seem to have been the gentleman farmer type, he would, no doubt, want any farm he owned to be a paying concern. There are credited therefore to the farm account sums received for oats and hay used at the Crown Street stable and for farm pasturage for the town horses. Profitable or not, the farm probably kept Trotter out of doors and out of the Front Street humidity some of the time. Occasionally his wife spent some time at the farm, during the heat of the summer, and Nathan drove out at night. "Mother wd. not be satisfied staying without me," he wrote his daughter.[36]

One aspect of Nathan Trotter's real-estate investment seems characteristic of the man. There is, in his real-estate purchases, none of that interest in western lands that was found among many other eastern capitalists early in the 1850's. Missouri, Iowa, Wisconsin, Minnesota, and other states had, apparently, no lure for him, though many of his fellow citizens in Philadelphia were taking fliers in the western states and territories. Trotter was clearly not one to invest his funds in the unknown.

He wanted his property under his own eye and management: and that it was, literally. From his counting room in the rear of 36 North Front he could look across the yard upon his Coombes Alley properties. If he walked through the large room just back of the open door (shown in the picture opposite page 174) and stood in the Front Street entrance, "38 on lease" was immediately to the north and 34 and 32 to the south. On his way to his home at 256 North Fourth, he could pass his Chancery Lane warehouse, and his stable on Crown Street.

Vine and Market, Front and Ninth bounded most of his real estate; and, on an afternoon, he could ride out a few miles to what was then the country to visit his Oxford farm and even before dark return with products of the season to be left with Edward, George, and Elizabeth.

SECURITIES

At the time when the Trotter partners transferred their investment accounts to private ledgers, securities were the most insignificant of their holdings.[37] Their portfolio consisted only of the following stocks:

Farmers Bank of New Jersey	$ 125.00
Pennsylvania Fire Insurance Company	1,000.00
Lehigh Coal & Navigation Company	2,500.00
Columbia Steam Boat Company	120.00
West Chester Rail Road Company	700.00
	$4,445.00

In the following three years, 1834–1837, the Trotters increased their investment in securities by ten times—to a total of $43,507.88. Then, with the equal division of the brothers' property, Nathan secured sole title to seven blocks of stock and a loan:

Stocks	No. of shares	Valued at
Pennsylvania Fire Insurance Co.	10	$ 1,000.00
Lehigh Coal & Navigation Co.	25	1,250.00
West Chester Rail Road	7	350.00
Reading Rail Road	72	3,600.00
Northern Bank Kentucky	50	3,814.74
Bank U. S. Stock	50	6,364.20
Philadelphia Gas Works	8¾	875.00
Loan		
Sandy & Beaver Canal		4,500.00
		$21,753.94

Securities rather than real estate seem to have been the concern of Joseph. Sometimes Joseph's status in the Bank of Pennsylvania put him in a position to turn a neat profit. On 2 August 1834, the private daybook of Nathan Trotter & Company records: "Thro Bk Pa we took 15 $\overline{\text{M}}$ of loan" of the State of Pennsylvania. The certificates were endorsed by Nathan Trotter & Company and left with Joseph Trotter. On 8 November 1834, Joseph "sold" the "stock" and got a brokerage fee; the Bank of Pennsylvania received $12.50 in "Int pd on 5 $\overline{\text{M}}$ borrowed a few days," and the firm gained $853.87 on the transaction. On the

$15,754.50 paid for the loan—one-third of which was borrowed from the Bank of Pennsylvania—the firm in three months made over $800. This is one of the many scattered items in the Trotter papers which indicate that the firm always enjoyed credit facilities at the Bank of Pennsylvania.

The banks and companies whose securities Nathan purchased were often those whose dividends were payable at the Bank of Pennsylvania.[38] The Sandy & Beaver Canal was one. On 8 August 1836, Joseph Trotter "on mutual ac[count]" subscribed for $10,000 of a loan to this company at 90 per cent. This particular investment turned out to be a total loss and was written off on 31 December 1853 as "considered of no value." The Planters' Bank of Tennessee, with dividends payable at the Bank of Pennsylvania, was another company whose stock Nathan Trotter held, doubtless through Joseph's influence. At the time of Nathan's death, his $3,000 investment in 30 shares of this stock was estimated as worth only $2,760.

Another losing investment in bank stock was one made by Nathan Trotter & Company in the Second Bank of the United States, purchased 5 February 1836 for $12,728.40. This purchase was made about two weeks before the charter granted the bank by the legislature of the State of Pennsylvania went into effect.[39] The firm received some dividends; but this bank, along with the other Pennsylvania banks, suspended specie payments in May, 1837, and finally failed in 1841.[40] A daybook entry of 31 December 1839 recorded that the stock had been sold at a loss of $1,364.20, and the Trotters were probably relieved that the loss was as small as it was. On 27 February 1841, Nathan Trotter wrote to his English correspondents, Jevons Sons & Company, of Liverpool:

the stock of U S Bank has run down to 15 dolls pr share yesterday but yet no one can say if its a fair estimate of value—the article is like a foot Ball Kicked from one Broker to another who really seem to elevate or depress it at will— We have no doubt if the directors could make the best of their assets, without being compelled to force anything, the issue would be infinitely better than present rates.

Table 12—arranged under the general heading of stocks and loans and the subheadings of bank, transportation, mining, manufacturing, insurance, and municipal—records a total investment in 1853 of about $140,000, valued at original cost. The estimated market value of approximately $150,000 would seem to indicate that Nathan Trotter had

Table 12

Securities held by Nathan Trotter
31 January 1853

	No. of shares	Cost	Estimated value [a]
STOCKS			
Bank			
Planters Bank of Tennessee	30	$ 3,000.00	$ 2,760.00
Northern Bank of Kentucky	57	5,700.00	6,384.00
Bank of Pennsylvania	3	500.00	378.00
Total		$ 9,200.00	$ 9,522.00
Transportation			
Chesapeake & Del. Canal	2	$ 400.00	$ 280.00
Lehigh Coal & Navigation	25	1,250.00	1,825.00
West Chester Railroad	7	350.00	35.00
Pennsylvania Railroad	60	3,000.00	3,000.00
Schuylkill Navigation	200	4,110.00	4,000.00
Little Schyl. Nav. RR. & Coal	380	19,000.00	19,000.00
Schuylkill Navigation Prefd.	428	11,750.00	12,412.00
Union Canal	300	4,575.00	5,100.00
Monongahela Bridge	23	471.88	460.00
Total		$ 44,906.88	$ 46,112.00
Mining			
North West Mining Co.	300	$ 4.945.12	$ 6,600.00
Siskowit Mining Co.	110	1,595.00	110.00
Ontonagon Mining Co.	150	1,387.50	150.00
Bohemian Mining Co.	100	950.00	300.00
Charlestown Mining Co.	1000	7,500.00	5,000.00
Total		$ 16,377.62	$ 12,160.00
Manufacturing			
Lehigh Crane Iron Co.	200	$ 10,000.00	$ 20,000.00
Swede Iron Co.	100	10,000.00	10,000.00
Total		$ 20,000.00	$ 30,000.00
Insurance			
Pennsylvania Fire Ins. Co.	10	$ 1,000.00	$ 1,500.00
Total		$ 1,000.00	$ 1,500.00
Municipal			
Northern Liberties Gas	320	$ 8,000.00	$ 9,600.00
Total		$ 8,000.00	$ 9,600.00
TOTAL		$ 99,484.50	$108,894.00
LOANS			
Transportation			
Schuylkill Navigation		$ 6,045.00	$ 6,609.20
Reading Railroad		17,000.00	18,600.00

(*Table 12 continued*)

	Cost	Estimated value[a]
Lehigh Coal & Navigation	$ 8,883.00	$ 8,616.51
Lehigh Coal & Nav. Mortgage	5,561.25	6,166.05
Total	$ 37,489.25	$ 39,991.76
Manufacturing		
Lehigh Crane Iron Co.	$ 600.00	$ 600.00
Total	$ 600.00	$ 600.00
Municipal		
City of Philadelphia Gas 6%	$ 900.00	$ 945.00
City of Philadelphia Gas 5%	300.00	279.00
Total	$ 1,200.00	$ 1,224.00
TOTAL	$ 39,289.25	$ 41,815.76
TOTAL OF SECURITIES	$138,773.75	$150,709.76

[a] Value as estimated by Nathan Trotter's nephews a few weeks after his death.

better judgment in securities than was really the case, since at an earlier date, in December of 1852, he had already written off to profit and loss a total of $17,400 in worthless stocks.[41]

Transportation, which in Pennsylvania was often associated with coal mining, had the greatest attraction for Nathan Trotter. About two-thirds of his entire $138,773.75 investment in securities was in transportation stocks and loans. He had a number of associations with the Reading Railroad aside from a loan that he made to that company. Gihon & Company, merchants with considerable financial interest in the road, were from 1839 until 1843 his tenants at "38 on lease." Trotter also discounted the Reading's own notes as well as the commercial paper which the railroad had received in the course of its business operations.

In 1852, when the Reading Railroad was in a state of "Recovery and Prosperity," [42] after a difficult period, Nathan Trotter's private daybook records this incident:

1852 Feb 9
    Reading R Rd Stock dr to Cash
        paid TGH for 100 shares $3325
    I was influenced by J Tucker prest who
    called on me 7 inst & pourtrayed it in
    such colours as really induced me /with
    TGH efforts/ to try a little

Apparently, Thomas G. Hollingsworth, the TGH who seconded President Tucker's portrayal of the railroad's future did not paint the "colours" overbrightly, at least as far as Trotter's immediate profits would indicate. On April 28 of the same year his nephew, Joseph Hough Trotter, sold this stock for him at a gain of $525.

During the last few years of his life, especially from 1849 through 1852, Nathan Trotter invested substantial sums in mining securities. This is the only group of his securities which cost more than they were considered to be worth in the 1853 estimate. *Ulman's Pennsylvania Business Directory . . . for the year 1854–5* listed seven Lake Superior copper companies with Philadelphia offices, and Trotter invested in six of the seven. It was natural that Nathan Trotter should be interested in the domestic supply of copper, since the firm handled ingot copper as a commodity and since it sold copper for some of these mining firms. In addition some of the younger Trotters undoubtedly turned Trotter's attention toward mining stocks. Nathan's son George would shortly be president of the Siskowit Lake Superior Company and his nephew Joseph Hough Trotter was treasurer of the Ontonagon Mining Company.

A description of the Lake Superior copper region and the development and production of the mines, written at about the time Nathan Trotter was purchasing copper securities, may be found in J. D. Whitney's book, *The Metallic Wealth of the United States.*[43] Whitney felt that the Lake Superior district was not finally established on a firm basis until after the "copper fever" boom of 1845-1847—a period when speculation in copper stocks had inflicted a serious injury "on the mining interests of the country by the unprincipled attempts to palm off worthless property as containing valuable veins." In other words, Nathan Trotter had not speculated in the earliest period but was investing when some of the companies at least were going concerns if not paying ones.

Whitney had this to say about the companies whose stock Trotter purchased. The Northwest Copper Mining Company had been in operation since 1847 and its works were "so extensive as to be exceeded by few in the region." Concerning the Siskowit, the Ontonagon district, and the Bohemian Mining Company on the Piscataqua location, Whitney's findings were not so favorable; nor was the opinion expressed by the men who evaluated these stocks when they found them in Nathan Trotter's estate. Though Trotter had paid nearly

$4,000 for these stocks, his executors thought them worth not more than an eighth of that price.

In 1850 Nathan Trotter even invested in a gold mine. Since Joseph Hough Trotter was treasurer of the Eagle Gold Mining Company, in this purchase, also, it may well have been family influence which led Trotter to invest. However, the year following 1849 might well have seemed even to a sound and conservative businessman a logical time to buy stock in a gold mine.

Nathan Trotter was proud of Pennsylvania and eager for her to play a larger part in the economy of the United States and it was through his connections with a Pennsylvania company—the Lehigh Crane Iron Company—that he participated in an important pioneering enterprise. This iron company, promoted by the anthracite-owning Lehigh Coal & Navigation Company of which Trotter was a director, built "the first successful anthracite furnace in the Lehigh valley" at Catasauqua in 1839 and 1840.

Since, to quote James M. Swank, [44] the introduction of anthracite and of bituminous coal in the manufacture of pig iron "caused a revolution in the whole iron industry" of the United States, it is interesting to note that the usually conservative Nathan Trotter had a part in this revolutionary change.

In the fall of 1838, Trotter wrote to his friendly correspondents in Liverpool, Jevons Sons & Company, iron manufacturers: [45]

The Writer has been this afternoon engaged with the Board of Managers of the Lehigh Coal & Navigation Company and thot of smelting Iron with Anthracite Coal was the subject of much conversation and is one in which the interest of the Company is much involved.

A few months later he reported: "A Farmer on a small scale at Mauch Chunk, Lehigh, has been making Iron exclusively with Anthracite for some weeks. Take care Johnny Bull when Uncle Jonathan gets fairly under way in this matter." [46]

The smelting of iron with anthracite coal was still in the experimental stage in both England and the United States and Trotter kept the English iron maker, Jevons, informed about progress in this country. In 1840 the Lehigh company brought David Thomas "The Father of the American anthracite iron industry," from Wales to undertake the smelting of iron with anthracite. Shortly Trotter wrote: "Our friend David Thomas from Wales with the writer and others have been among the Coal regions for a fortnight and hope something may grow

Stores at 32, 34, and 36 North Front Street

Houses on Coombes Alley

out of it in the shape of iron." By 1840 Trotter thought—and time would prove him correct—there would soon be a "new era in the Iron business arising from Anthracite Smelting." Between 1839 and 1850 Thomas built five furnaces for the Lehigh Crane Iron Company at Catasauqua. The first had been in operation about two weeks when Trotter wrote "it runs off 7 tons in 24 hours—it is expected to make 60 Tons pr Week." The expectation was almost realized and the furnace came to produce at a weekly rate of 50 tons "of good foundry iron." [47]

Nathan Trotter's investment in the Lehigh Crane Iron Company proved unusually profitable. On 30 April 1839 he paid his first installment on 100 shares which carried a total par value of $5,000. Later, a daybook entry of 31 December 1845 records that, the business of the company appearing to justify it, the Lehigh company increased its stock 100 per cent out of profits. Trotter still held his 200 shares at the time of his death, and the appraisers estimated his $5,000 investment to be then worth $20,000.

In the midst of activities connected with the establishment of the Lehigh Crane Iron Company, Nathan Trotter had expressed the hope that Pennsylvania would yet, "by means of Coal & Iron take a more prominent rank among her Sisters in the sale of Manufactures." It must have been a satisfaction to him to watch the successful progress of this Pennsylvania enterprise, to which he seems to have given more time and thought than to any other activity outside his own business or family, and to note that it was definitely helping to bring Pennsylvania into a more prominent rank among the states.

The securities market in the first half of the nineteenth century presented a varied pattern. A number of men were acting as dealers: brokers, officers of companies, and bankers, to mention some. From about 1806 until 1834 the members of the Philadelphia Board of Brokers conducted their stock transactions in the Merchants' Coffee House. The Trotters dealt with some of the brokers mentioned in the first membership list, that of January, 1818. [48]

However, many persons who were not included in the Board of Brokers' official list dealt in securities. In answer to a request from the Baltimore McKims for the name of a Philadelphia stockbroker in whom confidence could be placed, Nathan Trotter replied, 31 August 1843: "In regard to a Stock Broker, Mr. Hollingsworth is not a member of the *Board* of Brokers, but informs us he often buys & sells

Stocks & we know is largely engaged in Money operations and a party with whom we have had large transactions, & *we* have great confidence in his integrity—we know many others & will think among the Members of the Hong—who will best suit our views."

One type of security was absent from Trotter's list, except when he purchased to make payments abroad: that was government bonds. I suspect that in the Quaker mind government bonds were associated with war finance in a period when the War of 1812 and the Mexican War were being paid for.

For the most part Nathan Trotter limited his purchases of securities to enterprises in Pennsylvania. When he ventured farther—when he favored banks toward which he may have been influenced by Joseph Trotter, or mines in which he had a natural interest even if his nephews had not been involved—he usually suffered financial loss.

In Trotter's investments, as in his other activities, the personality of a man who likes to manage his own affairs shows through. His interest in adventures, the form of investment managed in part by agents half the world away, had disappeared by the 1840's. His purchases of real estate and securities, investments he could keep under his eye, increased between 1840 and 1853 until they amounted finally to over $260,000. But it was commercial-paper discounting, combining in one activity the virtues of being manageable, profitable, and capable of increase almost without limit, in which his particular talents found the greatest scope.

CHAPTER X

Commercial-Paper Discounting

NATHAN TROTTER ended his career a discounter of commercial paper often at high rates of discount. He, as well as his contemporaries, seems to have regarded the rates as something to be arrived at mechanically. They were merely the result of calculations based on the current demand for money and the responsibility of the borrower. Rates of 6, 8, and 10 per cent were often recorded. For some reason, possibly because it was the custom of the times, high rates of 12 per cent and over were always stated in his accounts as the rates per month instead of the annual rates; thus 15 per cent per annum was quoted as 1¼ per cent—a rate at which he sometimes purchased the notes of his own son's partnership.

Trotter was engaging in a business activity which, while not open to those without capital, was engaged in by many contemporary merchants. The attitude of contemporary merchants is evidenced in this extract from a letter written by George Brown, of the famous Baltimore firm, to his brother William on 16 November 1837: "It would not suit me to give up my business entirely, and if I retired tomorrow I would employ my capital in discounting and doing a private banking business, but on a moderate scale." [1]

Of utmost importance for an understanding of the background of the discounting business was a Pennsylvania legal decision which specifically stated that "a fair *purchase* may be made of a bond or note, even at twenty or thirty per cent. discount, without incurring the danger of usury." [2] A straight loan, made between individuals or by a bank to an individual, seems to have carried only the legal maximum rate, 6 per cent. But when a man signed his name to a note and then "sold" the note to Trotter, for example, Trotter might pay whatever price was the current rate and, when money was scarce, he might be willing to buy the note only at a figure considerably less than the note's face value. The difference between the face value and the amount the maker received was the discount, or Trotter's profit. Discounts were not infrequently 12, 18, or 24 per cent.[*]

Banks were often forbidden to charge more than 6 per cent. The act of incorporation of the Second Bank of the United States, for example, stated that the bank should not take "more than at the rate of six per centum per annum for or upon its loans or discounts." [3] Even though banks evaded the law in ways enumerated by Condy Raguet and others,[4] Trotter's constant reference to 6 per cent as "bank rate" indicates that this figure was the normal one. Naturally the signers of notes would prefer to have their notes discounted at a rate as low as possible and would frequently apply first at a bank when "out of doors" or market rates were running higher than 6 per cent. Possibly some of the paper rejected by banks came to Trotter. It would be a mistake to think that the rejected paper was always a poor risk, however. Some notes may have been turned down because the bank already held substantial amounts of paper of that particular house; other notes because the total discounting quota which the bank had set for itself had been filled. On 17 December 1838, for example, Nathan Trotter wrote Church McVay & Gordon: "Owing to the peculiar state of our money market the offerings at our banks are probably in a three fold ratio of their ability to disct: . . . and the best paper out of doors has been selling from 1 to 1¼ p Ct disct a Month."

There were a number of reasons why the commercial-paper business appealed to Nathan Trotter. First of all it was profitable. Time

---

[*] "Both *loans and discounts* are designation applying to advances made by a bank [or other lender] to its customers. The chief distinction between them lies in the fact that in the case of loans interest is ordinarily collected at maturity, while in the case of discounts the interest is deducted in advance. In both instances, the interest is computed as a per cent of the total amount of the loan; hence, when the loan is discounted, *i.e.*, when the interest is deducted in advance, the rate charged is somewhat higher than the stated percentage." Theodore N. Beckman, *Credits and Collections in Theory and Practice* (New York, 1939), p. 52.

after time Trotter complained that he could make no more than 5 per cent on his metals business while his records show that his discounting business was bringing him much larger returns.

Then, too, Trotter was particularly well equipped to enter a business which required as its chief assets excess liquid capital and a knowledge of credit ratings. Trotter had excess capital because of his reluctance to push his metals business to the point of making it risky. His knowledge of the credit rating of his fellow Philadelphians was gained, in the natural course of his business, from association with his customers, from fellow merchants in other lines of business, and most certainly from his banking brother.

By temperament also Trotter was fitted for this activity. In Bagehot's book on the money market there is a penetrating description of the qualities needed in the discounting business. The description applies specifically to bill brokers (and a bill broker Trotter was not) but it fits equally well the man who bought the bill from the broker as an investment: [5]

Mercantile bills are an exceedingly difficult kind of security to understand. The relative credit of different merchants is a great "tradition"; it is a large mass of most valuable knowledge which has never been described. The subject matter of it, too, is shifting and changing daily; an accurate representation of the trustworthiness of houses at the beginning of a year might easily be a most fatal representation at the end of it. In all years there are great changes; some houses rise a good deal and some fall. And in some particular years the changes are immense. . . .

No one can be a good bill broker who has not learnt the great mercantile tradition of what is called "the standing of parties" and who does not watch personally and incessantly the inevitable changes which from hour to hour impair the truth of that tradition. The "credit" of a person—that is, the reliance which may be placed on his pecuniary fidelity—is a different thing from his property. No doubt, other things being equal, a rich man is more likely to pay than a poor man. But on the other hand, there are many men not of much wealth who are trusted in the market, "as a matter of business," for sums much exceeding the wealth of those who are many times richer.

Possibly there was another consideration which to Trotter made the discounting business attractive; the nature of the Philadelphia market. To the extent that it was a Quaker market, Philadelphia was probably an unusually safe place to take credit risks. Although religious precepts were no guarantee of a loan, Quaker practice certainly favored the prudent course, for it put pressure on good Quakers both to avoid contracting debts which they could not pay and to make every effort to meet obligations they had incurred.

The minutes of the Northern District Monthly Meeting of Philadelphia on "1 mo. 25, 1831," stated that the answer to a query made as to the business practices engaged in by Philadelphia Quakers, "upon careful deliberation" was: "Our members appear generally careful to live within the bounds of their circumstances [,] to keep to moderation in their trade or business [,] to observe punctuality to their promises and justice in the payments of their debts."

Sometimes Quakers were dealt with for "disregarding the advice contained in the discipline in relation to trade and business." On one occasion in the difficult times of 1841–1842 Trotter's former clerk, John W. Dixon, was called to task for nonpayment of debts. He gave assurance in writing to a committee of Friends that he fully intended to pay his just debts at the earliest possible opportunity. The committee was satisfied with his statement and decided that he should not be expelled from the Society of Friends.[6] The threat of expulsion was by no means idle. It was, in fact, carried out against none other than Trotter's brother-in-law, Ephraim Haines, when it became apparent to a specially appointed committee that Haines was "not in a disposition of mind to condemn his conduct" in contracting debts he was unable to pay.[7]

There was a great demand for capital in the expanding commerce and industry of the growing America, and there are indications that the banks were supplying neither the amount nor the period of credit required to finance the expansion. One bit of evidence is presented in "An Address to the Stockholders of the Bank of Pennsylvania," 22 December 1829. In this document the directors of the Bank answered the accusation that they had rejected $1,500,000 in bills offered for discount the previous year. They defended themselves by asserting that over $150,000 of these bills had been offered by brokers and commented that this was "a species of loan to which very great exception has been taken on the part of the State." Obviously they were not to be blamed for restricting loans to brokers who were thought to be speculating. Another group of potential borrowers whose request had been denied were the auctioneers who had offered more than $120,000 of paper. These same auctioneers were in turn "discounting for very large sums," and as a result of their operations "the specie in the vaults of the banks was rapidly diminishing." In addition to the paper of brokers and of auctioneers, over $200,000 of paper of other persons had been rejected "because the paper had more than four months to run." The directors concluded, therefore, "that less than $400,000 of unexceptionable paper was rejected during the year . . . which small amount is no evidence of a general want of funds." [8]

In view of the Bank's defense it seems significant that Nathan Trotter, during the period 1827–1833, was annually discounting thousands of dollars worth of notes for the auctioneers. This discounting was significant not only because these auctioneers were not allowed by banks all the credit they seemingly needed, but also because their notes ran for four months and from 1830 on usually for six months, whereas the banks were willing to discount only notes with no more than 60 days to run.[*]

Much of the time Nathan Trotter was supplying capital for periods of more than 60 days,[†] the normal term granted by the banks.[9] Businessmen other than auctioneers also needed discounts on notes running for four, six, and even eight months. Trotter constantly held *eight-months notes* of dry-goods merchants, for example. Merchants needed more time in which to turn their purchases into cash, and Trotter's discounts enabled them to do so. As early as 1811, James Mease had commented on the current financial situation in these words: [10]

> If some plan were adopted to accommodate those who possess good notes, at three, four, or six months . . . trade would not only be greatly benefitted, some of the evils of banking lessened, but above all, the practice of usury, which prevails to a disgraceful degree in most of our commercial towns, would be much diminished.

[*] "Discounts at all the banks are made for sixty days on endorsed notes," stated James Mease in 1811 (*The Picture of Philadelphia . . .* , p. 108).
On 7 June 1822, the Bank of Northern Liberties of Philadelphia "resolved no note be discounted having a longer time to run than 60 days, unless, under peculiar circumstances, the Board decide otherwise." (Lemuel C. Simon, *A Century of the National Bank of Northern Liberties of Philadelphia*, p. 19.)
[†] Out of 72 of the 100 receivables which Trotter purchased in 1833, only 6 were for so short a period as 60 days; the others ran for 3, 4, 6, and 8 months. Trotter purchased some notes a month or two after date and always held them until due.
A statement of Nathan Trotter's receivables on 30 June 1852 shows that he was still granting much credit for a period over 60 days—some up to 7 months:

Bills due 31 Dec. 1851 (overdue bills)	$ 38,762.97
" " July 1852	69,477.89
" " Aug.	69,535.66
" " Sept.	135,940.93
" " Oct.	143,159.46
" " Nov.	79,861.14
" " Dec.	53,321.84
" " Jan. 1853	35,410.24
Total	$625,470.13

With the growth of manufacturing another large group appeared which needed working capital for longer than a two months' period.

Commercial-paper discounting, as carried on by Nathan Trotter, falls rather naturally into four periods: (1) 1818–1826, when notes, amounting to not over $15,000 a year, were purchased chiefly from fellow merchants; (2) 1827–1833, when discounts increased from about $22,000 a year to probably $100,000 and represented in addition to purchases from neighbor merchants the purchase of notes from auctioneers, a hardware merchant, and a dry-goods merchant; (3) 1834–1840, when Trotter began to ask for collateral to back a signed note and when discounted paper amounted to over $225,000 in one year; and (4) 1841–1853, when Trotter's notes rose to about a million and a half dollars a year and his capital was financing a wide range of business activities (see Table 13).

The period 1818–1826 was, in general, one of money stringency. In 1818, when Nathan Trotter first discounted appreciable quantities of commercial paper, credit was being contracted, and widespread financial difficulty was resulting.* It was in this period, 1818–1819, that the Philadelphia branch of the Second Bank of the United States reduced its discounts by $3,500,000 [11] and the pressure for money consequently became very great. Money continued to be tight throughout 1819 and 1820 and was scarce again in the spring of 1822 and in 1825 and 1826.[12] During this period Trotter loaned to his brother-in-law, Charles C. West, who was a tailor, or to his neighbor merchant by discounting 60- or 90-day notes which they drew in his favor. These notes were in some cases renewed year after year. Interest rates were frequently high: 10, 12, 20, and even 30 per cent. West, however, had his notes renewed continuously from 1823 until 1830 and, perhaps because of his family connection, paid only 6 per cent.

The firm whose notes Trotter discounted most often in this period was Thomas & Martin, neighboring merchants at 51 North Front Street.† In fact he held their notes throughout the 1830's and 1840's.

---

* Actually Nathan Trotter had been discounting ever since he became a partner in William Trotter's firm but the amounts had been small and the transaction had often been entered into as a favor. William Trotter may well have inherited the idea of discounting as a use for idle funds from the Sansoms—a family whose connections with the Bank of Pennsylvania had been close.

† The first loans at this time may have been made as a friendly gesture rather than as a money-making proposition. The cash book—and that book alone—records over a series of years (1808–1820) a great many temporary accommodations. The Trotters were sometimes lenders and sometimes borrowers, never for more than a

Table 13

Discounting Record of Nathan Trotter
1818–1853

Year	Total receivables [a] for the year	Receivables on Dec. 31	Yearly profits (interest balance)	Commission earned in the year	Cash on hand Dec. 31
1818	$ 13,794.92	—	$ 568.50	—	$18,211.26
1819	9,270.38	—	257.99	—	100.63
1820	1,245.38	—	96.34	—	12.86
1821	—	—	85.08	—	2,314.70
1822	—	—	62.88	—	634.39
1823	6,464.57	—	—	—	200.89
1824	1,994.00	—	—	—	77.53
1825	7,454.58	—	—	—	887.88
1826	11,577.30	—	412.91	—	1,561.09
1827	22,244.40	$ 10,981.75	888.71	—	226.13
1828	42,867.15	14,285.93	717.18	—	3.63
1829	—	—	—	—	1,520.79
1830	—	23,867.01	—	—	559.11
1831	96,603.89	33,494.53	—	—	3,260.77
1832	—	—	—	—	7,758.48
1833	—	—	4,336.62	—	—
1834	—	47,435.27	4,550.00	—	3,716.35
1835	—	59,763.57	3,782.42	$ 381.66	7,706.51
1836	—	79,897.43	9,430.90	4,725.17	2,689.09
1837	—	56,619.88	6,914.31	4,166.90	19,699.70
1838	—	58,010.48	4,086.71	1,353.40	11,340.67
1839	225,168.00	79,513.28	11,493.53	294.37	153.45
1840	138,681.52	52,197.77	8,247.93	—	57,184.09
1841	265,679.74	124,448.54	14,620.70	—	40,187.33
1842	347,824.08	172,665.18	26,922.10	—	2,692.27
1843	331,780.25	125,707.15	12,198.12	—	58,158.42
1844	380,304.30	184,989.44	15,072.54	—	5,868.16
1845	543,716.57	237,707.77	23,483.32	—	2,871.73
1846	669,826.96	242,796.54	28,960.61	—	22,959.82
1847	782,745.97	360,905.88	33,188.81	—	2,381.75
1848	1,156,050.75	408,646.86	54,011.09	—	1,850.14
1849	1,068,705.88	420,248.23	37,735.57	—	16,754.38
1850	1,336,434.66	488,132.21	43,079.56	—	12,683.51
1851	1,480,794.81	599,913.50	63,927.78	—	12,761.49
1852	1,494,684.47	—	55,564.87	—	—
1853	—	528,357.43 [b]	—	—	—

[a] Receivables was the term Trotter here used for the commercial paper which he discounted.

[b] Receivables, Feb. 1, at the time of Nathan Trotter's death.

few days at a time, and never with interest being charged. Gradually the firm of Nathan and Joseph Trotter began to discount notes of the same persons to whom they were lending free of interest and such items as "Recd on loan of 1000 Drs to Thomas & Martin a few days $1.33" appeared. Then, from 1820 on, either because the firm had excess cash, or because lending profits were large—or for both reasons —interestless borrowing disappeared from the accounts.

As far back as the Trotter records go, some member of the Trotter family was usually engaged in a shipment or a venture in trade with a Thomas. Discounting the note of a Thomas was merely the 1820 variation of an 1810 venture. The Martin of this firm was a friend of such long standing that he had attended a Westtown reunion with Nathan in 1808 and had been, like Richard Oakford, one of the signers of Susan and Nathan's wedding certificate.

By purchasing notes from Thomas & Martin, Trotter was contributing his capital to financing the distribution of American manufactured cotton goods. Among the many activities of Thomas & Martin was the sale of cotton yarn, hand weaving being important in the Philadelphia area throughout the first half of the nineteenth century. In addition to yarn these merchants sold cloth which was manufactured in New England's Blackstone Valley and was shipped to them apparently by coastal vessels sailing from Providence. They had "constantly for sale" Blackstone shirtings and sheetings which they "received on consignment from the manufactory." [13] Undoubtedly they had to advance money on these consignments, and the proceeds of their discounted notes were probably used for this purpose. Trotter also took off their hands some of the notes they received in the course of disposing of their goods.

In this early period Trotter's discounting was reserved principally for those years when money was tight and interest and discount rates high. From 1820 to 1822 he did almost no discounting. What notes he did discount were chiefly renewals. He was busy buying real estate and building a house.

It was, I believe, Trotter's activity as administrator of his brother's estate which gave him his initial interest in a major discounting business. In 1827 and 1828 certain bonds and mortgages of the estate were paid off and Trotter was faced with the necessity of reinvesting these funds. Finding no long-term investment of suitable quality and limited risk, he decided to lend the funds to himself at 5 per cent interest. He felt that he could invest the funds in commercial paper at a return of at least 6 per cent. Though on the surface he seemed to be profiting at the expense of his wards, actually he was being ultraconservative for he thought it inappropriate to risk guardianship money in the commercial-paper market.[14]

From about 1827 on, commercial-paper discounting became more of a business with Trotter. Thereafter he kept orderly lists of "Receivables" (which was the ledger designation for his commercial-paper purchases), with information under such headings as "Date of note," "Indorser," "From whom purchased," "Rate," "When due," and "Amount."

During the period from 1827 to 1833, Trotter continued to buy the notes of his neighbor merchants but added three new types: he bought notes in batches from a Philadelphia firm of auctioneers, from the Philadelphia branch of an English hardware firm, and from a dry-goods merchant. In 1833 over 70 per cent of the notes he purchased were from these three sources.

The auctioneers, Jennings & Thomas and their successors, extended a great deal of credit, for they not only advanced money to the people from whom they received goods on consignment but they also accepted notes for the goods they auctioned off. These goods might be British, French, or domestic dry goods, Oriental imports, or furniture, books, and even groceries. The people who bought the goods and gave notes for them were usually Philadelphia merchants. A batch of a dozen notes or so, endorsed by the auctioneers, might amount to $7,000, $8,000, or even $12,000.[15] Nathan Trotter usually purchased the notes a month or two after the date they were drawn and held them until due. All the notes in any lot were discounted at the same rate.

From A. Harrold, representative of the Birmingham house of William Harrold & Sons (through whom the Trotter firm purchased English hardware), Nathan Trotter purchased batches of notes given Harrold by his American customers. Often, naturally, they were Nathan Trotter's customers, too, and their credit rating was well-known to him. These Harrold customers—hardware and saddlery dealers and watchmakers—usually drew notes which ran for 60 to 90 days. It was Harrold's custom to take the notes to Trotter for discounting as soon as he received them.

Henry Farnum & Company, whose place of business was at 45 North Front Street, at that time just next door to the Trotter firm, and whose senior member was a particular friend of Nathan Trotter, was the third firm whose notes Trotter bought in batches. Farnum dealt in domestic goods from Providence and in imported fabrics from England. The notes which Trotter purchased from Farnum were four, five, and six months' notes, signed by Philadelphia merchants. There were also some eight months' notes. Whenever one finds an eight months' note in this period one can be sure it belonged to a firm handling dry goods.

The period from 1834 to 1840 was one of money stringency. Comments in Thorp's *Annals* run: [16]

> 1834. "Money very tight, easing slowly."
> 1835. "Money easier, but tightens late in year."
> 1836. "Money extremely tight."
> 1837. "Money very tight."
> 1838. "Money eases."
> 1839. "Money market tightens to panic and bank failures, October."
> 1840. "Slowly easing money market."

Much of this early stringency was related to the difficulties encountered by the Second Bank of the United States. President Jackson, in the course of his war on the Bank, had presented, on 18 September 1833, a paper prepared by his then Attorney General, Taney, giving the reasons why the charter of the Bank should not be renewed. On the twenty-sixth of the month, Taney, newly appointed Secretary of the Treasury, ordered that public money thereafter be deposited in certain state banks. This "precipitated a panic in a market already stringent on account of the reductions in bank accommodations due to the hostile relations between the administration and the bank." [17]

On 14 December 1833, Nathan Trotter had written his English correspondent, Newton Lyon & Company, about financial conditions in the United States:

The pressure in our money market is without parallel and great distress is the consequence of the serious allegations against Bank United States, removing Government deposits, &c. The Subjects are now claiming the attention of congress which it is hoped will act promptly and do justice to an institution which has been very unjustly assail'd.

In this period while money was generally tight, Trotter dropped some of his old discounting connections and took on some new ones. In general he became more selective. He stopped buying notes in batches from the dry-goods merchants and he declined to handle the notes signed by customers of the auctioneers—although he did purchase the auctioneers' personal notes. For a time he continued to discount the notes of the English hardware exporter's representative, but after 1835 he dropped these also.

During these years, and these years only, Trotter entered in his private daybook a series of transactions which, while difficult to explain, seemingly served a need when there was "a most severe pressure for money." Here is an example:

1837			
Apl 20	Thomas & Martin dr to Bills Payable		
	for my note 6 Apl 5 mos for	12000	
	To Comm: act		
	chg. com: issuing said note	863.50	
	Sundries dr to Thomas & Martin		
	Bills Recd. for their note in my favr		
	Apl 6 5 mos—	$12000	
	Cash		
	recd. Com: chgd	863.50	
	Bills Payable dr to Sundries		
	To Cash pd for my note T & M 12000	$11686.—	
	To Int a/ct		
	disct off Ditto	$314.—	

It appears that when money was tight Trotter exchanged notes with the borrower, charging a commission for doing it; then he discounted his own note charging the bank rate of discount. The purpose of this transaction was not, I believe, so much the discounting of commercial paper—permitting *any* rate of discount to be charged—as it was the lending of money, for which only 6 per cent interest could be charged under the laws of Pennsylvania. In order legally to obtain a higher rate—a rate which the borrower would gladly pay—Trotter observed the fiction of exchanging notes, for which a commission was charged, and the reality of discounting his own.

Although Trotter charged both commission and discount (or interest) on the above transactions, the borrower must have considered it a favor since Trotter did it only for such particular friends as Thomas & Martin, Henry Farnum, or Richard Oakford with whom he was at the time sharing some ventures to Calcutta and Canton. The profitable nature of the exchange transactions is indicated by the commission figures in Table 13. In 1836, for example, Trotter received $9,430.90 in discounts * and $4,725.17 as commissions "chgd for Exchg" to quote the daybook.

Beginning with this period, 1834 to 1840, the account books men-

---

* Discounting rates were high during those years. In 1836 the daybook records discounts of 12, 15, 18, 21, and 24 per cent (in terms of 1, 1¼, 1½, 1¾, and 2 per cent monthly, of course).

tion the deposit of collateral as security for notes that Trotter discounted. For instance, sometimes when Trotter discounted a note he required the borrower to deposit as security additional notes with a total face value in excess of the face value of the note he had discounted; by such means Trotter strove to protect himself should the discounted note be defaulted. In other cases Trotter accepted the following as collateral: shares of stock of the Western Bank of Baltimore and of the Bradford Coal Company; loan certificates of the Sandy & Beaver Canal; certificates of deposit in the Agricultural Bank of Mississippi and in the Commercial Bank of Natches; and even a bill of sale of the ship *Washington*.

Safe investments in this period were often scarce. Here we see the cautiousness of the Quaker overcoming the money-making desire of the lender who wished to keep his capital active. At the close of the depression year 1841, Trotter had a cash balance of $57,184.09 on his private account books. Ordinarily one would have expected him to keep this money employed in commercial paper, but a glance at the receivables account shows him investing only $33,494.53 in that fashion. He had, it is true, just been withdrawing considerable amounts from Nathan Trotter & Company and his discounting business had not yet reached its peak. He may have been following the conscious policy of putting his capital out on loan only in gradual amounts; but most certainly he was also being cautious about lending in times of business distress.

In the period from 1841 to 1853 Nathan Trotter's annual purchases reached about a million and a half dollars. In this period Trotter's two eldest sons, Edward and George, as their father's partners handled much of the routine of the merchandising business up to the close of 1849, when they and their younger brothers took over the metals business entirely. Nathan Trotter was, therefore, able to devote more time and money to discounting.

Among the types of paper which Trotter had purchased before this period and which he continued to purchase were receivables, in lots of a dozen or more at a time. A single lot might contain only grocers' notes or dry-goods dealers' notes, or a manufacturer's receivables. Such receivables bulked largest in the number of notes discounted although not in the dollar volume in this period.

During the 1841–1853 period the types of paper became more varied. Previously Nathan Trotter had merely sampled an occasional note of local manufacturers. Now he purchased them regularly. The notes of railroad, canal, and coal companies were also added, while those of grocers, dry-goods merchants, commission merchants, auctioneers, dealers in leather, and plain "merchants" continued to be purchased. Of this group the manufacturers tended to pay the highest discount rates and the dry-goods merchants the lowest.

Since Philadelphia was a center of the textile industry and *the* center of printed calico manufacture, it was natural that the notes of textile manufacturers should be discounted by Trotter. He usually held the notes of Joseph Ripka, outstanding manufacturer of cottons in the area,[18] and the notes of David S. Brown, a dry-goods merchant and the founder of a cotton-printing firm, the Gloucester Manufacturing Company. He also frequently held notes of J. &. W. Horrocks, dyers and finishers of cotton goods.

Other manufacturers whose notes were regularly discounted were Joseph L. Lovering & Company, "steam sugar refiners"; Israel P. Morris & Company, iron founders; Reeves, Buck & Company, manufacturers of nails and railroad iron; Baldwin & Whitney, locomotive manufacturers; the Lehigh Crane Iron Company; and F. & W. Perot, brewers.

One of the manufacturers whose notes were discounted by Trotter was Samuel Comly, founder of the Comlyville Power Loom Factory—later called the Frankford Woolen Mill. Comly had been a fellow student with Trotter at Westtown in 1801. He was also Philadelphia agent for the Barings of London. Neither of these circumstances prevented Trotter from discounting Comly's notes at 21 per cent in the spring of 1837—or from suffering a loss of $3,000 when Comly went bankrupt in the crash of 1837. Trotter's daybook entries record the loss philosophically: that of 21 April of 1837 ran "little or no probability of ever getting any thing," and the final one of 30 December 1843 concluded, Comly "took benefit Bankrupt Law & will never pay any thing I guess."

Nathan Trotter also helped finance the Philadelphia & Reading Railroad. This railroad, chartered in 1833 and begun in 1835, was for years in financial difficulties,[19] in spite of the fact that the road was so well constructed that operating costs were low and freight tonnage was increasing. Conditions improved after John Tucker was elected president of the road about 1844 and adopted aggressive measures to better its financial standing. Throughout the period from 1843 to 1852, Trotter discounted notes of the road; * the larger notes were signed by Tucker and often endorsed by a firm which had financial interests in the Philadelphia & Reading, Gihon & Company.† In addition, Trotter bought some notes signed by Gihon & Company directly. Large amounts of collateral were often held by Trotter in these transactions— securities of the railroad and business notes received from its customers being among the types noted in the accounts.

Although the Reading road lacked working capital and had to borrow to meet current expenses, it granted credit on freight in return for the acceptances of shippers. Trotter also assisted the road by discounting these acceptances. A typical lot, purchased in February, 1847, amounting to $10,688.02, included notes of Rogers, Sinnickson & Company, coal merchants; Jaudons & Mason, dealers in nails; and John R. White, president of the Mt. Carbon Rail Road Company and of the Delaware Coal Company.

Notes of the following transportation and coal companies were also discounted: the Union Canal Company, the Buck Mountain Coal Company, the Lehigh Coal & Navigation Company, the Hazelton Coal Company, and the Little Schuylkill Navigation Rail Road & Coal Company.

The bulk of the notes which Trotter purchased were those of Philadelphians or of Pennsylvania companies. However, the batches which he purchased from the Philadelphia & Reading Railroad and the Lehigh Crane Iron Company included notes of such out-of-state firms as Horner & Company and Corning of Albany, Peter Cooper of New York City, and the Fall River Iron Works of Massachusetts.

This study of Trotter's discounting indicates the importance of the private financier in a period when commercial banks were inadequate to finance current business needs. In this period, before the National

---

* At one time in 1850 Trotter held four 60-day notes of the Reading Railroad amounting to $50,000. The notes were obtained through Thomas G. Hollingsworth —who seems to have been a broker used extensively by the Reading—at a discount of 7 per cent, and on this occasion Hollingsworth divided his commission with Trotter.

† This firm rented a Philadelphia store from Trotter, dealt in dry goods, and is spoken of as a New York banker: "The road also built up a New York banking connection in John Gihon & Company, whose interest was at least partly based at first on a loan to a client, secured by Reading securities, which had been defaulted. The New York bankers in this way became involuntary owners of Reading securities, at the time unsaleable, and they thus had an interest in helping the line to completion and success." (Jules I. Bogen, *The Anthracite Railroads*, pp. 24–25.)

Banking System was established in 1863, "the great bulk of the borrowing on the part of merchants & others was accomplished through the brokers," declared Jay Cooke. He went on to say: [20]

I have seen & passed through periods extending over two or three years at a time when the bulk of negotiations of business paper was discounted through a medium of the brokers at from nine to 18 per cent per annum—and during these periods we had frequent suspensions of specie payments when all exchanges would be thrown into utter confusion. . . . It was a grand time for brokerage & private banking. The Nat B. sys[tem] has done away with all this confusion & as I have said above resulted in saving at least $50 mill per annum to the people.

Nathan Trotter must have been but one of many men with capital who assisted the brokers in their business, and the amount of business done by this one merchant—reaching almost a million and a half dollars in some years—is impressive.

Something of the mechanism of discounting at the time also appears, although only part of the whole system is presented in the Trotter papers. The records of brokers are needed to round out the picture. There does appear, however, the change from direct lending to indirect lending through a broker as Trotter became a larger factor in the commercial-paper market. A few examples will indicate how this process took place.

Trotter's first discounting was direct. Friends and acquaintances, knowing that Trotter had money to lend, approached him in person or through a mutual acquaintance to sell him their own notes or the notes they had received in their business. Here is an explanatory statement written by Trotter's old friend Samuel Archer, in which Archer reveals how he helped an acquaintance, Allen Key, obtain money from Trotter at a rate of interest which, while higher than that charged by a bank, was nevertheless a going rate among private lenders.

On or abt the 28 of May 1836 Allen Key one of the firm of Key & Biddle Called on me—Said he wished to obtain abt. $5,600 I remarked that it was a scarce Article and told him I think it was worth 12 @ 15% pr ann—he said K & B had some Silk Hkfs and thought of giting *Edward* [Biddle] to obtain a note   I said that wold be verry good and thought I knew where the money could be had for it at the current rate of Interest (out of Bank)   in a day or two he Called again bringing Foster & Co note or one purporting to be theirs. I took said Note to Nathan Trotter who agreed to discount it and named the time the money wold be ready which was accordingly paid to me and by me handed to Allen Key, he being little acqunted with monied men I surpoes was the cause of his Calling on me, and to oblige him procured the amt wanted free of any charge whatever

Parenthetically it might be added that Trotter had considerable difficulty in collecting the note of Foster & Company.[21] Apparently it was not said without reason that Samuel Archer, who had recommended this transaction to Trotter, was one who "made fortunes as easily as he lost them, but his great error was placing too much confidence in others." [22]

It is easy to imagine, though I have no information on this point, that notes were sometimes offered to banks, and by them turned down, before being offered to Trotter. Quite naturally a merchant would prefer to sell his notes to a bank if by so doing he would pay no more than 6 per cent. We see something of this in the business records of a firm in which one of Trotter's sons was a partner—the commission dry-goods house of Iddings, Wells & Trotter. This firm sent, probably a day or so before the days regularly set aside by these banks to do their discounting, to the Bank of Northern Liberties and the Bank of Pennsylvania batches of notes which they had received from customers.* The banks selected the notes they were willing to discount and returned the rest. Occasionally the Iddings, Wells & Trotter partners sent these rejected notes to a second bank, and frequently the second bank returned them also. Apparently the banks used something like a uniform measure of value by which they arrived at a decision whether or not to discount. On a second rejection the commission firm might simply hold the note to maturity. But if it desperately needed cash it might turn to a private investor even at a much higher rate of discount. As early as 1828 the Bank of Pennsylvania had rejected during the year notes amounting to $1,709,746 either because "they were not deemed good by the board" of Directors or "because they had a longer term to run, than the board thought it advisable to discount for." [23] When the function of the private investor is looked upon as supplementing the bank's discounting business, it is easier to understand why, in certain instances, a sale of paper to an individual was of crucial importance to the borrower and why the borrower was willing to accept a rate he might never have been able to pay for the bulk of his borrowing.

As Trotter's capital increased, he needed more notes than were coming to him directly. The transition from direct to indirect pur-

* "Notes are presented the day before discount days," states Mease (*op. cit.*, p. 108) in 1811. They are listed in the Iddings, Wells & Trotter books as "offerings" to the Bank of Northern Liberties and the Bank of Pennsylvania.

chases was easy, however, for the volume of notes in the market was growing so rapidly that business was seeking him out. In these later years it was the note broker who called on Trotter to offer him a batch of receivables, whereas in earlier times it had been the merchant or friend. Indeed one of the attractions of the discounting business to Trotter must have been the fact that it required no selling effort: borrowers and brokers came to him.

Thomas G. Hollingsworth, from whom Trotter obtained the largest number of his receivables between 1841 and 1853, was one of the note brokers who regularly called on Trotter. Hollingsworth was a merchant who had turned to the brokerage and securities business. His original enterprise, listed as S. & T. G. Hollingsworth in the Philadelphia directories of 1816 and 1837, advertised such goods as wines received from Marseilles, olives, and anchovies. His new business was commenced some time between 1837 and 1842, when he moved from 73 South Wharves to the brokerage district on Walnut Street.

Although men like Hollingsworth were beginning to specialize in the brokerage business in the 1830's and 1840's, there are indications that there existed an established marketing organization for the purchase and sale of commercial paper in Philadelphia long before Hollingsworth's time. In the early years this business had been carried on by men whose interests were spread among a number of other activities. Some advertisements in the 1790's informed the public that Isaac Franks, a stock and foreign exchange broker, negotiated "notes of hand" and "acceptances," [24] and also that Solomon Lyons bought and sold bank stocks and bills of exchange and discounted approved notes.[25] Varied activities were carried on by one Thomas Goodwin, commission merchant and broker, who advertised on 14 December 1803: "He continues to buy & sell public securities, lands, bank stock, Bonds and approved notes discounted at the shortest notice, money loaned on deposits and business generally transacted on commission." [26]

In Hollingsworth's time a number of men were turning their attention to the brokerage business.[27] At Bank Alley, South Third Street, Dock Street, and Walnut Street were to be found the men from whom Nathan Trotter purchased notes: Morgan Ash, C. P. Bayard, William H. Newbold, H. P. Truefitt, and about a dozen others. Now and then Trotter also bought notes from "Sol" and Isaac Moses. Some of these brokers still appeared in the Philadelphia directories, not as brokers or note brokers, but as merchants. Seemingly they carried on both activities at once or perhaps there was a quality about being a "merchant" that men did not like to forsake.

A broker's commission of ¼ of 1 per cent was charged by Hollingsworth, as a few references in the Trotter papers indicate. Occasionally, when discount rates were low, Hollingsworth divided this commission with Trotter. If this was not sufficient evidence of Hollingsworth's strong desire to co-operate with his friend Trotter, the following example should be. When rates were low and Trotter thought they might go higher, Hollingsworth sometimes agreed in advance to buy back six or eight months' paper so that Trotter could put his money into better-paying investments.*

Hollingsworth almost never endorsed the notes he sold to Trotter and therefore never assumed responsibility for their payment.† He did, however, on a voluntary basis, sometimes do what he could to speed up payment when there were collection difficulties. One sample daybook entry reads: "I hold protested notes of E Levick Co. . . . amtg. to $3900. & thro T. G. Hollingsworth I recd. of him from Wm Neal assignee a dividend of $396.45   T G H representing the debt."

Ordinarily notes which Trotter bought were paid at the Bank of Northern Liberties or the Bank of Pennsylvania. Occasionally notes purchased from Hollingsworth were paid to him. Rarely were payments made directly to Trotter. Although the records are not clear on this point, I assume that Trotter was not the means by which the signer of the notes knew where to render payment when the notes came due. There is evidence that Trotter "did not appear" in the transactions. Instead, as in the case of one collection difficulty (14 April 1842), "Tom" arranged it: Trotter was "not known in the matter."

Trotter had losses on his discounting business but they were usually small and not so easy to total as his gains, since profits, or his income from "interest" to use the ledger heading under which discounts were

---

* This was a common practice among friends and relatives. Nathan had agreed to do the same with his nephew Daniel Haines back in the 1820's. On 28 June 1839 Nathan bought back from his brother Joseph Trotter a couple of notes he had sold him at 10½ per cent, noting: "on the 23d May I sold these notes to J. Trotter for Foster & Co & pd. them 5051.61 agreeing to take them of him if he did not wish them—and this day he sold them to me on same terms as he paid" and concludes with the explanation of the repurchase—"money being now worth 1 to 1¼ prCt a Month." Joseph could then make 12 to 15 per cent on capital which had been tied up at 10½ per cent.

† One of the few exceptions was recorded in the private daybook, 2 Sept. 1848, in these words: "Tom recommended this as good as any note in Philad. & said he wd pay it if no one else did—I have no knowledge whatever of him."

entered, were estimated annually, while on the other hand a loss was often carried along year after year. Only by checking each item could one find whether an unpaid note of one year had been eventually paid off or was omitted from the following year's list as hopeless.

Losses on some notes of the New Yorker, S. A. Halsey, purchased of John L. Newbold, 27 October and 6 November 1841, were continued in the list of unpaid receivables for many years. Trotter was bitter about these particular notes which, so he wrote, "were discounted in good faith to oblige Mr Newbold under the assurance that it was for Coal actually sold & delivered   therefore a perfectly legitimate transaction." However, Trotter came to believe that these acceptances were only "Kites" which Halsey never expected to pay "but got up to raise Money." In fact, Trotter concluded in a letter (19 February 1842) to his Van Antwerp relative, "it is the laxity of moral principles that had led into the lamentable state of things as we now witness them."

Aside from these Halsey acceptances, amounting to $4,566.78, Trotter's other overdue notes which he believed probably never would be paid totaled $10,181.94 in 1844. However, one acceptance on the list, of $530, *was* paid before the following December with the result that the unpaid notes entered on 31 December of the next three years amounted to but $9,651.94.

The bills receivable charged to profit and loss as "considered of Little or no Value" reached $28,400.18 on 31 December 1852 only because the item included an unpaid balance of $21,137.21 on a total of $25,000 loaned the firm of Iddings, Wells & Trotter. Trotter's son William Henry was in this firm, and Nathan may well in his own mind have charged the amount up to his son's business education rather than to losses on the discounting business. If this debt, incurred some years before, is subtracted, then Trotter's loss was but $7,262.97 as of 31 December 1852—a year in which he discounted $1,494,684.97 worth of receivables. Considering Trotter's overcautious practices in allowing for bad debts, it may well be that even some of that $7,262.97 was later paid.

As one observes Nathan Trotter at his discounting business, one gets the impression that here was a man well suited to his time. The man: alert, calculating, shrewd in his appraisals; possessed of ample fluid capital; and with a liking for diversified, short-time, profitable, manageable risks. The time: an economy rapidly expanding and in great need of capital, particularly capital which was available for longer periods than the banks provided.

When one has recovered from the first shock of discovering the high discount rates which prevailed during periods of stringency before the Civil War, one can look objectively at the function performed by this merchant discounter. As a result of his metals business and economical way of life, he built up a reservoir of lending capital. With this, he could get in or out of the money market as he chose. When he chose to get in, his capital enabled the merchant, manufacturing, mining, and transportation interests to operate in a period when, without his capital—or that of some other such person or institution—they could not have carried on their business. The wheels of the Industrial Revolution were powered with his capital: manufacturer Ripka could build up his textile establishments and the Reading Railroad could carry on its operations because the conservative merchant Nathan Trotter risked adventurously in these enterprises.

PART IV

Epilogue

CHAPTER XI

Changes from 1853 to 1953

PERHAPS it was a sense of order but it was also the feeling of making an accounting that led Nathan Trotter to keep detailed records. The following entry in his personal daybook, the book in which his moneylending transactions appear, reveals his sense of the importance of strict accountability. It also indicates possibly, in the last nine words, a feeling that the Trotter collection might one day be the subject of a study. The entry reads:

1845   Dec. 31 Bills Recd. Dr
          The debit to Bills R on Ledger is $237,707.77
          & amot notes on hand   237,819.47
             making more notes than called for   111.70
          Profit & Loss Dr
             there is yet required to Bal Ledger a
              debit of   16.62
          these two amots equal 128.32 is what the
          Ledger required more debit to balance it,
          and I have *forced* it in this way, much
          against my wishes, but really I had not
          time to go thro' a thoro' examination which
          would extend back thro' '43 & '44 and as
          the matter lies solely at issue with myself
          I must reconcile it—had the Books been
          Kept by me for others I never would have
          given up an investigation till I found the
          error and rectified it. And the constant em-
          ployment with my own, N T. & Co & farm
          affairs must be the apology to myself & any
          others who subsequently may look over my
          Books

The man who wrote the above entry sounds like a tired man, weary with the "constant employment" of business affairs. Yet for seven more years he continued to attend to his various activities. In the correspondence of 1849 and 1850 there were references to his poor health. In January of 1849 the McKims expressed their sorrow that Nathan Trotter had "again suffered annoyance from the strain of his back." They hoped he had recovered enough to be out again since it obviously did not "suit his taste to be confined to the house." A year later a member of the Jevons firm wrote: "We regret that your prior has been indisposed." Then, on 13 January 1853, the Philadelphia *Public Ledger* printed this item:

Died   On the 11th inst., NATHAN TROTTER, in the 66th year of his age.

His friends and those of the family are particularly invited to attend his funeral, from his late residence, No. 256 North Fourth street, on Sixth day morning, 14th inst., at 10 o'clock, without further notice. To proceed to Laurel Hill.

When Nathan Trotter died, his wife and children inherited his property.* Over half of his estate, that is, more than $500,000, was in commercial paper the cash from which, after maturity, was divided among the heirs; real estate, securities, and certain other properties valued at nearly half a million made up the remainder of the young Trotters' inheritance. Quite aside from the metals business, therefore, Trotter was able to leave his children independently well off.

The metals business had, three years before their father's death, been turned over to the sons. In 1850 the two elder brothers, Edward Hough and George, had admitted into partnership their other brothers, William Henry and Charles (see Table 14). Except for George, these brothers were to manage the business for the next quarter century and no reorganization took place until 1878. George withdrew from participation in the profits at the close of 1854, but remained with the firm on salary for another ten years. Since, on his departure, George took out his partnership balance of $86,700 and since his inheritance was well over $150,000, it is possible, other evidence considered, that his brother became a managing investor as his father had been before him.

Under the direction of the three sons the most notable aspect of Nathan Trotter & Company was the firm's remarkable continuity in

* See Appendix 2 for a copy of Nathan Trotter's will.

Table 14

Nathan Trotter & Company
Changes in Ownership, 1850–1953

1850	1855	1872	1879	1880	1883	1884	1886	1890	1891	1894	1895	1896	1898	1901	1912	1915	1928	1947
EHT	EHT																	
GT																		
WHT	WHT	WHT	WHT	WHT														
CWT	CWT	CWT																
			NT	NT	NT	NT	NT	NT	NT	NT	NT	NT	NT	NT				
			EFN	EFN	EFN	EFN	EFN	EFN		EFN								
				EHT[2]	EHT[2]	EHT[2]	EHT[2]	EHT[2]	EHT[2]	EHT[2]	EHT[2]	EHT[2]						
					WSB[3]													
							JCB	JCB	JCB									
								WHTjr.	WHTjr.	WHTjr.	WHTjr.	WHTjr.	WHTjr.	WHTjr.[a]	WHTjr.	WHTjr.		
									JD	JD	JD	JD	JD					
															WMW	WMW	WMW	
																	WTN	WTN
																	JMR	JMR

[a] In 1901 William H. Trotter, Jr., alone bore the losses.

Key to Code: Edward H. Trotter, George Trotter, William H. Trotter, Charles W. Trotter, Nathan Trotter, Edward F. Nivin, Edward H. Trotter [2] (son of William H.), William S. Boyd[3], James C. Burton, William Henry Trotter, Jr., Jason Davis, William M. Weaver, William T. Newbold, James M. Reilly.

Note: Only those years are shown when there were changes in the ownership; e.g., Edward H. Trotter was a partner from 1850 to 1872, etc.

both merchandising and investment practices. The firm continued to deal in a variety of nonferrous metals with, however, increasing emphasis on tin plate and therefore on importing. Idle funds continued to be put to work by the purchase of commercial paper, and Thomas G. Hollingsworth continued to be one of the men through whom the notes were bought. Somewhat surprisingly the firm even made occasional investments in ventures to Calcutta, but as in former times the ventures as a whole were not profitable. Their father's training, their native caution, and in addition, possibly, the uncertainties of war and panics influenced them to put aside extremely large sums in the contingent fund. Ample capital remained a source of strength as during year after year the firm earned nearly as much through its ability to buy for cash, sell on credit, and discount commercial paper as it earned through the skills and services of wholesaling. Prior to the 1870's total profits rose to two and, in one year, even three times the highest figure they had ever reached in Nathan Trotter's day. Only in the depression year of 1857 were the profits less than the highest of the 1803–1849 period.

Among the few changes which occurred in this period were experimental purchases of pig tin from the Malayan Straits region. The first was made in 1860 from Behn Meyer Company of Singapore. Then followed the Civil War. A second purchase was made from the same company in 1866. Subsequent purchases of tin were made from Boustead & Company, a British firm with offices in London and on the island of Penang, off the west coast of Malaya. The time would come when pig tin and the House of Boustead would figure importantly in the firm's business.

Use of the Atlantic cable speeded up communication with English correspondents. The firm had a code book printed and sent off such unintelligible messages as "Along Agape," which being deciphered meant that the Trotters had—for the price of but two words—informed their English supplier: "We cannot accept your offer at price quoted Plates are selling on this side below your quotation."

Other changes began in this period also. Toward the close of the period, because of the need to sell increasing imports of tin plate, the firm began to use traveling salesmen.* From 1875 until 1896 these

---

* The connection between tin plate and traveling salesmen is clearly shown in the following extract from the firm's letter of 11 January 1898 to John H. Rush, Concordville, Pennsylvania: "We are not in want of a travelling man at this time as we are about closing out the Tin Plate branch of our business."

employees of the firm sent orders and gave shipping and credit information from as far afield as Illinois, Iowa, Minnesota, Wisconsin, the Carolinas, and Georgia. The firm also sold on commission for a number of producers: Vieille Montagne Company, of Liege, Belgium (sheet zinc and spelter); Catasauqua Manufacturing Company, of Pennsylvania (puddled and bloom sheet iron); and the Pennsylvania Mining Company, of Michigan (ingot copper). No innovation, I suspect, would have chagrined father Nathan so much as the firm's frank statement in its advertising that it was selling on a commission basis.

The depression of the 1870's and the increasingly keen competition in the sale of tin plates brought difficult times for the company. The high premium on gold in the period of the resumption of specie payment was a great drain on a company which required gold, particularly for payments of bills of exchange and customs. The charge against profit and loss for premiums on gold amounted in the one year of 1873 to $27,863.87. Another outstanding financial item, this one on the profit side, however, in these years of national hardship, was the firm's income from interest and the relation of this item to the business as a whole. In the year 1877, when the metals business was operating at a loss, the interest account was earning $24,900, or a return of about 6 per cent on the firm's capital of $415,000.

By the close of 1878 the eldest of the brothers had died and the youngest, fifty-one-year-old Charles, had withdrawn.* The firm was therefore dissolved and was reconstituted with William Henry as senior partner. Between 8 January and 27 April 1878, Charles drew from the firm his partnership share of $88,000 after having divided with his brother, William Henry, certain of the firm's stock, bond, and mortgage holdings worth a total of nearly $100,000.

Under William Henry the new partnership had as its junior members William Henry's son Nathan † as well as an employee of the firm since 1863—Edward F. Nivin. Nivin was the first non-Trotter to be a partner although there would soon be others. In 1880 another son, Edward H. Trotter, was admitted (see Chart XII). The new group continued but a short time, however. The year 1882 was again a year

---

* About 1903 Charles W. Trotter was president of the Connellsville Gas Coal Company of Pennsylvania (picture and identification statement in the 1903 publication, *Souvenir History. Philadelphia Stock Exchange*).

† Nathan was employed on a salary as early as 1872 and went, in 1874, on the usual young Trotter tour to Europe in which pleasure and business education were mingled.

of marketing loss, and the elder partner decided the time had come to
retire. This year 1882, with the retirement of William Henry, marked
the close of a 33-year span under the management of one or more of
Nathan Trotter's sons and the close of almost three-quarters of a century under the combined management of Nathan *and* his sons.

In a sense the period from the time of reorganization at the close
of 1878 to the late 1890's was in marked contrast with the preceding

Chart XII

ABBREVIATED GENEALOGY OF NATHAN TROTTER'S DESCENDANTS

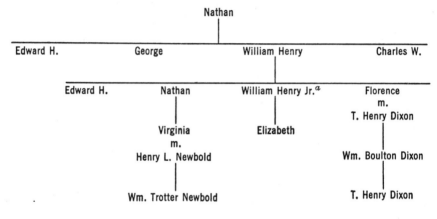

Nathan

Edward H.	George	William Henry	Charles W.

	Edward H.	Nathan	William Henry Jr.[a]	Florence m. T. Henry Dixon

Virginia m. Henry L. Newbold   Elizabeth   Wm. Boulton Dixon

Wm. Trotter Newbold   T. Henry Dixon

[a] Donor of the Trotter collection to the Baker Library.

quarter century of prosperity. It was characterized by low profits and
sometimes even losses, a discontinuance of the former investment
policy of the firm, and the most revolutionary change in the firm's
business in a period of ninety years. Partnerships were formed only
to be dissolved and reformed. Employees were given a share in the
earnings—but only twice in the losses.

The new firm started in a depressed mood: frankly they had lost
so heavily in the previous few years, they declared in a letter of 22
November 1878, that they were "naturally timid and careful" in their
operations. Summing up the laments concerning tin plate, the era of
the 1880's and early 1890's was one of overproduction in England,
keen competition in America, constantly decreasing prices, lessened
demand for good quality and increasing call for only fair quality
and cheap tin plate. There was much in the period to remind one of
the situation facing the first Nathan Trotter in the 1820's. Economies

were stressed and shipments often came to be made directly from Swansea although irregular sailings and inferior ships made this a not entirely satisfactory solution for high freight rates. Calculations showed that New York was often the better place for bargains and also revealed that Phelps Dodge & Company frequently sold below Trotter's importing costs.

The firm realized that unless they bought "intelligently and with rare judgment" they could not hope to compete with the larger concerns who were "so powerful in the trade, both as regards buying and selling."

Buying intelligently came to mean taking advantage of New York bargains and in England depending upon the London firm of Goring Hanlon & Company. Once again, from 1884 until 1895, London and the commission merchant became the chief source of Trotter's English tin plate. Goring Hanlon & Company bought on commission a great variety of fair quality tin plate and frequently were able to get the best prices by arranging for monthly contracts on the Trotter firm's behalf. With all their efforts, so the Trotter firm declared, the great aim and object of an importer's life was not "to make money on his goods, but to reduce his losses to a minimum."

Then in 1890 came the McKinley Tariff which placed a high duty on tin plate, a product which made up from one-half to two-thirds of the Trotter's inventory in some years. The business which this firm had for many years proudly put at the head of their advertising and letterheads—Importing—was at an end. By 1892 Nathan Trotter & Company wrote their English suppliers: "We have made up our minds that we must either get into the manufacture of Tin-plates or give up that branch of the business."

"The question of their manufacture in this country is settled"; they concluded, "it is already an accomplished fact; works are springing up in all parts of the country & within twelve months our output of roofing-plates will be sufficient to supply our entire wants.

"Bright plates are also being made and we can buy today American Coke plates superior to the imported @ $5.40 pr bx, 108 lbs."

Their prediction, "In three years we shall not be importing a box," was realized. With other references, such as, "we, as importers, are prepared to bow to the inevitable," and "We have recognized for some time that the days of the importers are numbered and already see the business drifting away from us," the firm turned to new endeavors.

Almost as soon as the tariff had gone into effect, Nathan Trotter made a short visit to England to make arrangements with the firm of Sanders & Company about speculations on the London metal exchange and importations of pig tin. A cable code and methods of payment were arranged; and the speculations in copper and tin begun at this time continued with varying but on the whole profitable results.

By 1894 the Trotter firm was convinced that the McKinley bill had started the manufacture of tin plates in the United States and that "nothing now can stop it." "We regret the loss of our business as importers," they mourned "and only wish we had started manufacturing at an earlier date." The manufacturing to which they referred was a tinning plant in which they tinned black plates imported from England. It was not a successful undertaking, however, and, 19 February 1898, they wrote none other than James M. Swank, historian of the iron and steel industry, as follows:

> In reply to your favor of the 18th inst. we beg to advise that you may consider our Tin dipping works as an abandoned enterprise, and there is no prospect of our ever resuming operations unless the present state of affairs should be considerably changed. We might add, however, that the works are still intact and we do not expect to dismantle in the immediate future.

Nathan Trotter, grandson of the man who gave his name to the firm, seems to have been the dominating manager of the firm at the turn of the century. He it was who went to England when new contracts were to be formed and his return was awaited before important decisions were made. He and his partners were feeling their way toward new methods of making money and their efforts resulted in fairly stable profits. Except for depression years, income ran about $20,000, that is about the level of the 1880's—not so high as the prosperous years under the first Nathan's three sons, but not so profitless as the transitional years of the 1890's.

To show the firm in its new business pattern, I have selected the year 1913—the last full year before the war and the sixtieth year after Nathan Trotter's death. The year was one of depression not only for the firm but for industry as a whole. The firm's volume of business was off about a third and so were its profits. But with this difference, the year was not unlike those which immediately preceded it.

Having dropped one specialty, tin plate, the firm had turned to another, pig tin. In 1913 two-thirds of the total purchases—$1,198,403 out of $1,768,117—was accounted for by this one commodity.* Straits was the principal type of tin handled and it was obtained chiefly from New York agents of London houses: James W. Phyfe & Company representing Boustead & Company of London, Penang, and Singapore; and Emil Baerwald the representative of the London house of Lewis Lazarus & Sons. Copper and lead were purchased from American manufacturers or their selling agents.

Aside from the products, the most striking changes appear in the company's capital accounts. Where the firm's net worth under Nathan's sons had been about $450,000 and as late as 1890 had been over $300,000, it was in 1913 only $150,000 (including $50,000 left in on loan by William Henry, Jr.'s, brother Nathan upon his retirement the year before). On this capital the partners had been earning a return of about 12 per cent. This return, as had been true in earlier periods, still resulted almost as much from the ability to pay cash as from profits on goods sold. However, the old practice of investing idle funds in commercial paper had ceased. There were few idle funds to invest. The firm was actively using its capital and was going to the banks to borrow for short periods if it wished to meet particular needs.

Transactions were fewer in number and larger in dollar amounts. The number of employees in the office and warehouse had therefore not changed much. Quality of goods was still an object of concern. Copper, by analysis, should be 99.88 per cent pure, Japanese antimony, 99.50 per cent, spelter at least 96 per cent, and that was considered low grade.

Everywhere the records reveal the speed with which business had come to be conducted. The ledgers reveal that cable, telephone, and telegraph charges were large items in the company's overhead account. Speed was required in accepting offers: the same day or at least the day following. Ninety-five per cent of the sales were for cash payment and many purchases were for spot cash. A regular exchange for deal-

* Pig tin	$1,198,403.59
Ingot copper	323,689.22
Pig lead	142,653.54
Sheet zinc	37,956.13
Spelter	35,135.84
Antimony	23,177.24
Aluminum	5,786.09
Nickel	1,315.74
	$1,768,117.39

ings in metals operated in New York, and great was the irritation
when the daily market reports from New York were late in arriving.
Even in the most casual business there was the pressure for speed,
speed, speed. The tension of business shows through in every phrase of
such letters as this: "We have your night telegram and wired you offering 2 tons Straits Pig Tin for prompt shipment at 33¼¢ lb. f.o.b.
Philadelphia, spot cash on receipt of invoice and B/L, wire acceptance to-day." As one looks through the records of 1913 with all their
indications of fast tempo and prompt payment, it seems slightly in-
congruous to chance on the accounts of a small Philadelphia handicraftsman who still settled his bills only once or twice a year.

Though continuing to deal in imported metals, Nathan Trotter &
Company had in fact ceased to be an importing firm. New York had
become the importing center and the best way to obtain metals was
through New York agents. The Trotters were, however, still metals
wholesalers—"the only really wholesale dealers in metals in Philadelphia" they claimed. The distinction lay in the fact that they did not
turn to being metals brokers. They bought the goods themselves and
sought a customer for them. In a sense they were using their capital
to run the risks of the market and their skill and experience in buying
enabled them to be right enough of the time to render them a profit.
The large-scale buyer was willing to pay them a profit because he
could count on their buying skill to contract for delivery when the
market was low. The small buyer paid a price slightly above the carload lot for the convenience of buying in the quantities he needed. In
the latter case the ingots passed through the Trotter warehouse, but in
dealing with large customers the firm frequently never saw its goods:
shipments, handled by telephone, telegraph, or mail, went directly
from the producer or New York dealer to the customer.

From 1915 until the close of 1927, William Henry Trotter and a
former clerk, William M. Weaver, were the chief partners of the firm.
On 1 January 1928 William Henry Trotter retired from the business,
although he left some interest-bearing capital in the venture until
his death in 1933.

To carry on the Trotter tradition the firm brought in, during 1928,
William Trotter Newbold—a grandnephew of William Henry Trotter—
as a junior partner. Also admitted to partnership at the time was
James M. Reilly, an employee of the firm since 1907. William M.
Weaver succeeded to the position of senior partner, a position which

he held until his death in 1946. For the first time in the firm's history "the senior" was not a member of the Trotter family. Gradually Newbold and Reilly acquired larger shares in the business until, on the death of Weaver in 1946, the enterprise became almost entirely the property of these two men. In 1951 a younger man was hired by the firm, T. Henry Dixon, a second cousin of partner Newbold. Both Dixon and Newbold are great, great grandsons of Nathan Trotter (see genealogy in Chart XII).

Unlike World War I, which had affected the business little—although it increased profits tremendously—World War II brought momentous changes. The all-out war effort reduced the business to a routine. All the metals it dealt in were put under allocation. Contacts with tin suppliers were severed. Dealers like Nathan Trotter & Company received specified quantities. Decisions as to allocations among dealers were made by the federal government and were channeled through such agencies as the Tin Sales Corporation. On the selling end, the firm's chief problem was to keep customers satisfied that they were being fairly treated. In the Trotter firm's office the former concern with market quotations was replaced by a concern with government reports. With no fluctuation in price and no opportunity for future buying, the firm's profits, while stable, did not spiral as they had in previous wars.

For Nathan Trotter & Company the war did not end with 1945. Tin remained in short supply and therefore under control until 1948. Malayan production was slow to revive and supplies still had to be obtained from Bolivia and the Belgian Congo. Consequently the government's Tin Sales Corporation continued in operation.

With the decontrol of tin in 1948 two unexpected opportunities presented themselves to Nathan Trotter & Company. The first came about as a result of the death of the American agent of Boustead & Company. This company of London and the Straits, with whom the Trotters had from time to time done business since 1877, found it advantageous to have a resident agent in the United States who regularly provided market information regarding the consumption pattern of tin in the United States and the prices for tin quoted in the New York market during the business day. This latter service was extremely important for Boustead.

Early in 1951 an exclusive agency arrangement was entered into between the Boustead and Trotter firms which for Nathan Trotter & Company had special advantages. Before World War II the firm had been buying its tin from New York importers and brokers. With an agency it could buy direct and gain some of the importer's margin of profit. Particularly important was the fact that the Philadelphia firm would have, through Boustead, a direct contact with London, the center of the world's pig-tin market. Tin was bought in London but was shipped directly from Singapore or Penang. Trotter's cable connections with Boustead were daily, with the speed of transmission so far advanced that an answer to a cabled inquiry could be received in less than 20 minutes.

Meanwhile, the firm of Nathan Trotter & Company had set up an office in New York. This action of late 1950 was related to World War II developments. During the war Russell Clark, an employee of C. S. Trench & Company, metal brokers and publishers of a daily news sheet called the *American Metal Market*, had served as head of the government's Tin Sales Corporation. In this capacity he had come to be acquainted with nearly all the large-scale tin buyers of the country —firms which bought in quantities of five tons or more, of which there were about a hundred. Clark's familiarity with the tin market in this country made him a valuable person, as Nathan Trotter & Company realized, and in 1950 it was arranged that he should set up and manage a New York office for the firm.

This office maintained the firm's daily contact with Boustead & Company. Each morning after obtaining Boustead's quotations for future delivery, Clark and his associates telephoned their customers (principally the large steel companies, ingot makers, collapsible tube manufacturers, and makers of solder and babbitt metals) and asked if they wished to buy at quoted prices. With purchase orders verbally received, the New York office then cabled London for confirmation. The business was one-part telephoning, one-part cabling, and one-part paper work. The tin traveled directly to the buyer without being seen by the personnel in New York. The arrangement worked even more favorably than anticipated and substantially increased the company's net profits. Not since the 1870's had the business been so profitable as it became in the late 1940's and the 1950's.

In the Philadelphia office business continued more or less as usual. The firm bought spot orders of pig metals in truck and carload lots and sold in smaller quantities at a slight mark-up in price. Both the New York and Philadelphia offices required large amounts of capital. Commission purchases from New York houses which were not competing with Boustead business were paid for immediately by the Trotter firm. Since their customers took from 2 to 14 days to pay, Nathan Trotter & Company might find it necessary to borrow for a short time as much as a million dollars from their bank. The Philadelphia business was a wholesale-retail operation with capital invested in warehouse stocks. Sales were for cash, with 10 days as the usual collection period, and profits came as much from skills in knowing when to buy as in rendering wholesale-retail service.

Service was nevertheless an important part of the business. With a warehouse immediately adjoining the Philadelphia office—a legacy of the original Nathan Trotter—the Philadelphia firm had certain natural advantages over New York dealers who, because of the high cost of rentals, usually maintained their stocks in public warehouses from which rapid deliveries were not always easy to effectuate. Consequently, with trucking costs approximately the same from Philadelphia as from New York, the firm was able to compete for business all the way from New England to Cleveland and south to Florida.

The commodities dealt in, with one exception, continued much the same as in 1913: pig tin, ingot copper, pig lead, antimony, and slab zinc. The only important departure from the regular line of business in Philadelphia was an exclusive agency negotiated by the firm with the Reynolds Metals Company. This agency made Nathan Trotter & Company the exclusive distributors of Reynolds ingot and pig aluminum for an area of about one hundred miles around Philadelphia.

In the century of the firm's history after Nathan Trotter's death, profit margins have grown constantly narrower but the total profits have mounted because of the increasing sales volume. The firm has made some of its profits as a result of dealing in futures on favorable terms. Some profits have been made in speculation on the London metals market; and in addition the commission business has increased until commissions make up about one-third of the total profits.

For the entire one hundred and fifty years of the firm's existence under the Trotter name, it has carried on a wholesaling business. It has survived four major wars and numerous depressions. The company during this period has adapted its business to changing conditions. From the early importation of English woolens, leathers, and metals, it shifted in 1815 to specialization in metals. Then from both the importation and domestic purchase of quality semimanufactured metals required by handicraftsmen, it moved to dealing in the fair-quality and semimanufactured metals and the pig metals which were required by the growing industries of young America. The 1890's saw one of the most revolutionary changes in the firm's history when the manufacture of American tin plate induced the Trotters to give up tin-plate importing entirely. Since then Nathan Trotter & Company has continued its specialization, but the specialization has come to be in pig metals—metals which, while used by manufacturers in relatively small quantities, are nevertheless indispensable in the modern industrial age.

Appendixes

APPENDIX 1

Nathan Trotter's Letter of Guidance to his Son Edward on the Eve of the Latter's Visit to Europe about the First of December 1835

I had but little expectation a week ago that the day which completes thy twenty first year, and ushers thee into manly Estate, should be the eve of thy leaving thy parental roof for a foreign Land, but as such has been the conclusion, with the consent of thy parents & Friends, I trust a Father's advice at the separation, with his feelings of solicitude for thy Welfare will not be unheeded—

I hope I have always evinced a desire that my children should be brought up in the principle of sound morality and feeling thankfull in believing that thy general deportment has hitherto been consistent with such principles, I feel exceedingly desirous that after the[e] has left the pile of our enclosure, thee should not depart from that line of strict rectitude of conduct, which thy own sense of propriety, and the witness within will not fail to point out—

as the price of a passage in the packet ships for England is very high, I suppose the provisions is very ample & the inducements to indulge the appetite offered in profusion, and doubtless many passengers too much indulge in paying homage to Backus—now I beg thee will not let the influence of Company induce thee to partake with them of ardent spirits or lead thee beyond *one* generous glass of wine p day

this will be a salvo to any charge of parsimony, having thyself paid for & as much right to a free indulgence as others—that the moderation I recommend will enure more to thy benefit and evince that thee is governed by something other than appetite—during the passage be Courteous and polite to all—touch not on politics—Study thy remarks upon any subject before thee utters them—be an attentive listener at all profitable conversation, retaining in thy recollection whatever usefull can be discerned from it—and this course I think will be most likely to conserve a good feeling with the other passengers—thee will be careful to clothe thyself warm & not expose thyself too much on deck, and be attentive to the rules of the ship in regard to speaking with the crew or strange passengers—in short conciliate the good opinion of every one without being too familiar with any, and maintain that Self respect which will conserve its [illegible] I desire that you will pay every respect to the advice of our highly esteemed Friend J W R[ulon] who I am sure will do all in his power to make all your movements pleasant and agreeable and you will throut all your travels endeavour to Continue in that good feeling with each other in which you leave us—The ship will probably stop off Portsmouth where you will most likely land and proceed to London in Coaches when J W R will judge the most suitable place to stop and you must always be careful of your baggage that you lose nothing prevent [?] of proper Care on your part—at a suitable time you can deliver any or Such letters as you may deem expedient and where you appear to be well recd. you can if so disposed renew your Calls, and probably Such [illegible] and advice may be—tended as will facilitate your views [?] in seeing [?] things interesting in that great Metropolis and becoming a little acquainted with some of its respectable residents as well as relates to any further movements you may wish to make—the letter to T. Wiggin & Co—will I presume enable you to obtain such Funds as may be needful in defraying your expences and in which I desire that such economy is observed as will be creditable to yourselves & such as your parents cant reasonably object to—*keep a regular a/c of all monies recd. from Mr Wiggin and of your expenditures*—I wish the advice now given throut this letter to extend & apply at all times during your absence *and I most particularly desire and request that from your embarkation until you return a daily memo: is kept of your travels and of whatever interesting or profitable has presented itself—so that subsequently your memories may be refreshed and the advantage of observations be newly applied to your subsequent benefit as well as for the Satisfaction & pleasure of your Friends*   It is difficult for me to Say how your movements must be limited but my feeling is that after seeing all the most conspicuous & interesting parts of England particularly among the Manufactg Districts you will take a peep at Paris and return home by way of Liverpool so as to arrive here in April next—wishing you every possible enjoyment and that you may be [illegible] in conscious rectitude of Conduct and return Safely to your Fds

I remain affectionately

NT

APPENDIX 2

Nathan Trotter's Will

I, Nathan Trotter of Philada do make this my will and dispose of part of my property as follows and the residue to be equally divided among my children. I give and bequeath to my wife Susan Trotter all my household and kitchen furniture of every kind all Horses Carriages & harness to be disposed of from time to time as she may think expedient and she to have the free use and privileage of the stable on Crown Street during her pleasure. I also give her all the rents and income of my farm in Oxford township Philada County for and during the term of her Natural life.

I further give unto my said wife the sum of Ten thousand dollars to be paid when she may require it after twelve months after my decease and which she may subsequently dispose of as she may think proper. I also direct the annual payment to her of Three thousand dollars per annum or as much thereof as she may desire and request and in such payments as she may need and require, this Annuity to Commence six months after my decease and to continue during her life. I also devise and bequeath to my said wife my house and a lot No. 256. North fourth street Philada where I reside for her proper use and benefit during her life which premises shall be kept in good order with the necessary repairs at the expense of my Estate and all taxes on said Estate to be paid out of my estate. All the above to be in lieu of dower at Common Law.

I hereby appoint my Brother Joseph Trotter and my Sons Edward H. Trotter, George Trotter & William Henry Trotter Executor of this my last will and testament.

Philada 1st Mo 4, 1853

Nathan Trotter [seal]

Witnesses
the name of Edw H Trotter
above the 3rd line

from this (?) written
interlined (?)
Newbold H. Trotter
Francis Hart
Mary H. Trotter
Newbold H. Trotter & Francis Hart two of the subscribing witnesses
to the foregoing last will of Nathan Trotter were affirmed Jan 21 1853
and Jos Trotter & George Trotter affirmed same day in presence of
                                        Saml Lloyd   Dep. Regr.

Source: City Hall Philadelphia. Wills, no. 30. Register, p. 168, no. 13.

APPENDIX 3

Annual Expenses of Nathan Trotter and His Accumulated Balance of Profits

Date	Expenses of Nathan Trotter's Family	Accumulated Balance of Profits (Personal Wealth as of 31 December)
1815	$1,456.57	——
1816	1,619.25	——
1817	1,636.81	——
1818	1,904.09	——
1819	1,330.28	——
1820	1,227.40	$ 12,960.36
1821	1,395.96	——
1822	1,242.06	——
1823	1,355.46	——
1824	1,197.55	——
1825	1,333.12	20,183.47
1826	1,278.41	——
1827	1,370.69	——
1828	1,724.69	——
1829	1,546.46	——
1830	2,074.02	94,627.52
1831	1,892.30	112,943.72
1832	2,090.08	——
1833	2,161.98	——
1834	2,304.41	——
1835	1,972.90	——
1836	1,853.05	——
1837	1,901.66	260,768.85
1838	2,794.46	——
1839	2,754.18	334,377.11
1840	2,341.05	350,000.00

(APPENDIX 3 continued)

Date	Expense of Nathan Trotter's Family	Accumulated Balance of Profits (Personal Wealth) as of 31 December
1841	$2,723.76	$350,000.00
1842	2,687.74	375,000.00
1843	2,707.38	405,000.00
1844	2,704.97	430,000.00
1845	2,112.58	475,000.00
1846	2,893.33	520,000.00
1847	3,313.79	568,184.00
1848	3,247.82	640,000.00
1849	4,115.55	——
1850	2,040.98	750,000.00
1851	3,111.00	800,000.00
1852	3,669.34	——
1853 [a]		836,537.86

[a] On 31 January.

APPENDIX 4

Warehouse Inventories

31 December 1815

			Per Cent
Steel		$ 1,470.00	12.4
Tin plate		1,026.00	8.7
Copper			
raised and flat bottoms, copper sheets, bolts, and sheathing	$4,550.04		
rivets	174.40	4,724.44	40.0
Brass cocks		16.00	——
Wire		2,207.00	18.7
Sheet iron		740.00	6.2
Spelter		559.68	4.7
Lead, pig and bar		117.00	0.9
Solder, spelter		86.40	——
Hardware			
anvils	247.83		
bright and black vices	394.38	642.21	5.4
Felting		202.95	1.7
Total		$11,791.68	

31 December 1825

			Per Cent
Steel		$ 1,232.53	3.8
Tin plate	$3,318.25		
Block tin	1,637.60	4,955.85	15.4
Copper			
braziers	13,804.80		
sheathing	5,508.16		
cake	493.46		

(APPENDIX 4 continued)

			Per Cent
old	$ 1,145.20		
nails and rivets	417.25	$21,368.87	66.7
Sheet brass	979.70		
Brass kettles	12.00	991.70	3.0
Iron wire		1,493.87	4.6
Russia sheet iron		163.83	0.5
Sheet zinc		41.37	0.1
Spelter		696.52	2.1
Bar lead		65.38	0.2
Spelter solder		22.80	——
Antimony		152.04	——
Borax, crude and refined		111.54	——
Hardware			
rivets	354.52		
ears	125.40		
scale beams	218.57	698.49	2.1
Old metal		30.24	——
		$32,025.03	
"deduct from above"		1,186.48	
Total		$30,838.55	

31 December 1850

Steel		$ 2.60	——
Tin plates	$29,428.25		
Banca tin	13,774.68	43,202.93	52.2
Copper			
braziers and bolts	10,899.69		
sheathing	2,444.97		
tin'd copper	83.82		
kettle bottoms	223.00		
old	1.65		
nails, tacks, rivets	713.85	14,366.98	17.4
Sheet brass	68.62		
Brass stamped kettles	16.75		

(APPENDIX 4 continued)

			Per Cent
Brass cocks	$ 6.70	$ 92.07	——
Wire, iron, spring, etc.		6,508.47	7.9
Sheet iron			
Russia	3,884.65		
English	6,602.48		
American	50.14	10,537.27	12.7
Round iron	1,024.25		
Hoop iron	1,513.74		
Malleable iron castings	191.36	2,729.35	3.3
Sheet zinc		647.48	0.78
Spelter		199.87	——
Lead, pig and sheet		187.38	-——
Solder		121.80	——
Antimony		282.78	——
Mica		145.00	——
Bismuth		214.87	——
British lustre		66.00	——
Babbitt metal		20.80	——
Tinman's machines	580.50		
Tinman's tools	618.68	1,199.18	1.43
Hardware		2,218.55	2.7
Total		$82,743.38	

APPENDIX 5

Nathan Trotter & Company: Summary of Annual Purchases, Sales, Profits, and Inventories, 1815–1849 (Cents Omitted)

Year	Sales	Gross Profit on Merchandise Sold	Income from Interest	Net Profit	Purchases	Inventory
1815 a	$ 96,656	$11,430	$ 225	$10,673	$ 97,017	$11,791
1816	87,275	9,164	1,608	11,557	93,045	26,725
1817	73,273	12,167	2,312	13,000	64,573	30,192
1818	86,431	13,291	3,328	18,000	84,223	41,276
1819	50,284	6,178	1,203	7,300	35,701	32,870
1820	54,019	7,378	631	7,000	35,769	22,000
1821	77,263	7,583	3,167	12,000	81,848	34,169
1822	51,852	11,536	1,921	13,561	29,471	23,325
1823	88,830	6,615	2,656	8,602	88,628	29,737
1824	102,252	12,475	3,068	14,556	78,673	18,634
1825	120,740	14,449	4,632	19,000	118,495	30,838
1826	150,000	13,758	5,616	20,000	135,320	29,917
1827	74,573	12,635	6,414	20,000	63,688	31,667
1828	132,862	9,165	7,242	14,000	122,750	30,721
1829	100,030	9,532	6,353	14,000	95,584	35,809
1830	112,593	10,397	7,663	15,983	108,108	41,721
1831	87,409	16,447	7,295	22,000	72,674	43,433
1832	168,231	15,215	9,287	25,000	161,120	51,538
1833	227,671	20,176	6,077	26,480	215,873	59,916
1834	140,238	13,818	7,055	21,260	113,287	46,784
1835	206,165	22,769	5,428	26,080	163,768	27,156
1836	242,171	35,323	5,790	38,995	204,690	25,000
1837	216,293	25,000	3,388	29,341	195,331	29,037
1838	246,294	25,000	5,040	31,082	238,245	45,989
1839	241,747	30,000	9,126	35,129	231,525	65,766

(APPENDIX 5 continued)

Year	Sales	Gross Profit on Merchandise Sold	Income from Interest	Net Profit	Purchases	Inventory
1840	$214,533	$24,578	$2,886	$20,000	$171,876	$47,689
1841	243,991	26,363	?	20,000	217,761	47,822
1842	139,565	10,000	4,473	10,000	147,022	65,279
1843	173,572	23,537	3,289	27,287	134,809	50,053
1844	218,712	25,777	713	24,402	198,880	56,000
1845	290,661	32,817	9,904	37,999	246,523	44,679
1846	319,829	31,820	10,281	39,693	321,887	78,556
1847	376,403	42,061	3,547	42,000	307,161	51,377
1848	372,682	34,398	16,613	41,087	346,970	60,063
1849	268,852	45,707	14,773	60,000	244,082	81,000

[a] March to December only.

Notes and References

MANUSCRIPT SOURCES

The Trotter collection, in Baker Library, Graduate School of Business Administration, Harvard University, consists of thousands of items. The collection includes Daybooks, Ledgers, Cash books, Invoice books, Foreign Exchange books, copies of domestic and foreign letters sent, letters received, books of commission sales, credit reports, traveling salesmen's letters, as well as a variety of other account books of the Trotter firm, of Nathan Trotter, and even of firms with which some member of the Trotter firm was associated. The collection was catalogued by Margaret Ronzone (now Mrs. James Cusick) and her classified list of materials is an invaluable guide to the researcher.

The study of Nathan Trotter's business is based primarily on these records. Unless otherwise indicated, the Trotter business records used are in Baker Library. Letters written to Nathan Trotter or the firm or by him or his firm are referred to in the footnotes as NT or NT & Co.

The Trotter-Newbold papers to which references have been made are in the Thompson collection, Historical Society of Pennsylvania, Philadelphia.

NOTES AND REFERENCES

CHAPTER I. Nathan Trotter: The Man and His Career

1. "An early petition of the Freemen of the Province of Pennsylvania to the Assembly, 1692," *The Pennsylvania Magazine of History and Biography*, XXXVIII (1914), 498.

2. Included in the muster rolls of Philadelphia, 1776–1782, are the following: Daniel Trotter, Joseph Sidons, Henry Drinker, Conrad Gerrard [Conrad Gerhart], Leonhard Snowdon [Leonard Snowden], and Michael Dawson. All of these men paid the double tax in 1779 in the Mulberry Ward, East Part, imposed on those who failed to take the oath of allegiance—an oath which the tax records indicate the Friends were loath to take. I do not think that the above entry nullifies the statement that none of Nathan Trotter's ancestors participated in the War of Independence, since I question whether any of the above actually performed any military service. See "Muster Rolls of Militia and Frontier Rangers—1776-1782. City of Philadelphia. Captain Andrew Geyer's Company. A return of Company of Militia that Were Notified to Turn out into Actual Service under the Command of Colonel Wm. Will, Third Battalion, September 20, 1781," *Pennsylvania Archives*, 3d series, XXIII, 401.

3. Two years *before* Nathan was born, Daniel Trotter was listed at Elfreth's Alley and at Water above Arch Street (*The Philadelphia Directory* by Francis White for the year 1785). *The Philadelphia Directory* by Clement Biddle for 1791—four years *after* the birth of Nathan—lists Daniel Trotter still at Elfreth's Alley, No. 30, and at 61 North Water Street.

The North Water Street address was the location of Daniel's shop. There is today in the Trotter firm's office a picture of this shop, entitled: "East side of Water St. above Arch St. occupied by Daniel Trotter as a cabinet-maker shop from about the year 1774 to 1797 at a rent of £5 per annum. Taken down Aug. 28, 1848."

The Directory for 1795 places Daniel Trotter at 100 North Front—his address and naturally his son Nathan's, until Daniel's death in 1800—and gives 11 Elfreth's Alley as the location of his shop. There is material in the Trotter papers indicating that Daniel owned both a shop and a residence in the Alley.

Herbert G. Moore, in an article entitled "Colonial Alley: old street in Philadelphia to mark more than 200 years of history Saturday" (*The New York Times*, Sunday, 27 May 1951), states that each year, on the first Saturday in June, the Elfreth's Alley Association with the residents of the Alley stage what is known as Elfreth's Alley Day.

The Alley, one block long, "is said to be the oldest street of colonial row houses in North America—thirty-three little brick homes, each over 200 years old, once occupied and still occupied by just average citizens. . . . The quaint little alley is rich in historic lore, even though no important events ever happened here. Tradition does have it that Stephen Girard lived for a time at 111 Elfreth's Alley, and Talleyrand is said to have sought refuge here after his flight from the French Revolution. But except possibly for these two, the residents were just average people. According to the earliest city directory, they included William Atkinson, shipwright; Daniel Trotter, cabinet-maker; Lewis Cress, shallopman (boatman); Edward Brennan, porter; John Broomstone, pewterer; Adam Rees, cordwainer; Thomas Tracy, sea captain; Isaac Donaldson, hatter."

4. The school at Westtown had been founded in 1799. It was established as a result of the activities of James Pemberton, John Dickinson, Owen Biddle, Joseph Sansom, and other Quakers of the Philadelphia Yearly Meeting. The school was intended to give "Friendly youths a chance to come in contact with a better

type of scholarship than they had been used to and was the beginning of better days" in Quaker education. Joshua Sharpless was the first superintendent of the school, and the first matron was Ann Sharpless.

5. *List of Students at Westtown School 1799–1872; A brief history of West-town Boarding School with a general catalogue* . . . (2d ed.; Philadelphia, 1873); Helen G. Hole, *Westtown through the years, 1799–1942* (Westtown, 1942), pp. 47, 72, 89, 104, 171.

6. *Journal of the Life and Religious Labours of John Comly* . . . (Philadelphia, 1853), chap. v, "West-Town Boarding-School, 1801."

7. Trotter-Newbold papers, "A list of Sundry Books, Plate &c. had by Joseph Trotter, at the appraised value." These items were purchased by Joseph from his father's estate.

8. NT private daybook, 19 Jan. 1808.

9. Trotter-Newbold papers, exercise book labeled "N. Trotter's Arithmetic Book."

10. NT private daybook, 23 Jan. 1808.

11. There is no direct reference to the date of William's apprenticeship, but several circumstances lead me to select 1789. William was fourteen in that year, a customary age for a young man to begin an apprenticeship. The fact that he did not appear in the Philadelphia directories as a merchant until 1800 indicates that he was working for someone else before that time, and it is known that he worked for the Sansoms before forming a partnership with Joseph Sansom. In the 1890's the letterhead of the Trotter firm first read: "Established in 1789, Nathan Trotter & Co., importers of and dealers in metals. . . ." From this letterhead I infer that the more recent members of the Trotter family were extending the date of origin of the family business to the year when the first family member engaged in the importing business. Letterheads of the 1870's and 1880's did not use this statement.

12. Unless otherwise indicated, the material which I quote from the Minutes of the Monthly Meeting was obtained from the records on deposit at the Fourth and Arch Street Center, Philadelphia.

13. William Trotter's immediate business was not his only concern. He was one of the Guardians of the Poor from Nov., 1811, until Nov., 1812. Scattered items show that he was a contributor to the Philadelphia Society for the Establishment and Support of Charity Schools with its school at Walnut above Sixth; and in 1804 he purchased the Estate's—Daniel Trotter's Estate, presumably—share in the Philadelphia Library for the sum of $40. Another indication that he was interested in more than his mercantile affairs was the fact that he spent $12 for a ticket of admission to the Chemical lectures given in the winter of 1812. Records from the Trotter papers.

14. Alfred Coxe Prime, collector, *The Arts and Crafts in Philadelphia, Maryland and South Carolina Gleanings from newspapers*, series 2, 1786–1800 (Topsfield, Mass., 1929), p. 2, prints a copy of this advertisement from the *Federal Gazette*, 8 May 1800: "TROTTER & HAINES.—Adv. of estate of Daniel Trotter, Cabinet Maker, deceased. The Partnership of Trotter & Haines, Cabinet-Makers, being dissolved by the death of Daniel Trotter.—All persons indebted to said firm, are requested to make payment, and those having demands to present their accounts for settlement to William Trotter, Ephraim Haines. The Cabinet Making business in its different branches, will be continued as usual by Ephraim Haines, at the old stand, Nos. 100 north Front street, and 11, Elfreth's alley."

15. Trotter-Newbold papers, ltr., Mary Jane Trotter to Elizabeth Trotter, 20 May 1850. Susan Hough Trotter was born 13 Mar. 1785 and died 31 July 1867. See *Genealogical and Memorial History of the State of New Jersey*, Francis B. Lee, ed. (New York, 1910), IV, 1448.

16. Ltr., John W. Rulon to NT, 16 Aug. 1836.

17. Ltr., Edward Trotter to Elizabeth Trotter, 14 Jan. 1836.

18. Ltr., NT to John W. Rulon, 18 June 1832.

19. Trotter-Newbold papers, ltr., NT to Elizabeth Trotter, 29 July 1844.

20. Trotter-Newbold papers, ltr., Mary Jane Trotter to Elizabeth Trotter, 20 May 1850.

21. NT private daybook, 31 Dec. 1852.

22. "From our Preparation Meeting was introduced the case of Edward H. Trotter who has been visited for violating our discipline and Christian testimony by accomplishing his marriage by the aid of a hireling minister; to treat further with him Benjamin H. Warder and Joseph Kite are appointed." See Minutes, Northern District Monthly Meeting, 1838–1846, 12th mo. 26, 1843.

The Minutes of 1st mo. 2, 1844 report that Edward freely admitted the truth of the charge. Not qualified at present "to condemn his violation of our discipline and Christian testimony, on consideration no benefit being likely to result from delay, the committee is continued to prepare a testimony of disownment adapted to his case and produce it to our next meeting."

On 2nd mo. 20, 1844 Edward was disowned.

23. "Pray has our Ed: H. Trotter called to see you—he must have been so engaged with his new Bride as to have forgotten home—he had not written us—did he submit a Memo: for Copper we wanted sent by Steamboat thro' Can, 12 Sheets 14" say fourteen lb each to make up an order & must have them on Friday if at all   in haste." See ltr., NT & Co. (endorsed by George Trotter) to Wm. & H. McKim, 25 Oct. 1843.

24. E. Keble Chatterton, *The Mercantile Marine* (Boston, 1923), pp. 173–174.

25. Trotter-Newbold papers, ltr., NT to Elizabeth Trotter, 29 July 1844.

26. Based on material in the Trotter collection and Robert G. Cleland, *A History of Phelps Dodge, 1834–1950* (New York, 1952), pp. 7–12.

27. Ltr., NT to Wolcottville Brass Co., 14 Aug. 1845.

28. Ltr., NT to Rodenbough Stewart & Co., 19 July 1845; Cleland, *op. cit.*, p. 32.

29. Ltr., NT to J. E. Smith, 12 June 1839.

30. Ltr., NT to C. Hager & Son, 18 June 1847.

31. Ltrs., NT to Phelps & Peck, 26 May 1834; Phelps Dodge & Co. to NT & Co., 24 Sept. 1838; NT to Phelps Dodge & Co., 27 Sept. 1838.

32. Cleland, *op. cit.*, pp. 15–16, 26–29.

33. Ltr., NT to Anson Phelps, 8 May 1832.

34. Ltr., NT to Anson Phelps, 12 May 1837.

35. Ltr., Anson Phelps to NT, 13 June 1838.

36. Ltr., Anson Phelps to NT, 23 June 1838.

37. Ltr., NT to Anson Phelps, 3 Sept. 1836.

Once in reviewing what he considered a somewhat unfavorable contract for wire, Trotter asserted: "this Seems too much like having the whole matter and convenience to suit one side. . . . We want to be democratic in our operations but not Loco Foco" (Ltr., NT to Rodenbough Stewart & Co., 4 Nov. 1844). The Loco-Focos were the radical reformers who suddenly came into prominence in 1836.

On one occasion Trotter sent some notes to a bank cashier to be collected from an S. R. Christian, and could not refrain from commenting: "If he is a good *Christian* he will pay it" (Ltr., NT to F. J. Hinkson, 2 Mar. 1843).

38. Ltr., Newton Keates & Co. to NT, 2 Mar. 1843.

39. Trotter papers, box labeled Vol. Y–b.

40. Ltr., J. & E. Walker to NT & Co., 11 Feb. 1853.

41. Ltrs., NT & Co. to J. & E. Walker, 24 Sept. 1842; J. & E. Walker to NT & Co., 17 Oct. 1842.

42. NT private daybooks: 13 Jan. 1819 recd. for Jury Services, Dist. City & County $8.00; 14 Dec. 1824 recd. for Jury Services 29 Nov. to 10 Dec. $12.00; 30 Sept. 1825 in U. States Circuit Ct., Mar. term 1825 $12.50. In a letter to

Rodenbough Stewart & Co., 6 Oct. 1840, Trotter reported: "The writer has been so much engaged in Jury service that he had not had time to answer your letter of 29 Sept to hand 1st inst."

43. Trotter papers, box labeled Vol. Y–2a.

CHAPTER II. Family Antecedents

1. City Hall, Philadelphia, Deeds, Book G4, p. 429: "Benjamin Trotter, 6 July, 1731, turner, one of the sons of William Trotter Senr late of the said city Sawyer," and Joseph Trotter for 5s. released quit claims on land in Chestnut Street.

2. *Publications of the Genealogical Society of Pennsylvania*, IV, No. 2 (Mar., 1910), 169–170; William Wade Hinshaw, *Encyclopedia of American Quaker Genealogy* (Ann Arbor, 1938), comp. by William Worth Marshall (referred to hereafter as Hinshaw), II, 670.

The Society of Friends numbered the months with March the first, April the second, etc. The new year began on March 25; the week began on Sunday. The great Law or the Body of Lawes of the Province of Pennsylvania, 35th section, read: "And Be it further enacted . . . that the dayes of the Week and ye months of the year shall be called as in Scripture, & not by Heathen names (as are vulgarly used) as the first Second and third days of ye week and first second and third months of ye year and beginning with ye Day called Sunday and the month called March."

The change from this custom came in 1752. The Minutes of the Yearly Meeting held at Philadelphia for Pennsylvania and New Jersey for Friends (14th to 18th, 7th mo. 1751) ordered "that the first day of the Eleventh month next, shall be deemed the first day of the Year 1752, and that the month called January shall be successively accounted the first month of the Year." Spencer Bonsall, "Computation of Time, and changes of style in the Calendar," *The Pennsylvania Magazine of History and Biography*, II (1878), 399–401.

The Sansoms in their accounts continued for some time to begin the new year on March 25th. I was told at the Philadelphia Contributionship that Samuel Sansom continued the practice with the Contributionship accounts. William Trotter, brought up in the Sansom tradition, used March 25th as the beginning of the year in some of his early accounts.

3. "The First Tax List for Philadelphia County," *The Pennsylvania Magazine of History and Biography*, VIII (1884), 94.

4. Frank Willing Leach, "Old Philadelphia Families," *The North American* (Philadelphia), 8 June 1913. Leach quotes from a letter written by Isaac Norris, 11 Sept. 1699, to Jonathan Dickinson, Jamaica, describing the current yellow fever epidemic, and stating: "There is not a day nor a night has passed for several weeks but we have the account of the death or sickness of some friend or neighbor. . . . About ten days ago, there was reckoned nine persons lay dead at the same time, and I think seven or eight this day lay dead together." Norris then enumerated those "we have buried of our friends," and the list included William Trotter.

5. City Hall, Philadelphia, Deeds, Book G4, pp. 425–426, recorded 7 June 1744: William Trotter owned 100 Acres in White Marsh, Philadelphia County. *Publications of the Genealogical Society of Pennsylvania*, I, No. 4 (Dec., 1898), 177.

6. Harold E. Gillingham in his article, "The Philadelphia Windsor Chair and its Journeyings," *The Pennsylvania Magazine of History and Biography*, LV (1931), 306, gives this information about Benjamin Trotter (1699–1768), who "styled himself a Chair maker in his will, proved April 1, 1768, and the inventory of his estate shows he made all kinds of chairs. Windsor chairs are listed as well as 'a quantity of Chair Rounds.' The versatility of his craftsmanship is likewise

evidenced by the inventory which included '8½ Doz. Walking Sticks & Rodds' and '3½ Doz. Straw Hatts, some platt &c.' "

7. *The Pennsylvania Gazette*, 24 Mar. 1768, contains Benjamin Trotter's obituary.

8. *Ibid.*, 13, 20 Jan., 3 Feb. 1741/42; 26 Oct., 2, 9 Nov. 1749.

9. One of the copies which I have seen, in the Boston Public Library, is entitled: "Facsimile of the Autographs of the Merchants and other citizens of Philadelphia as subscribed to the non-importation resolution, October 25, 1765."

10. Trotter-Newbold papers.

11. Hinshaw, *op. cit.*, p. 648; "Early Minutes of Philadelphia Monthly Meeting," *Publications of the Genealogical Society of Pennsylvania*, VII, No. 2 (Mar., 1910), 187.

12. *Extracts from the Journal of Elizabeth Drinker, from 1759 to 1807, A.D.* (edited by Henry D. Biddle, Philadelphia, 1889; referred to hereafter as Drinker, *Journal*), p. 3. The house of Martyn Jervis, Elizabeth's grandfather, was "on the west side of Second street, between Market and Chestnut streets, at the upper corner of an Alley leading from Second street to Strawberry Alley," which is exactly where the Philadelphia directories locate Trotter's Alley—west from South Second to Strawberry Alley.

In 1757–1760 John Jarvis and Joseph Trotter are listed side by side on the west side of Second Street, "A Directory of Friends in Philadelphia, 1757–1760," *The Pennsylvania Magazine of History and Biography*, XVI (1892), 226.

13. *The Pennsylvania Magazine of History and Biography*, XXIII (1899), 400.

14. *The Pennsylvania Gazette*, 29 May 1755.

15. *The Pennsylvania Magazine of History and Biography*, XIV (1890), 414.

16. Anne H. Cresson, "Biographical sketch of Joseph Fox, Esq. of Philadelphia," *The Pennsylvania Magazine of History and Biography*, XXXII (1908), 180.

17. *Pennsylvania Archives*, 8th series, Vols. III–V (III, 14 Oct. 1726–22 Sept. 1741; IV, 14 Oct. 1741–11 Sept. 1753; V, 15 Oct. 1753–24 Sept. 1756).

18. Isaac Sharpless, *A Quaker Experiment in Government* (Philadelphia, 1898), p. 225.

19. 17 Sept. 1719 his widowed mother, Rebecca, deeded Joseph land on Chestnut Street for the sum of £40 (City Hall, Philadelphia, Deeds, Book G4, pp. 427–428). On 25 November 1727 he purchased land on Second Street (Deeds, Book F5, p. 258), and on 23 May 1735 he purchased at sheriff's sale ground and a tenement between Delaware Front Street and Kings (now Water) Street (Deeds, Book F8, pp. 185–187).

20. *Pennsylvania Archives*, 3d series, XIV, 154.

21. Hinshaw, *op. cit.*, p. 428; "The Elfreth Necrology," *Publications of the Genealogical Society of Pennsylvania*, II, No. 2 (May, 1902), 213.

22. Elizabeth's grandfather, named Caspar Hoodt, was undoubtedly the Causper Hoote who appeared in the first tax list of Philadelphia—the list in which the first of the Philadelphia Trotters also appeared. Causper Hoote paid 10 shillings on property assessed at £120, or four times that of his Trotter contemporary. See "The first Tax List for Philadelphia County," *The Pennsylvania Magazine of History and Biography*, VIII (1884), 94.

It is recorded that Hoodt was a German who had been naturalized in Philadelphia in 1701. He appears in the Minutes of the Philadelphia Monthly Meeting of 1701, when on 27 April he was "left at liberty to marry" Sarah Coleman. I presume that the Daniel Hoodt "reported married to Esther Oldman," on 31 March 1719, is their son and the father of Elizabeth who appeared later in the Monthly Meeting records in this entry: "1742, 8, 28, Elizabeth Trotter (late Hoodt) reported married contrary to discipline." There is, however, no indication as to why or how she had violated the Quaker discipline and no record that she was disowned. See George Morgan, *The City of Firsts: Being a Complete History of* the City of Philadelphia from Its Founding, in 1682, to the Present Time (Philadelphia, 1926), p. 532. See also Hinshaw, *op. cit.*, p. 552.

Elizabeth's father, Daniel Hoodt, a cooper, presented a petition to the House in 1747 "praying to be appointed the Officer for putting in Execution the Act for preventing unfair Practices in the Packing of Beef and Pork for Exportation." His petition was unsuccessful and the post was given to another cooper. See *Philadelphia Archives*, 8th series, IV, 3130–3133.

23. "A Directory of Friends in Philadelphia, 1757–1760," *The Pennsylvania Magazine of History and Biography*, XVI (1892), 226.

24. Hinshaw, *op. cit.*, pp. 428–429; Elizabeth Drinker recorded in her *Journal*, p. 8, on 30 January 1759: "were invited to ye Burial of Wm. Trotter."

25. *The Pennsylvania Gazette*, 17, 24 Oct. 1751, contains the advertisement of a schoolteacher "opposite the shop of Nathan Trotter, Blacksmith, in Second-street, between Market and Chestnut-street."

26. "A Directory of Friends in Philadelphia, 1757–1760," *The Pennsylvania Magazine of History and Biography*, XVI (1892), 225–226.

27. The 1814 Directory (Kite's) lists Trotter's Alley from 22—which would be on the west side—South Second to Strawberry.

28. Hinshaw, *op. cit.*, p. 493.

29. In Mulberry Ward, Daniel Trotter, a Benjamin Trotter, and a Joseph Trotter were all reported paying in 1779 the double tax exacted of those who did not take the oath of allegiance required by law. *Pennsylvania Archives*, 3d series, XIV, 806; John Bach McMaster in *The Life and Times of Stephen Girard* (Philadelphia and London, 1918), I, 14–16, explains that the Assembly of Pennsylvania, 13 June 1777, passed an act requiring all male white inhabitants over eighteen years of age "on or before the first day of July, 1777, [to] take and subscribe an oath of allegiance. . . . All who did so renounced allegiance to George Third, King of Great Britain, swore to bear true and faithful allegiance to the Commonwealth of Pennsylvania, never do anything prejudicial to the freedom and independence thereof, and discover and make known to some justice of the peace all treasons or traitorous conspiracies whereof they were cognizant."

On 1 April 1778 a new Act for the Further Security of Government "required all who had not hitherto taken the oath of allegiance to do so on or before the first of June, 1778, or suffer all the penalties of the Act of June 13, 1777, and in addition be rendered incapable of suing at law, or acting as administrator or guardian, of receiving any gift or legacy, of making a will or testament, and be forced to pay double the taxes which, on the same property, would be required of one who had sworn allegiance to the Commonwealth."

The Benjamin Trotter mentioned above could not have been Daniel's great uncle since the latter died in 1768.

30. Gillingham, *op. cit.*, p. 332.

31. Trotter-Newbold papers, "N. Trotter's Arithmetic Book."

32. Elizabeth Drinker, one of "Becky's" neighbors, recorded in her diary for 25 February 1797: "A boy came in a hurry to enquire for Danl. Trotter said his Wife was dead—Sister went there, found it likely to be the case—she had been much better for some days past than since her lyeing-in, and to day was setting up discorseing with her family &c.—she was suddenly taken sick at stomach, fainted and appeared gone. the Docr. was sent for, who thought, when he saw her, it was to no purpose.—he however advised friction &c. poor Daniel came home while Sister was there, she left him in very great distress, several women were there continuing their efforts to recover Becky—but it proved without effect!"

I am indebted to Dr. Cecil K. Drinker for the entries in Elizabeth Drinker's Diary of 25, 26, and 28 February 1797. Since these were not in the published portions of Elizabeth's *Journal*, Dr. Drinker sent me a copy from the manuscript which is in his possession.

33. Trotter-Newbold papers, "N. Trotter's Arithmetic Book."

34. Trotter-Newbold papers. Joseph Trotter, four years older than Nathan and therefore for whom less would be spent, received the following legacies: $250 from his sister Rebecca and the rest from his father's estate.

Esther Hoodt's Est.	28.50
Personal Est.	494.68
Real Estate	800.00
do	264.28
Ch (?) Springfield	44.00 [Conarroe legacy, N. J.?]
Legacy R. Trotter	250.00
Total amt of Legacys recd by J T to 1816	1,881.46

CHAPTER III. Business Antecedents

1. Albert Cook Myers, *Quaker arrivals at Philadelphia, 1682–1750* . . . (Philadelphia, 1902), p. 97. Samuel's certificate of removal reads: "Samuel Sansom, unmarried, dated 6 mo. 14, 1732, from Two Weeks Meeting at Devonshire House, London, England. Certificate signed by John Sansom . . . Received 11 mo. 26, 1732."

2. Typescript material which Mr. T. Morris Perot, III, permitted me to use.

3. 1 and 8 Dec. 1737.

4. Letter from Mr. T. Morris Perot, III: "Sarah, wife of Samuel Sansom, Sr., was . . . Sarah Johnston, born in Pennsylvania 1706, died in Philadelphia 11/19/1762."

5. *The Pennsylvania Gazette*, July, 1738. This advertisement also announced that Samuel had goods for sale both at his new place of business "over against the Work-House in Third Street" or at Rees Meredith's store on William Fishbourn's Wharf.

6. The advertisements appear in *The Pennsylvania Gazette*, 8, 15, and 22 Nov. 1739. They announce that Sansom's place of business is now "next door to Peter Stretch's in Second-Street."

7. City Hall, Philadelphia, Deeds, Book G7, pp. 332–333 and 337–340. The first piece ran between Front and Second Streets, near Arch, and was purchased of "The Honorable John Penn by his Attorney Thomas Penn, Esqr." The second was bounded by Sassafras [Race] and Fifth and, on the north and west by "vacant ground."

8. *The Pennsylvania Magazine of History and Biography*, XXIV (1900), 213, and XXV (1901), 119 and 123.

9. *Ibid.*, XXIII (1899), 399.

10. "A Directory of Friends in Philadelphia, 1757–1760," *The Pennsylvania Magazine of History and Biography*, XVI (1892), 230.

11. The remainder of the obituary, which appeared in *The Pennsylvania Gazette*, 2 Mar. 1774, reads:

> The Patience and Satisfaction which he manifested in his last painful Disorder, were the happy consequences of having passed through Life with a proper Sense of moral and religious Duties, and a Course of Conduct consistent with the necessary Injunctions thereof.—
> To him the Approach of Death was not with Terror; his Dissolution was effected without a painful Grace [?] and his End 'the End of the just Man,' was crowned with *Peace*. He survived an amiable Woman, his Wife, about five years, whose Virtues were truly such, as to intitle their possessor to the most respectful Rembrance.

From Elizabeth Drinker's *Journal*, p. 39, we learn that on 20 December 1773, Samuel Sansom, Sr., "was in a bad way with a sore toe which has lately mortified," and that on 23 February 1774, he "departed this life this morning."

12. For taxes paid by Samuel Sansom see *Pennsylvania Archives,* 3d series, XIV, 198 for 1769; XIV, 301 for 1774; and XV, 317 for 1789. Of course 1780 was a period of inflation.

13. Drinker, *Journal,* entries of 11 and 15 Aug., 1 Sept. 1759 and 4 May 1760.

14. *The Pennsylvania Gazette,* 18 Sept. 1760.

15. Typescript material which Mr. T. Morris Perot, III, permitted me to use; Hinshaw, II, 416.

16. After settling in America, Callender married Katharine Smith of Burlington, New Jersey. About 1740 he purchased a farm four miles from Philadelphia on the Delaware. His daughter described this "Richmond Seat," as it was called by the family, in an entry in her Diary on "8th mo. 4th day," 1759 when she went with her father to the "Plantation." It contained "60 acres, 30 of upland and 30 of meadow. . . . Half the upland is a fine woods, the other orchard and garden." There were fruit trees, "honeysuckle on the fences, low hedges to part the flower and kitchen gardens, and a fine barn just at the side of the wood. . . . The whole a little romantic rural scene."

The farm was possibly profitable to the father, as well as a "romantic rural scene" to the daughter, since in February, 1747/48, Callender advertised for sale "at his plantation at Richmond, alias Point-no-point, good English hay . . . and several draft horses, with a large bay mare, a natural pacer, new with fole, and a colt by her side."

See George Vaux, "Extracts from the Diary of Hannah Callender," *The Pennsylvania Magazine of History and Biography,* XII (1888), 447–448. Also see *The Pennsylvania Gazette,* 9 Feb. 1747/48; 8 Jan. 1756, and *The Pennsylvania Magazine of History and Biography,* XXIII (1899), 502; XXIV (1900), 109, 353, 358, 514; XXV (1901), 561.

17. John F. Watson, *Annals of Philadelphia* . . . (enlarged by Willis P. Hazard, Philadelphia, 1881 [referred to hereafter as Watson's *Annals*]), I, 225.

William Callender was not only a businessman—and a successful one—but a member of the Pennsylvania Assembly from the 1753–1754 session until he, along with five other members, resigned in 1756 because, as they reported to the House:

> as many of our Constituents seem of Opinion that the present Situation of Public Affairs call upon us for Services in a military way, which, from a Conviction of Judgment, after mature Deliberation, we cannot comply with, we conclude it most conducive to the Peace of our own Minds, and the Reputation of our religious Profession, to permit [persist?] in our Resolutions of resigning our Seats, which we accordingly now do . . . . Philadelphia, sixth month, 1756

JAMES PEMBERTON	WILLIAM PETER
JOSHUA MORRIS	PETER WORRAL
WILLIAM CALLENDER	FRANCIS PARVIN

Joseph Sansom would follow in his grandfather Callender's steps to the Pennsylvania legislature, but in that body he would never be associated with anything as dramatic as his grandfather's resignation. See *Pennsylvania Archives,* 8th series, V, 4245–4246.

18. Sansom & Swett in *The Pennsylvania Gazette* of 16 July 1761 and 6 May 1762; Samuel Sansom, Jr., in 21, 28 May, 4 June, 29 Oct., 12 Nov., 1767; 11 Apr., 26 May, 13 Oct., 1771; and 16 Sept., 21 Oct., and 11 Nov., 1772.

19. Historical Society of Pennsylvania, Vaux Papers.

20. Ms. copy, Officers of the Philadelphia Contributionship for the Insurance of houses from loss by fire, from its institution March, 1752, p. 15. This book is in the possession of the Contributionship.

21. Since there were such close associations between the Drinker and Sansom families, it is not surprising that the oldest Sansom son, William, should be-

come an apprentice in Henry Drinker's iron store. He started his apprenticeship in January, 1782. Because William Sansom was twenty-one years of age in 1784, it is likely that the advertisements of Head & Sansom in *The Pennsylvania Gazette* in 1785 are those of William's partnership. Although the partnership continued but a short time, there were more lasting personal relationships: on 12 mo. 18, 1788, William Sansom married Susanna, daughter of John and Elizabeth Head; and William Sansom, along with Henry Drinker and Jeremiah Warder were made executors of the estate of John Head, merchant, at the time of Head's death in February of 1792.

The Head & Sansom partnership had advertised for sale "at their STORE, in Second-street, opposite the Church"—the Church being, of course, Christ Church—the usual assortment of cloth and also hardware.

By 1787 William Sansom was in business for himself and advertising for sale at his store "on the east side of Second-street, three doors below Arch-street, and nearly opposite the George Tavern. A GENERAL ASSORTMENT OF MER-CHANDISE, suitable for the season, part of which are just opened." This advertisement mentioned among the goods for sale red lead, silver watches, window glass, and sixpenny nails.

William Sansom and his younger brother Joseph soon went into partnership at 67 North Second Street, which was probably the "east side of Second-street, three doors below Arch-street," mentioned in the advertisement of 1787 and doubtless situated on the land their grandfather Sansom had purchased from the Penn family. See Drinker, *Journal*, entry of 16 Jan. 1782 (p. 138): "Billy Sansom, Isey Pleasants, and George Gordon tend at our Iron store as apprentices to H[enry] D[rinker]." See also typescript copy of the William and Susanna Sansom marriage certificate in possession of Mr. T. Morris Perot, III; *The Pennsylvania Gazette*, 29 Feb. 1792; *The Pennsylvania Packet and Daily Advertiser*, 23 Apr., 29 Sept., 13, 20 Oct., 3 Nov. 1790; 27 Apr., 4, 25 May, 1 June 1791.

22. This place on the Schuylkill was known as Par-le-ville and a Perot descendant advertised it for rent years later in these words: "A BRICK MANSION, WITH PIAZZA and back buildings, together with a stone coach and stabling, with a garden to the west and an inclosed lawn to the south" (*The National Gazette and Literary Register*, 24 May 1824).

Par-le-ville was once suggested as a rendezvous by Robert Morris, financier of the Revolution. When that Philadelphian's creditors were pressing him in 1797, he urged his partner Nicholson to return from Washington, "at least for a conference. As Morris did not wish his partner to enter Philadelphia until they had conferred on the situation and their policies, he suggested that Nicholson meet him at the 'little villa,' Sansom's place outside the city, and that he should order the Negro caretaker to start a fire and send Robert Morris word of his arrival" [Eleanor Young, *Forgotten Patriot: Robert Morris* (New York, 1950), p. 221].

23. Before turning to the young Sansoms in their more serious business aspects, observe Philadelphia Quakers at the wedding of Sarah Sansom and Elliston Perot. Ann Warder relates that first month 9, 1787, was

> a dull wet morning and bad prospect for Elliston Perot's wedding guests. . . . at the meeting house . . . Cousin Betsy Roberts first said a few words, then honest Robert Willis, soon after which Betsy appeared in supplication and William Savery followed with a long and fine testimony. The bride and groom performed, the latter exceedingly well, and the former very bad. Meeting closed early when the couple signed the certificate, the woman taking upon her her husband's name. We then proceeded to Elliston's house but a short distance from the meeting, where about forty-eight friends were assembled. We were ushered up stairs, where cake and wine were served, and Josy Sansom in helping with two decanters of Bitters, and glasses on a waiter, spilt the wine over his sister's wedding garments, much to his embarrassment.

The next disaster was, that some of the fresh paint ruined a number of gowns. At two o'clock we were summoned to dinner and all were seated at a horse-shoe table except Cousin John Head, Jacob Downing and Billy Sansom, who were groomsmen and waited on us. The bridesmaids were Sally Drinker, her cousin Polly Drinker, and a young woman named Sykes . . . . We had an abundant entertainment—almost every thing that the season procured. After dinner we adjourned up stairs, and chatted away the afternoon, the young folks innocently cheerful and the old ones not less so. Tea was made in another room and sent to us. At nine o'clock we were called to supper, after which the guests prepared to return to their homes.

Ann Warder's entry of the next day notes that she examined her clothes after breakfast and "spent near the whole forenoon in removing the paint of last night." See "Extracts from the Diary of Mrs. Ann Warder," *The Pennsylvania Magazine of History and Biography*, XVIII (1894), 58–59.

24. *Report of the Committee appointed to examine into the state of the Bank of Pennsylvania and Philadelphia Bank* (1829), p. 6.

25. Watson's *Annals*, III, 264, states: "William Sansom and others bought this property at sheriff's sale." Thompson Westcott in his *The Historic Mansions and Buildings of Philadelphia* (Philadelphia, 1877) p. 366, says: "The Bank of Pennsylvania was among the first creditors of Mr. Morris who brought suit. A judgment was obtained against him of $20,997.40. Execution was issued to Sheriff Baker in September, 1797. It was executed by Sheriff Jonathan Penrose, who on the 11th of December made deed-poll to William Sansom for the whole lot and building which was sold for $25,000, subject to a mortgage of £7,000, specie, due to Messrs Willink of Amsterdam. Mr. Morris in his bankrupt petition said that the purchasers of this lot were William Sansom, Joseph Hall, and Reed & Ford, and that they were under agreement that if they could dispose of the property for an amount beyond the purchase-money, they were to account to him for the surplus. This probably never was done."

William Sansom, in a letter quoted below (The Historical Society of Pennsylvania, Autograph Collection of Simon Gratz, "John Dickinson correspondence") states: "I purchased this Estate subject to thy demand at Sheriffs Sale on the 9th. Decr. last for a comparative low price—I have the title exclusively in me therefore the demand I have upon it is perfectly safe in any event—"

Philada. Jany. 16 1798

John Dickinson Esqr.
Respected Friend

The inclosed open Letter was sent to me under cover by Robert Morris Esq. under an expectation that I would have waited upon thee with it in Person; which I designed to have had the pleasure of doing, but the weather or rather the Roads have turned out so unfavourable that I must decline doing it for the present; and therefore now inclose the Letter to thee—

I am not now interested in the issue of the request made to thee by Robert Morris Esqr. further than by the feelings of compassion for the Family of an unfortunate and imprudent man; who have seen days of great splendour and apparent happiness & wealth: for which I am induced to take the liberty to second the contents of his Letter, and beg leave so far as may be consistent with propriety to urge thy compliance with his views—

For this freedom I can only apologize by observing that as thee well knows no Debt on Earth can be more positively secure than is the principal Debt in question the Judgement upon which may remain statu quo as at present this will leave it in thy power to act upon it with promptness when thee thinks proper—and as to the Interest & charges those I have offered & am ready to pay up to March next to whom thee pleases to order it—

As I have come forward in the theatre of Life in some measure since thee left this state it may be necessary to say that Providence hath indulged me with an ample fortune and I have no need of those applications for myself, but I expect thee knows how I stand in regard to this purchase yet lest thee should not I may inform thee that I purchased this Estate subject to thy demand at Sheriffs Sale on the 9th. Decr. last for a comparative low price—I have the title exclusively in me therefore the demand I have upon it is perfectly safe in any event—having a willingness that Robert Morris may receive the benefit of the purchase, so far as relates to me by merely paying my Debt which was only about 16,000 dollars; my Debt I thought it my duty to recover but equally as not [covered with seal—to make?] any thing by his misfortunes; he had & yet has the oppory—of recovering the Estate by paying off the Judgements, which would then leave a handsome property in the Estate & I believe he can accomplish [it] if thee will give time on the principle of thy Debt but which if not he must be infallibly cut off forever; as it is impossible he can raise the sum necessary & thine in addition—it is therefore clearly in thy power to do him an essential service without I hope rendering thyself any injury—

I shall be obliged by a line on the subject by the next Post and remain with sentiments of respect & consideration

Thy assured Friend
Wm. Sansom

To John Dickinson Esquire
Wilmington
Favor Saml Harvey

N.B. I have agreed to wait for my Debt also, having it assured—

26. See letter copied above.
27. Watson's *Annals*, I, 410.
James Mease, in *The Picture of Philadelphia* (Philadelphia, 1811), p. 21, lists the main streets and adds that others had been laid out "either by the state government or individuals, . . . Among these may be mentioned, that laid out by William Sansom, esq. situate between Chestnut and Walnut streets, and west of Seventh street.— It is sixty feet wide; the houses are built agreeably to his plan, strictly uniform in height and external appearance. In Walnut also between seventh and eighth streets, and Second above Callowhill street, rows of houses have been built, or caused to be built by him, which have greatly tended to ornament the city and accommodate the inhabitants."
28. Watson's *Annals*, I, 486; This was, I believe, Palmyra Square, which was above 10th from 10th and Vine to 10th and Callowhill (Directory of 1848).
29. Map in the Philadelphia Public Library, entitled "Improved and published by Wm McKeane Jan 1st. 1819."
30. See letter quoted above, note 25.
31. John A. Fowler, *History of insurance in Philadelphia for two centuries: 1683–1882* (Philadelphia, 1888), p. 50; [Thomas Harrison Montgomery], *A history of the Insurance Company of North America of Philadelphia: the oldest fire and marine insurance company in America* (Philadelphia, 1885), p. 79; Philadelphia directories; *The Philadelphia Gazette and Daily Advertiser*, 12 Jan. 1830; *Gazette of the United States and Philadelphia Daily Advertiser*, 2 Jan. 1798; *The Pennsylvania Magazine of History and Biography*, XLII (1918), 133; Poulson's *American Daily Advertiser*, 4 Jan. 1804.
32. Dunlap & Claypoole's *American Daily Advertiser*, 7 Jan. 1791.
33. *Friends' Intelligencer*, 7 mo. 19, 1813.
34. Clipping based on communication to Poulson's *American Daily Advertiser*, 16 Sept. 1826; Samuel Preston was the authority for this statement.
35. Among his published works were an article on "Outlines of the Life and

Character of William Penn," *Port Folio*, Mar., 1809; *Sketches of Lower Canada, historical and descriptive; with the author's recollections of the soil, and aspect; the morals, habits, and religious institutions of that isolated country; during a tour to Quebec, in the month of July, 1817*. By Joseph Sansom, Esq. member of the American Philosophical Society, author of Letters from Europe, &c. (New York, 1817); *Letters from Europe, during a tour through Switzerland and Italy in the years 1801 and 1802*. Written by a native of Pennsylvania [Joseph Sansom]. 2 vols. (Philadelphia: printed for the author, 1805). This last mentioned work will be referred to as Sansom, *Letters*.

An English edition of the *Sketches of Lower Canada . . . (New Voyages and Travels; Consisting of Originals and Translations*, III, London: printed for Sir Richard Phillips & Co., 1820), includes the following condescending editor's note:

> The Editor . . . has preferred to allow Mr. Sansom to speak for himself in his own words, conceiving that this would be more just towards him: and that, as a specimen of Americanisms, used by a man of good education, the work would thus be a greater curiosity to those English Readers, who are not aware of the deterioration which the language is suffering in the United States. For analogus reasons, many opinions of the Republican Author are retained, because they will add to the interest of the work, though they may sometimes offend by their coarseness, and evident want of discrimination.

36. Sansom, *Letters*, I, 381–383, 509.

37. *Ibid.*, I, 394; II, 282.

This Quaker's interest in art came to him by inheritance. His mother, Hannah Callender Sansom, reveals in her diary an appreciation of painting and architecture. Joseph's father, Samuel Sansom, Jr., brought home from England prints which were popular at the time. Joseph brought back from Italy prints and marbles and a mosaic copy of "Four Doves, sipping out of a bowl," the original of which was "as fresh as when it was described by Pliny as a Masterpiece, then existing, in the Villa of Adrian." See *Pennsylvania Magazine of History and Biography*, XII (1888), 433, 447–448.

Carl and Jessica Bridenbaugh, in *Rebels and Gentlemen* (New York, 1942), state: "In the seventies four other print shops competed with the Kennedys for the patronage of such inveterate print-buyers as Elizabeth Drinker and Hannah Callender, who, as soon as Friend Sansom had returned from England, rushed posthaste to his house 'to see Sammy's Prospective Views.'"

While Joseph Sansom was a member of the Pennsylvania House of Representatives during the 1805–1806 session, he served on committees dealing with education and he also presented a number of petitions in favor of turnpikes. Possibly his brother William and brother-in-law Elliston Perot were among the "sundry inhabitants" whose petition he presented "praying that a law may be passed authorizing the Governor to incorporate a company for making an artificial road from Berwick to North Pennsylvania." These relatives were also interested in the Philadelphia and Lancaster Turnpike whose petition Joseph presented—one in which the managers prayed "that the act, passed 11 Apl. 1799, making certain provisions for said Co. (which will shortly expire) may be made perpetual."

See *Journal of the House of Representatives*, 1805–1806, pp. 31, 33, 34, 42, 124, 151, 335, 357, 392–393. He also voted in favor of "an act to restrain the horrid practice of duelling," pp. 572–573.

38. Typescript copy in possession of Mr. T. Morris Perot, III.

39. Drinker, *Journal*, entries of 12 Feb., 5 Mar. 1799; 12 Nov. 1802; Joseph Sansom to Pieschell & Brogden, 18 Feb. 1799.

40. On 22 Nov. 1802, Poulson's *American Daily Advertiser* carried this advertisement to which no name was signed, but the address is that of the partnership and the goods undoubtedly belonged to the partners.

Tin in boxes,
T. Crowley Millington Steel,
T. Crowley   do
Single, double, & treble
roll'd Sheet Iron,
Black & coloured Morocco,
& kid Skins,
An assortment of Coatings,
Flannels, Forest Cloths,
&c.
For Sale,
Nov. 20 At No. 45 North Front Street

41. Ltrs., Joseph Sansom to Pieschell & Brogden, 13 Dec. 1803; William Trotter to John Waddington, 21 Apr. 1804.

42. The largest investors in the *Pigou's* cargo were William Sansom, Mordecai Lewis, and Jesse and Robert Waln. This venture was typical of Philadelphia's China trade, except that the *Pigou*, under Commander Richard Dale, had unusually short passages—as one might expect of a captain who, at the age of twenty-two, had been selected by John Paul Jones as his first lieutenant. The *Pigou* had arrived in Philadelphia on 7 Mar. 1796, and had sailed again on 12 Apr., making a quick passage of only 100 days to Canton. On 24 Nov. she cleared for Philadelphia and arrived in the Delaware on 13 Mar. just 108 days from Canton, thus completing a round trip in 11 months.

The outward cargo of the *Pigou* in Apr. of 1796 consisted of specie and a small amount of lead and ebony. The investment of the promoters, Lewis, Sansom, and the Walns, amounted to $89,520.11 and this with the investment of about 20 other persons or firms totaled $135,564. William Sansom's $35,000 in specie was the largest single amount and the next largest were $12,500 belonging to Archibald McCall, $12,000 to Penrose & Lewis, and $10,000 each to Sims & Brown, Moreton & Wells, and John Wharton.

Henry L. Waddell and William Trotter were the supercargoes, with William Trotter, probably because he was younger and the more inexperienced in the China trade, acting as clerk. Since William kept the account books as well as the accounts, the Trotter collection contains information about this venture and one on the *Woodrop Sims*. This vessel was in Canton at the same time and in her voyage Messrs. Lewis and Sansom and the Walns were also concerned.

Foreign trade in Canton was "as simple as any in the known world," at the time William Trotter spent over three months there. It was strictly regulated. Foreigners lived in residences, called factories, reserved for them. All business must be carried on with a member of the Hong or merchant group which controlled foreign trade. Provisions and ships' supplies were purchased from members of another organization known as compradors; and through a third group, known as linguists, any other business with the Chinese was carried on.

William Trotter and his group shared a factory with "Messrs [Charles] Haight and Swift"—probably supercargoes on another ship. There were about eight or ten in the factory although exactly how many is not clear from a furniture charge for 11 bedsteads, 11 curtains, 7 mattresses, 9 pair sheets, and 8 pillows. The "Account of provisions, necessaries &c. supplied the Factory by Aion Factory Compradore" records the bread, pots of milk, eggs, rice, beef, pork, fowl, shrimp, greens, onions, fruit, sugar candy, tea, water, segars, and liquors supplied the Factory from 28 July until 15 Nov. 1796, as well as the much less varied fare supplied the sailors when in Canton. A cook, two and sometimes three head servants, two boys, and two coolies served the residents at wages totaling never more than $34 a month.

The return cargo on the *Pigou* consisted of teas, nankeens, sattins, lutestrings,

Persian, Boglipores, silk handkerchiefs, sewing silk, chinaware, cassia, sugar, fans, and umbrellas. The supercargoes deviated from the instructions of Messrs. Lewis and Sansom, and the Walns, justifying themselves thus: since they obtained the greatest part of the teas on a credit, they were able to invest more than ordered in yellow nankeens which they "laid in on more reasonable terms than any purchases made by Americans this season"; also because very little young Hyson tea had come or was expected to come to market, and they thought it important to be the first ship back to Philadelphia, they decided not to wait to procure the specified amount of young Hyson tea but rather increased their purchases of Hyson skin, Gunpowder and Bohea teas.

Supercargo William Trotter had the privilege of some cargo space on board, as was customary, and this he filled with $3,097.68 worth of chinaware, teas, fans, cloths, and sattin-figured shoe patterns. In company with Robert Clay (possibly first mate on the *Pigou* since he was with her on this voyage and sailed as captain on her next) William Trotter invested in Boglipores and colored handkerchiefs. He used some of his space for four large landscape paintings for Robert Waln and for some umbrellas, citron, and a box of paints for William Sansom.

On 21 Mar. 1797, a week after the return from China, the cargo of the *Pigou* was first advertised by Lewis, Sansom, and the Walns. William Trotter doubtless assisted William Sansom in the sale of his share of the goods and sold his own small importation in William Sansom's store. See Trotter collection, "W. T. List of Fgt 15 Nov 1796 to 12 March 1806" and "Book containing Factory Expences at Canton Ship Pigou arrived July 26, 1796."

CHAPTER IV. An Introduction to the Business

As will be obvious from the nature of this and succeeding chapters the bulk of the information is drawn from the account books, balance sheets, and such material in the Trotter papers. Since the typewritten list of materials with the Trotter collection is a serviceable guide to the various types of records, I have not given separate footnote references to such materials as the Ledger for 1830, etc.

1. *Abstract of the Report of Joint Committee of the Legislature appointed to examine into the state of the Bank of Pennsylvania* (Philadelphia, Nov., 1829); George Morgan, *The City of Firsts* (Philadelphia, 1926), p. 533. Morgan, who used some material which I have not seen, states that in an old memorandum book of Joseph Trotter's is an entry dated 9 June 1830, "setting forth his appointment that day to the cashiership of the Bank of Pennsylvania."

2. John Thom Holdsworth, *Financing an Empire: History of Banking in Pennsylvania* (Chicago, Philadelphia, 1928), I, 153–154. During the crisis of 1857, the bank became insolvent through "peculations and frauds of some of the officers, including Thomas Allibone," Joseph Trotter's successor as president.

3. "We sadly have been put out in consequence of attaching limits to our orders," ltr. to Bainbridges & Brown, 15 Nov. 1824. He admitted his error and promised "we shall not hereafter define prices so exact, but leave it a little more to your judgment," ltr. to J. E. Smith, 30 Oct. 1840, and the same idea was expressed in ltrs. to Jevons Sons & Co., 9 Oct. 1840 and to J. & E. Walker, 19 Nov. 1840.

4. A typical example is a letter to Josiah Wilcox, 28 Sept. 1841; Trotter regretted that Wilcox had drawn on Nathan Trotter & Co. and stated "it cannot be accepted without a departure from our practice for many years   it has been near 20 years since we issued any notes & therefore shall not commence yet awhile or until we fail to meet our payments   if your a/c is due we are ready to pay it & if you draw let it be thro one of the banks or we will remit you if you prefer it deducting exchange."

5. Albert C. Applegarth, *Quakers in Pennsylvania.* Johns Hopkins University

Studies in History and Political Science, 10th series, VIII–IX (Aug., Sept., 1892), 17–18.

6. Customer George Trissler wrote on 16 Dec. 1820: "and Sir I must in form you To write me a plaine hand for I cant make out your Running hand." I have sympathized with Trissler often.

7. In the Directory of 1816, R. B. Rand was listed as professor of penmanship, 34 South 6th. By 1830 (*The Philadelphia Gazette & Daily Advertiser*, 2 Jan. 1830) Rand's Writing Academy is advertised at No. 36 South 6th St., and four years later the notice appeared: "Rand's Introduction to Penmanship, in 8 parts. Just published." (*The National Gazette and Literary Register*, 1 Oct. 1834.)

8. Ltr., Daniel Haines to NT & Co., 15 Dec. 1821.

9. Ltr., NT to Wm. and Hazlett McKim, 29 Dec. 1843.

10. A picture of John L. Conarroe in the office of Nathan Trotter & Co. contains a note reading: "John L. Conarroe Died Jan 1st 1908 Age 85 years connected with Nathan Trotter & Co. from 1845 to the time of his death 62 years." The account books indicate that John L. Conarroe came to work for the firm in 1847 and not 1845. Even so, 60 years is a long time to be employed in one firm.

11. Based chiefly on Kite's *Philadelphia Directory* for 1814 and Abraham Ritter's *Philadelphia and her Merchants . . .* (Philadelphia, 1860).

12. Kite's *Philadelphia Directory* for 1814.

13. Trade card in the possession of Nathan Trotter & Co.

14. Ltr., NT & Co. to Bainbridges & Brown, 18 Nov. 1815.

15. Ltr., Bainbridges & Brown to NT & Co., 9 Mar. 1816.

16. Ltr., NT & Co. to J. McKim, jr., & Sons, 25 Sept. 1826.

17. Ltr., NT & Co. to Mather, Parkes & Co., 10 Apr. 1824.

18. Ltr., NT & Co. to A. Broadwell, 5 Nov. 1827.

A price list from agents Samuel Baily & Co., Sheffield, 22 Mar. 1827, of prices of tinned plates at Gospel Oak Tin Works quotes 1C 10½ × 13⅜, wt. 1 Cwt, 225 sheets in a box and 1X the same size as 1C, weight 1 Cwt. 1 Qr. and 225 sheets in a box.

An undated list in the Invoice Book for 1827–37 gives the sizes for 1C and 1X as 13¾ × 10 inches. The weight of 1C was 112 to 115 pounds and of 1X was 140 to 143 pounds. Both were 225 sheets to a box.

19. Ltr., NT to J. Bradlee & Co., 28 Apr. 1840.

20. Ltr., NT to F. D. Musselman, 18 July 1835: "about 24 or 25 in. wide, size no. 10 or thinnest—90 sheets in a cask is most desirable."

21. David Pingree, Salem, 3 June 1846, wrote William Turrell: "you can say to him [Nathan Trotter] that the Tin that has the 'Rajah Mark' on it is the best, and the reason that it was not melted over, and the Revely mark put on, was its well known reputation—whereas the doubtful marks Messrs Revely & Co. *melt* over—all of it passed through their hands."

CHAPTER V. Merchandise Procurement

1. Ltr., Wm. & Jno. Walker to Wm. Trotter, 10 Feb. 1804.

2. George Bainbridge entered business in 1768. He later formed the firm of Bainbridge, Ansley & Co. with John Ansley, John Bainbridge, and Thomas Brown. This firm became Bainbridges & Brown on 31 March 1807, with George Bainbridge, his son John, Jr., his nephew John, and Thomas Brown as partners. Bainbridges & Brown were located on 45 Bread Street, London, and were called merchants and drapers. George Bainbridge died in 1827 whereupon the partnership was dissolved. The business was carried on for several years, however, by George B. Brown, a relative of Thomas. John Bainbridge, in testimony given before a Parliamentary committee in 1808 calls himself a merchant trading both to the Continent and to America solely on account of persons residing in America

from the time of the commencement of the house, nearly forty years before. Again in testimony before the Select Committee on the foreign trade of the country, 1821, he stated that his firm was engaged in business "as a general merchant, particularly with the United States of America and the British colonies"; and that they were "commission merchants entirely, both export merchants and importing from the Colonies on commission."

See ltr., Geo. Bainbridge to Wm. Trotter, 26 Jan. 1807. See also *Minutes of evidence before select committee on the foreign trade of the country, Reports of Committees,* VI (1821), 45, 51 (17 Feb. 1821). The 1808 testimony is from *Parliamentary Papers, Evidence of Merchants, 1808.*

3. In 1805 the firm was Pieschell, Brogden & Co. In 1809 it became Pieschell & Schreiber.

4. The information about this firm has been taken chiefly from two sources: W. A. Young's "Works organization in the seventeenth century, some account of Ambrose and John Crowley," *The Newcomen Society . . . Transactions,* IV (1923–1924), 73–101; and William Bourn's *History of the Parish of Ryton, including the Parishes of Winlaton . . .* (Carlisle, 1896), pp. 116–148.

5. *Holden's Triennial Directory* (for 1804) lists "Crowley, Millington, and Co. iron-merchants, 151 Upper Thames st. & Greenwich." "Crowley, Millington & Co. Wholesale Iron-mongers, 151 Upper Thames-street," is given in *The Post-Office London Directory* for 1816 and in *Pigot's Commercial Directory* (London, 1823–1824).

6. This firm was known as Capper, Startin & Co. before becoming Capper, Perkins & Whitehouse. In 1810 H. Perkins withdrew and a new partnership was formed by Walter W. Capper and James Whitehouse. In 1815 the firm became Capper, Whitehouse & Hawker.

7. The cloth merchant controlled the last stages of manufacture. He purchased in the great Cloth Halls and also had cloth woven according to his directions. In the merchant's own working room the cloth dressers or croppers carried on the finishing processes. The dyeing was done in one of the independent dye houses on the merchant's order. See William Bunting Crump, *The Leeds Woollen Industry, 1780–1820* (Leeds, 1931).

8. The firm of Cookson & Waddington, so far as I can learn, was composed of John Waddington, a merchant residing in Philadelphia, and William Cookson, merchant and twice mayor of Leeds (in 1792 and 1806). See *Report and Minutes of Evidence, on the state of the Woollen Manufacture of England* (ordered to be printed 4th July 1806).

9. This shift of trade is also noted in Norman S. Buck, *The Development of the Organization of Anglo-American Trade, 1800–1850* (New Haven, 1925), p. 121.

10. On March, 1822, Bainbridges & Brown wrote N. Trotter & Co.: "We think by a recent conversation with Messrs. Crowley's people that they have ascertained in the completion of a new furnace some of their steel was too highly converted the early part of last year as they have had some other complaints besides those of our friends."

On 19 Oct. 1822, N. Trotter & Co. wrote Bainbridges & Brown: "We most exceedingly regret the cause of our returning this steel, inasmuch as we were conspicuous in selling the article, our house having we presume imported for these 20 years back, more of the article than any other in this city, and the prejudice of many purchasers was such that they would not buy elsewhere, even of the very same Steel. This preference very often led us into the sale of other goods, and so sensible do we feel the effect of what has occurred in relation to it that the whole value or amot of what's now returned would not remunerate us for the disadvantage in loss of custom &c."

11. ". . . really our profit is so small that a saving of even a small commission is an object." See ltr., NT & Co. to Mather, Parkes & Co., 4 Sept. 1822.

12. John Crosby Brown, *A Hundred Years of Merchant Banking . . .* (New York, 1909), pp. 71–72; Frank R. Kent, *The Story of Alexander Brown & Sons* (Baltimore, 1925), pp. 129–131.

13. [S. N. Winslow] *Biographies of Successful Philadelphia Merchants* (Philadelphia, 1864), pp. 183–184.

The Trotter firm used all three lines into the 1830's at which time Welsh's and Walker's were withdrawn, but Trotter preferred Brown & Co. packets which he considered "vastly superior."

14. Ltr., George B. Brown, Liverpool, to NT & Co., 7 Nov. 1822: "on the subject of tin Plates it is to me the most extraordinary thing how P & P can sell at the rates you mention—they have as you are aware I dare say a contract with the Ponty Pool Co. but upon what terms of Course is a secret but the impression is not under 37/— one thing I do know that on the very day when I last bought for you this house gave an order for 1000 boxes at 37/— & 43/— *& paid Cash at the Wharf* this I pledge my word of for one of the Partners who is a [cousin— written over] friend of me shew'd me the order—"

15. A letterhead, dated 2 Oct. 1847, of the Walkers reads: "John & Edmund Walker, Ironfounders, and Manufacturers of Iron Ordnance and Ordnance Stores, Tin Plates, and Sheet Iron, and of Morewood and Rogers' Patent Galvanized Tinned Sheets, Plates, Hoops, Strip Iron, Bar and Angle Iron, Wire, Nails, etc., etc."

16. Ltr., J. & E. Walker to NT & Co., 23 Sept. 1846.

17. Ltrs., J. & E. Walker to NT & Co., 18 Aug. 1841; 17 May 1843. Nathan Trotter warned the Walkers not to sell to Mr. Phelps when Phelps went to England, chiefly, so he said, because Phelps would depress the price (July, 1841). J. & E. Walker wrote NT & Co. on 17 May 1843: "After all we have said on the subject it is hardly necessary to assure you that the 'Mountain' has *not had any of our tin direct from us*—he may possibly have had some at second hand, but we think not, because we find, on looking through our order book for the last 2 years, that our sales have been (except to yourselves) almost exclusively for home consumption—perhaps in that period 500 boxes, not more, of our mark have left the country—divided between Spain, Portugal, Germany, & New South Wales,—there were also 50 boxes that may have gone to the United States, but we are almost certain they went to Canada— We receive very many inquiries for Tinplates intended for the United States, but we always decline giving a quotation if we think they can interfere with you—"

18. Ltr., Wm. Llewellyn & Sons to NT & Co., 22 Feb. 1849.

19. Ltr., NT & Co. to Bainbridges & Brown, 1 Aug. 1821.

20. Ltr., NT & Co. to John McKim, Jr., & Sons, 28 May 1825: "We notice your remarks that you would be pleased to Supply us with copper—we cant however help feeling a good deal disappointed that we are unable to have occasional small orders executed— We could not expect you to furnish us with any considerable quantity during the fulfilment of heavy engagements with others—but really hardly expected to be so entirely cut off— We now want a few sheets but fear to order them."

21. Ltr., Bainbridges & Brown to NT & Co., 30 Dec. 1817.

22. Ltr., NT & Co. to Bainbridges & Brown, 22 Mar. 1822.

23. Mather, Parkes & Co. had a lead, copper, and tin warehouse on the west side of the Salthouse Dock Gates, Liverpool (Cornhill). Robert Mather of the firm had been in Philadelphia, probably soliciting orders, shortly before Nathan Trotter sent his first order. The Mather, Parkes method of doing business is explained in this letter to N. Trotter & Co., 31 May 1822:

On receipt of your orders we always secure the sale at what we consider the lowest price at the time unless we see a prospect of its going to be had lower by waiting. The Sale is then advised to our principals: if a remittance comes with the order, at the Nett price, & if not, on credit of 3 mos. When the Sales are thus completed, if in the interval of 1 or 2 months a remittance comes, we are not able to make a deduction being only Commn. Agents, unless at the loss to ourselves of the difference in the price.

The firm became Samuel Parkes & Co., and later Parkes, Ashton & Co.

24. The firm later became Newton, Keates & Co.

Newton, Lyon & Co., of Liverpool, were copper and lead manufacturers as early as 1805. They had manufactories at Greenfield and at Bagillt, near Holly-well. They were also agents to the Marquis of Anglesey, for the sale of ingot copper. "Mona," the classical name of the Island of Anglesey, was usually stamped on each sheet of their copper sheathing.

25. Ltr., Edward Trotter to NT, 15 June 1836.

26. Ltr., David T. McKim for Jno. McKim, Jr., Copper Co. to NT & Co., 29 Jan. 1822: "Our Mr. Hollingsworth, who attends personally at the mill is at present in N. York, he proposes on his return to Phila. to call on you."

Ibid., 2 Sept. 1822: "I did hope that your Boiler plates would have been ready the last of this week, but in consequence of the death of Mr. Hollingsworth, (my Fathers partner) which took place last night, I fear it will be some time next week before they are ready. . . ."

27. Ltr., E. T. Ellicott to NT & Co., 28 Mar. 1828.

28. *Dictionary of American Biography.*

Mr. Louis McKim of Queenstown, Maryland, sent me this information copied from the "black book" of his grandfather:

> Isaac McKim, son of John McKim, July 21, 1775 in Phila. died April 1st. 1838 in Washington, D. C.
>
> In 1820–21 he built a large steam grist mill in lower end of Smith's Wharf, at a cost of about $75,000—besides the ground. The Engine was imported from Bolton & Watts, England. After running it 3 or 4 years during which time flour was very low, and the business unprofitable, it was abandoned, and the steam power applied to a copper Rolling mill which he erected on adjoining property. The Flour Mill in the meantime standing idle & unproductive, and so continued until after his death. This Rolling Mill cost him about $50,000—and was more profitable than grinding flour. It commenced running in 1828 and was continued until after his death by him, and afterwards by his nephews Wm. & Haslett McKim, who purchased it.

29. Ltr., NT & Co. to Wm. Harrold & Sons, 31 Oct. 1831; William G. Lathrop, *The brass industry in the United States* (Mount Carmel, Conn., 1926), p. 74.

30. Ltr., NT & Co. to F. Lucas, Agt., Baltimore Type Foundry, 20 June 1834.

31. Ltr., NT & Co. to Wm. Harrold & Sons, 19 Aug. 1834.

32. Lathrop, *op. cit.*, pp. 57, 63.

33. Ltr., NT & Co. to Wolcottville Brass Co., 14 Aug. 1845.

34. Here are the ways in which Nathan Trotter & Co. secured pig and ingot metals:

English pig tin was secured through English commission merchants and through English selling agents.

Banca and Straits tin were secured through English commission merchants; through Rotterdam commission merchants who purchased through brokers at Dutch government sales in Holland; through New York freight-renting importers; and through shipowning importers of Boston and Salem who sold to Trotter either directly or through Boston and New York brokers.

English ingot copper was purchased of the English refiner or through his selling agent (and was one of the products which Trotter at times sold on commission).

Cuban ingot copper refined in Baltimore was procured from the McKims (and was sold by Trotter on commission for the Baltimore refiners).

Lake Superior copper was procured usually from the McKims (and was sold on commission for them by Trotter).

Pig lead was purchased of the English refiner and through the New York and Philadelphia merchant and broker.

Spelter was purchased through Philadelphia copper merchants, New York merchants and brokers, and the New York selling agent of the Belgian manufacturer.

Regulus of antimony was purchased through an English commission merchant and New Yorkers who imported it from London and Havre.

35. The British government "issued an order in council on July 27 [1825], interdicting trade in American vessels with *all* British colonies with the exception of British North America, the order to take effect regarding the various colonies on successive dates from December 1, 1826, to May 1, 1827." This order in council excluded American vessels from the British West Indies and most other British colonies. (F. Lee Benns, "The American struggle for the British West India Carrying-Trade, 1815–1830," *Indiana University Studies*, No. 56 (Bloomington, 1923), pp. 119, 121.

36. Ltr., NT & Co. to Jevons Sons & Co., 15 Sept. 1837.

37. Ltr., Edward Trotter to NT, 15 June 1836.

38. Ltrs., Morrison, Cryder & Co. to NT & Co., 14 Jan. 1836; NT & Co. to Morrison, Cryder & Co., 31 Mar. 1836.

39. Ltr., NT & Co. to E. F. Sherman & Co., 24 Sept. 1841:

> We have concluded to order a few Rivets from you. . . . but do not wish your label placed on the difft packages for obvious reasons it is not necessary for us or any other dealers in goods to inform all our various customers where we procure our goods by having the makers name and place designated by Labels or otherwise upon them because we Should become merely the medium of informing the various consumers & purchasers in the different places we might sell to where they probably could procure them on as good terms as ourselves & hence our orders become abstracted we therefore wish them labeled only with the Size and kind and in rather larger letters Say 1000—2 in Black Rivets & this mode may not abridge your Sales and we may continue to be the means of an increased dissemination of them relying that the quantity [quality?] and finish will be rigidly maintained.

40. For example, by 7 Sept. 1833, so much sheathing was located in Philadelphia on English account, so Trotter stated, that he was determined to import but little unless he could sell on consignment.

41. There is evidence in the Trotter Papers that Nathan Trotter did protect some of his wholesale customers. In 1824 he sold tin plate through his customers Ehler & Rine of Lancaster at the same time that he was selling directly to C. Hager, a merchant of that town. Trotter wrote Ehler & Rine 30 June 1824:

> We feel anxious that the price of the Tin plate sent you sometime ago to sell for us, should not be put so low as to shut out all profit to some of our customers in Lancaster who buy considerable lots of us and are induced to drop you a line in consequence of Mr. Hager stating to us that some were detailing it there at 12 dollars ⅛ 1X—he did not say *you* were, but inasmuch as the price he paid us would not admit of its being sold to advantage at that price, we should feel ourselves very unpleasant after selling the article to stand as a block in the way of his even getting a com by it—you will appreciate our views in relation to it as we wish to act fair and honourable in our dealings, and should regret that he should think that we were endeavouring to undersell him—you will recollect there was no fixed price to it

except that it was to nett us not less than 12 dolls ⅛ 1X tho' more to be realized if possible.

This arrangement with Ehler & Rine, made before Hager became a Trotter customer, was ended shortly.

Nathan Trotter not only protected C. Hager & Co. in the matter of price, but he discouraged the trade of Hager's handicraft customers, unless for cash. "Since we have commenced our dealings with yourself," Nathan Trotter wrote Hager 4 Oct. 1832: "it has been our wish to have no applications for Tin Copper &c from any of the workers of those articles in Lancaster nor have we made any sales of consequence to them." He continued this policy and the correspondence of 1832, 1833, and 1834 contain refusals to sell Lancaster handicraftsmen on credit.

Once when Nathan Trotter had sold a Mr. Gable of Lancaster about $20 worth of goods more than he paid for, C. Hager replied to Trotter's letter informing him of the fact in these words:

I was aware at the time I recd your favour that Mr Gable had sent for copper although I knew nothing as [to] the quantity he had ordered nor the amts he remitted—

I did however suppose he would purchase a larger amt than he paid as such has been his policy with me uniformly unless I put a stop to it which I did several times—I doing so about a month since I [he] stoped dealing with me and left a balance of upwards of $800 unpaid— I informed you when down of the particulars and therefore think it unnecessary to say anything further upon the subject except to do him the Justice to say that whilst I was absent and since my return he has paid me near half the amts and to myself that I shall be much pleased when I receive from him the balance— Mr Gables custom until within the six or eight months was entirely unimportant he being one of the smallest of my customers— He is not a coppersmith but a Tin smith by trade, although he has done a little at the copper for several years— He has now stepped into a part of Mr. Getz business by employing a set of hands which were discharged from Mr. G. shop— His Foreman is Mr Weitzell whom I think I have heard you speak of— I am satisfied from what you informed me whan I was with you and from your letter now before me that you are disposed to do what is right and satisfactory to me in this business so far as it may comport with fair dealing— So much I conceive I have a right to expect from you inasmuch as I have for years given you a preferance at equal prices— More I hope you do not consider me capable of asking—

In Mr Gables business I do not intend to advise anything, I wish you to exercise your Judgment with a view to your own interest exclusively— I am sure you will acceed to me the priviledge of doing the same— How much the difference in your favour would be wether you wish to sell to him or me— or how long his business may continue as it now is brisk It does not become me to say— In Baltimore none of them can purchase without the cash or old copper— McKims have some knowledge of their way of dealing and they have paid for it— With regard to Mr Ehlers recommending Mr Gable I can say nothing further than we disagree in opinion although there may appear from the amts I have stated he owed me to be an inconsistency on my part which I can only answer by saying that I generally had a knowledge who the Jobs were for and when they would be paid for and in this way had an advantage of managing him which you cannot have— I do not believe Mr Ehler would recommend a man unless he believed him to be trustworthy—

Mr. Ehler does sometimes guarantee to me the payment of bills to coppersmiths and it is but a few weeks since I gave him a notice that a bill which he had answered to me for a friend of his was unpaid and that I should have to look to him for the payment of it as we were unable to collect it from the person— Your letter will of course be confidential— In dunning him for the amt of his a/c I have said to him /but without mentioning your name/ that as he now went abroad for his goods I had a right and would expect him to pay off his a/c without much delay.

The business of a well-established merchant like C. Hager, whose capital was adequate and credit A–1, and whose trade was likely to continue was preferable to handicraft custom. Nathan Trotter had found this out to his sorrow in the difficult period 1817–1822, when he lost by bad debts to some of the very men whom Hager designedly mentioned in the above letter. Of course Hager knew that Trotter would recall the $300 which Getz had never paid and the $207 which foreman Weitzell still owed.

42. Trotter sold metals on commission somewhat according to the following pattern, during the years 1828–1849. (A indicates sales for an American manufacturer; B indicates a Belgian manufacturer; E is English; and I is an American importer.)

	Copper			Tin Plate	Steel	Sheet Iron	Zinc
	braziers	sheathing	ingots				
1828	A	A		I			
1829	A	A		I			
1830				I	E		
1831					E		
1832					E		
1833					E		
1834		E			E		
1835		E			E		
1836		E			E		
1837		E	E		E	A	
1838			E		E	A	
1839				E	E	A	
1840				E	E	A	
1841		A		E		A	
1842		A				A	
1843		A				A	
1844		A				A	
1845		A				A	
1846		A				A	
1847						A	B
1848			A			A	B
1849	A		A			A	B

Some articles were sold on commission chiefly to be assured of a supply, I believe. Sheet iron was a seasonal article. The manufacturer turned to its manufacture from rolling other iron late in the season and the supply was frequently inadequate, especially in a dry season. Beginning in 1838 the Trotter firm arranged with a manufacturer to sell on commission. During some seasons the manufacturer gave Nathan Trotter & Co. exclusive selling rights in the Philadelphia area. The selling agreements with the Belgian firm, the Vieille Montagne Zinc Co., for whom he sold on commission, and with William and Hazlett McKim for whom he sold ingot copper on commission gave Trotter exclusive rights in the Philadelphia area also.

Joseph W. Roman & Sons of the Octoraro Mills made the following proposal, 17 May 1838, to Trotter for the sale of their sheet iron:

1st. We to send you sheet Iron of such numbers and in such quantities as you may order /provided we are able to supply you/ at the full, fair, whole-

sale market price of American Sheet Iron in Philada. payable in six months
from the delivery upon the payment of which we deduct five Dollars per
Ton. If earlier payments are required and paid Interest to be allowed—
2nd. We to Sell no Sheet Iron to any of the merchants in Philada. at less
price than we charge you without discount and none to the stove fitters or
sheet Iron workers at any price after this arrangement shall have been
agreed upon—
3rd. We will send no sheet Iron to Philada. to be sold on commission except
to Omick Noble & Fox in Broad street (who generally sell to the Western
end of the City and small Towns on the Rail Road and canal)
4th. All heavy or single rolled Iron we may sell when and where we can
5th. You are not to sell any American sheet Iron except ours unless we are
unable to supply you
6th. This arrangement to last for one year or as long as the parties may be
satisfied with it—
43. Trotter's income from commission sales was as follows (1835–1848):

1835 —	$1,164.42	1842 — $	735.04
1836 —	688.77	1843 —	495.80
1837 —	723.70	1844 —	605.51
1838 —	592.97	1845 —	855.20
1839 —	747.95	1846 —	1,490.29
1840 —	531.06	1847 —	823.50
1841 —	621.95	1848 —	1,085.09

CHAPTER VI. Sales, Trends, Customers, and Market Areas

1. Tench Coxe, *A View of the United States of America, in a series of papers,
written . . . between the years 1787 and 1794* (Philadelphia, 1794), pp. 334–335.
2. Morton L. Montgomery, *History of Berks County in Pennsylvania* (Philadelphia, 1886), pp. 664, 675.
3. For example, customer Henry Kelcher, of Milton, wrote on 23 July 1824
that he wanted the best tin—"pont pool used to be very good tin—I used to get
very good tin of Keim in Reading and I believe he used to buy all of you. I used to
get from 25–30 Boxes from him at the time and never got any bad tin likely I
shall buy all of you after this."
4. Tench Coxe, "Digest of Manufactures," *American State Papers Finance*,
II, 688.
5. Ltr., J. M. Bowes to NT & Co., 8 Oct. 1847.
6. Robert Sutcliff, *Travels in Some Parts of North America in the Years 1804,
1805, 1806* (2d ed.; York, England, 1815), p. 278.
7. Historical Society of Pennsylvania, Manuscript Collection.
8. Tench Coxe, compiler, *A Series of Tables of the Several Branches of
American Manufactures . . . So Far as They Are Returned . . . in the Autumn
of the Year 1810. . . .* [U. S. Treasury Dept., Tabular statements] (Philadelphia,
1813), p. 52.
9. *Lancaster Journal*, 24 Dec. 1803.
10.   Number and Production of Distilleries

County	1810			1840		
	no. of distilleries	gals.	av. gal. per still	no. of distilleries	gals.	av. gal. per still
Philadelphia	11	466,096	42,374	11	505,032	45,912
Berks	250	324,230	1,296	29	59,814	2,062
Dauphin	104	222,642	2,140	17	147,040	8,649
Lancaster	316	1,438,484	4,552	102	1,459,232	14,306
Northampton	160	170,670	1,066	16	407,300	25,456

The figures for 1810 are taken from Coxe, *A Series of Tables . . . in the Autumn of the Year 1801 . . .*; those for 1840 are from *Compendium of the Enumeration of the Inhabitants and Statistics of the United States* [U. S. Census Office, 6th census, 1840] (Washington, 1841), p. 150.

11. "Here [in Berlin, Connecticut] the Pattison brothers, Edward and William, fashioned the first tin ware made in America (1740) . . . ," *Connecticut, American Guide Series* (Boston, 1938), p. 504; George L. Clark, *A history of Connecticut: its people and institutions* (2d ed.; New York and London, 1914), p. 190.

12. Ltr., Chester Beckley to William Trotter, 19 Nov. 1807.

13. Ltr., NT & Co. to E. D. Cheyney, 10 Oct. 1818.

14. The turnpike era in Pennsylvania had begun with the building of the 62-mile Lancaster turnpike in 1792–1794. Between 1801 and 1815, 47 turnpikes were started in Pennsylvania. A 25-mile stretch between Germantown and Perkiomen was constructed, 1801–1804; and after the 29-mile pike between Perkiomen and Reading had been completed, 1811–1815, there were better transportation facilities with Reading, an important Trotter market. Radiating out from Lancaster were a number of new turnpikes to sections in which the Trotter firm had customers: the Lancaster, Elizabethtown, and Middletown, 1805–1812; the Lancaster and Susquehanna, 1801–1803; and the Susquehanna and York, 1809–1810. Wilbur C. Plummer, *The Road Policy of Pennsylvania* (Philadelphia, 1925), pp. 46, 52–53.

Communication services over the turnpikes facilitated marketing, of course. As early as 1794 there was a stage to New York every day but Sunday; two land stages left for Baltimore on Mondays, Wednesdays, and Fridays; stages for Lancaster set out on Tuesdays and Fridays and for Reading and Hamburg on the same days; the Bethlehem stage left every day in the week but Sunday. Benjamin Davies, *Some account of the city of Philadelphia . . .* (Philadelphia, 1794), pp. 30–31.

15. An example follows: "If you was to call at Spread Eagle Tavern you might find some teams to send it [sheet iron] this week. The Teams generally make inquiry with us for loading on Saturday and I was not at home therefore I had no chance to send for it this week." Ltr., D. D. B. Keim, Reading, to William Trotter & Co., 26 Oct. 1812.

16. "Waggoners name Daniel Norrier [?] will want the goods by 10 oclock leaves at Spread Eagle in 3rd St." Ltr., Peter Shenfelder & Cathcart, Reading, to NT & Co., 26 Sept. 1818.

John Getz, Lancaster, ordered two boxes tin sent to the Black Horse Tavern in Market St. with request to have it sent on as soon as possible by some of the Lancaster waggoners (10 May 1814).

Jacob Boas, Harrisburg, wrote on 28 Aug. 1809: "send wire to Mr. Gratz's in Market St immediately as there is a waggon to be there in a few days—or about the time this letter come to hand."

Information about John Jordan & Co. taken from S. N. Winslow's *Biographies of Successful Philadelphia Merchants*, pp. 27–28, and the Trotter papers.

17. Thomas B. Searight, *The Old Pike: a History of the National Road, with Incidents, Accidents, and Anecdotes Thereon* (Uniontown, Pennsylvania, 1894), pp. 110–111.

18. Plummer, *op. cit.*, p. 35.

19. Ltr., Daniel D. B. Keim, Reading, to NT & Co., 10 Nov. 1821; Searight, *op. cit.*, p. 111, says that "the whip used by old waggoners was apparently five feet long, thick and hard at the butt, and tapering rapidly to the end in a silken cracker."

20. "Geo. W. Bush & Sons Company, Transportation and Coal Shippers, Wilmington, Delaware," *Centenary firms and corporations*, p. 57; Elizabeth Montgomery, *Reminiscences of Wilmington . . .* (Wilmington, Delaware, 1872), p. 166.

21. Chester Lloyd Jones, *The Economic History of the Anthracite-Tidewater Canals* (Philadelphia, 1908), pp. 15–16.

22. *Ibid.*, p. 18; Avard Longley Bishop, *The State Works of Pennsylvania*. Reprinted from the *Transactions of the Connecticut Academy of Arts and Sciences*, XIII (Nov., 1907), pp. 149–297, 163–164.

23. L. & F. Stoughton, Milton, wrote Nathan Trotter & Co., in 1828: "send goods by Schuylkill Canal to Mount Carbon by White & Coombe's boats They leave Phila every Tues, Thurs, & Sat. Write us when goods start so that we may know when to send the wagon after them."

24. Jones, *op. cit.*, p. 130.

25. Ltr., H. Dehuff, Lebanon, to NT & Co., Sept., 1828.

26. *Tabular Statement of the Cost, Revenue and Expenditures of the Several Finished Lines of the Canals and Railroads of the Commonwealth* (Prepared by John W. Hammond and printed in Harrisburg in 1841), Columbia and Philadelphia Railway, first year of revenue, 1832–1833.

27. *Ibid.*, Eastern Division, from Columbia to Duncan's Island, first year of revenue, 1829–1830.

28. *Ibid.*, Juniata Division, Duncan's Island to Hollidaysburg, first year of revenue, 1830–1831.

29. *Ibid.*, Allegheny Portage Railway, first year of revenue, 1834–1835.

30. *Ibid.*, Western Division, first year of revenue, 1829–1830.

31. *Ibid.*, Extended from Northumberland to Lackawannock, a distance of 73 miles. The first year of revenue was 1832–1833.

32. *Ibid.*, Extended from Northumberland to Dunnsburg, 72 miles. The first year of revenue was 1834–1835.

33. *The Register of Pennsylvania*, ed. by Samuel Hazard, VII (July, 1831), 415.

34. Clerk McCune wrote, 25 May 1843, from Wheeling, West Virginia, that he had been to Cincinnati. "I called on Lawsons who complain very much of persons in their city buying Tin Plates in New York and selling it at such reduced prices that they are unable to make any thing by it. . . . I told them we would sell them on as favourable terms as they could buy elsewhere and they admitted a preference for dealing with you but are compelled to buy as low as they can to compete with others."

35. Joseph Jackson, *Early Philadelphia Architects and Engineers* (Philadelphia, 1923), pp. 145–146.

36. R. A. Smith, *Philadelphia as it is, in 1852. . . .* (Philadelphia, 1852), pp. 381, 383, 385.

37. Ltrs., NT & Co. to the Commissioners of the New Jersey Penitentiary, 11 July 1834, 24 Mar., 12 July 1835.

38. Jackson, *op. cit.*, p. 13; ltr., NT & Co. to Commissioners for erecting the New Almshouse, 25 Oct. 1833; Ledger.

39. Jackson, *op. cit.*, pp. 193, 196; ltr., NT & Co. to Isaac McKim, 13 June 1832. On 26 Mar. 1833 Nathan Trotter & Co. wrote to Isaac McKim about an advertisement for copper for the new prison and after seeing it: "our young man Mr Dixon had however an interview with Mr Walter the architect from whom he learnt that the terms of payment would be cash upon delivery reserving 10 pr ct from amt of bill as a guarantee for the performance of the contract."

40. Smith, *op. cit.*, p. 297.

41. Ltr., Eli F. Cooley, Commissioner for Building N. J. State Lunatic Asylum at Trenton, N. J., to NT & Co., 1 Oct. 1846.

42. Ltr., Luke Reed to NT & Co., 12 Sept. 1834.

43. *Seventeenth Exhibition of American Manufactures, Held in the City of Philadelphia . . . 1847, by the Franklin Institute*, p. 510.

44. *J. F. Kimball & Co.'s . . . Business Directory* (Cincinnati and New York, 1846), p. 405.

45. M'Elroy's *Philadelphia Directory*, 1837.

46. Edwin T. Freedley, *Philadelphia and its Manufactures* . . . (Philadelphia, 1858), pp. 321–323.

47. Smith, *op. cit.*, pp. 407–411.

Radiating out from Philadelphia were the Philadelphia and Trenton, completed in 1834; the Philadelphia, Germantown, and Norristown, which was constructed as far as Germantown in 1832 and completed to Norristown in 1835; the Philadelphia and Columbia and the Allegheny Portage—important links in the State Works—which were completed in 1834; the Philadelphia, Wilmington, and Baltimore, opened in 1838; and the Philadelphia and Reading, 58 miles of which were laid down in 1839 and which was considered completed in 1842 when it reached Mount Carbon. Henry V. Poor, *History of the Railroads and Canals of the United States of America* (New York, 1860), pp. 415–417, 480, 482, 486, 487–488.

Between 1829 and 1849 the following miles of railroads were opened in Pennsylvania:

1829	4.0	miles	1836	20.5	miles	1843	–	miles
1830	12.73	"	1837	40.25	"	1844	8.5	"
1831	20.5	"	1838	142.0	"	1845	–	"
1832	27.0	"	1839	83.0	"	1846	–	"
1833	48.7	"	1840	63.45	"	1847	–	"
1834	127.0	"	1841	–	"	1848	42.0	"
1835	–	"	1842	35.0	"	1849	72.0	"

Ibid., pp. 415–417.

48. An order for a "suit" as it was termed, called for three weights of copper. John Devereaux ordered for the Barque *Globe* 700 sheets of 24, 26, and 28 oz. This, with 375 lbs. of composition nails, amounted to $1,320.91.

CHAPTER VII. Selling Methods

1. Ltr., NT to Edward Trotter, 19 Mar. 1836.

2. Ltr., Samuel Effinger to NT & Co., 9 Apr. 1822.

3. Ltr., Christian Luckenback to NT & Co., 26 Oct. 1818.

4. Ltr., NT & Co. to Isaac McKim, 6 Aug. 1831.

One reason Nathan Trotter was satisfied with Isaac McKim as a source of copper is indicated by the following letter from Baltimore, 23 Dec. 1835:

Your favor of the 21st was received this morning, in reply I beg leave to state that I have concluded the contracts with the Steam Boat Company for the furnishing the 60000# boiler copper at 26 cents per lb and on examining my stock of pig copper I am afraid that I shall hardly be able to meet that engagement, still, as you have promised to furnish the 85 pattern sheets ordered in yours of the 11th, and as I am exceedingly anxious that you should not be disappointed, I must try and make the copper which I expect to do in all next week, as soon as it is ready I will let you know and in meantime remain

> yours truly
> Isaac McKim
> by William Spear

5. Ltr., to NT & Co., 14 Sept. 1835.

6. In a letter to C. Hager & Son, 15 June 1847, Nathan Trotter described the practices of Phelps Dodge & Co. and continued:

This course with the full determination to engross the trade has arisen the greatest monopoly that exists in that article by one extensive concern.— yet notwithstanding all these things to contend with, the writer has pursued one course for about 40 years, of mainly importing all we sell of a *good article* & have established a set of customers, who have stuck to us thro' evil report & good report, & in the aggregate have expressed themselves as well served & satisfied, but many times we assure you, our measure of profit has been brought down to a feather edge.

Again, in a letter of 17 May 1839, Nathan Trotter & Co. had written to J. Elnathan Smith: "P D & Co must have recd. at New York near 10 M boxes [tin plates] within a month and have also heavy lots at New Orleans from whence they supply many Western orders—our sales however have been more extensive than usual this year and if we are enabled to contend with them in price we shall go increasing in the amot. of our sales." And then Trotter continues with the same complaint referred to earlier: "They import various brands and blend them together in Sales— we find our customers more particular & choose a brand, and none seems to please better than Walkers or Cookly K. the MC latterly has improved and we hope will continue to be good quality— We have had RG but not deemed satisfactory."

7. Ltr., NT & Co. to Phelps & Peck, 7 July 1829.

On 7 Apr. 1843, Nathan Trotter & Co. wrote to M. Leech & Co. of Pittsburgh: "We therefore now offer you 300 Boxes or More ⅓d X at 7¾ Cash—it is all in prime order & of best brands & fully tallyd with NYk rates there they often ship [slip?] in a portion often that costs Stg 4/- pr box less equal to One Dollar— this acts for some large sales at a nominally lower rate."

8. Ltr., NT & Co. to King & Holmes, 11 Aug. 1843.

9. Ltr., NT & Co. to James Black, 12 Sept. 1823.

10. Ltr., NT & Co. to Halderman & Cotrell, 1 Aug. 1839.

11. Ltr., M. Leech to NT & Co., 21 July 1837.

12. Ltr., NT & Co. to F. Lawson & Bros., 5 Apr. 1848.

13. Ltr., NT & Co. to C. & J. Marshall & Co., 12 Feb. 1846; also a letter (13 Feb. 1844) reading: "We should like to hear from you on the rect. of this letter whether we may calculate on being supplied by you with Sheet Iron on Sale as usual—our object in asking now is, that in a few days some persons will be on from the West who we know buy largely and we have sold them of English 20 to 30 Tons at a time—of course we cannot do that now—but shall we contract to sell them say as high as 600 Bdles or any portion of it and shall we take anything less $120—we wish to be prepared in case we have an opportunity of selling, and if we contract we must of course deliver—the quality must also be defined— we would not sell an article for the best without its being such—how soon could you deliver that quantity—"

14. Ltr., NT & Co. to C. & J. Marshall, 22 Jan. 1847: "You will be kind enough to advise as what rate we may engage to supply say to the extent of 25 Tons of your Sheet Iron, Equal in quality to what we have been getting of you. Some customers or consumers are now as usual about making their arrangements for Sheet Iron, and we must be early to meet them, or others *will* Supply them therefore you will please say definitely what descretion you will give us for delivery in the Spring. And write by an early Mail."

15. Ltr., NT & Co. to E. T. Ellicott, 5 June 1828.

16. Ltr., NT & Co. to Isaac McKim, 4 May 1831.

17. Ltrs, NT & Co. to Isaac McKim, 19, 26 Mar., 3, 11 Apr., 14 May 1833. The bid read as follows:

To the Commissioners for Erecting New County Prison &c

Gentlemen

We will agree to furnish the Copper for the new prison at twenty four cents and ninety mills pr # of the sizes and weights mentioned in your advertisement of 9 inst and of the best quality Copper, equal to that furnished by us for the new Alms House, and which perhaps came under the notice of Mr. Walter, the Architect for the Building of which you now have the charge

Or should the Commissioners prefer we will agree to furnish all the Copper that may be required for the Building, of the best quality, at one eighth of a cent pr # *less* than any other offer they may have received, provided the Copper is of equal finish & quality—and that they are as well satisfied of punctuality in the performance of the contract—an early answer would very much oblige us, and as we feel very desirous that the terms we propose may only be known to the Commissioners we respectfully request that they may be confined to themselves—

Philada. 30 March 1833
NT & Co

A note from Trotter on the same date to the Commissioners shows how both McKim and Trotter could save face by blaming the error on "our young man." The note reads: "In the proposals for Copper handed in this morning by us, our young man says he is under the impression that in Copying he inserted twenty four cents & 'ninety mills' instead of *nine* mills—we meant 24 90/100 cents pr #."

But in a letter to Isaac McKim, 3 April 1833, Nathan Trotter wrote: "yourself & us both overlooked an error in the proposal—24 & 90 mills was the offer you knew equal 33¢—the error occurred to me as returning from dinner and the same afternoon a note was sent correcting it & stating 24c 9 mills or 24 90/100 cents was meant."

18. Ltrs., NT & Co. to E. T. Ellicott, 21 July 1828 and 31 Mar. 1829.

CHAPTER VIII. Credit and Collections

1. On 16 Dec. 1818, Nathan Trotter had written Shultz Hixson & Co.: "We are not in the habit of dunning our customers."

2. One per cent was charged for the collection of some notes (ltr., NT & Co. to J. O'Connor, 23 Nov. 1841). The daybook includes such items as "allowed Bk of Northern Liberties 68¢ for collecting 2 notes amtg to $273.01" (21 Jan. 1843).

3. Ltr., NT & Co. to Lyne & Thompson, 9 Oct. 1816.

4. Ltr., J. & J. Arter to NT & Co., 13 Apr. 1847.

5. Granting credit to new customers in such periods was out of the question. In reply to a Louisville, Kentucky, request from a prospective customer, Nathan Trotter wrote (17 July 1837): "There has been no period for many years back that we should not have been much pleased with the acquisition of a new customer and even now have the disposition to sell on time yet owing to the sad change of commercial affairs and having large amts outstanding which it is impossible to collect we are compelled from the necessity of the case to confine our sales for cash and hence you will excuse us doing what under a different aspect of things we should be pleased to embrace."

6. Ltr., NT & Co. to Bainbridges & Brown, 19 June 1819.

7. Ltr., NT & Co. to George Miltenberger, 8 July 1819.

8. Ltr., NT & Co. to Joseph Cooper, 6 Sept. 1838.

9. Ltr., NT & Co. to S. E. Craig, 30 Aug. 1842.

10. Ltr., John Bollinger to NT & Co. 29 Feb. 1840, 4 Jan. 1842.

11. Ltr., NT & Co. to Jacob Weitzel, 16 Nov. 1816.

12. Ltr., NT & Co. to F. Lawson & Bros., 24 Nov. 1841.

13. Ltr., Edward Trotter to NT, 17 June 1843.

14. Ltr., NT & Co. to Harvey & Birch, 2 Mar. 1844.

15. Ltr., NT & Co. to D. M. Brautigan, 6 Feb. 1843.

16. Daybook, 1 June 1847.

CHAPTER IX. A Merchant Turns to Investment

1. McMaster, *The life and times of Stephen Girard* . . . , I, 112.
2. *Ibid.*, II, 59.
3. Private daybook, 4 Aug. 1843.
4. Nathan Trotter as "investor" borrowed this money from Nathan Trotter as "guardian" allowing 5 per cent for the guardianship money.
5. Ltr., NT to Edward Trotter, 19 May 1836.
6. Ltr., Edward Trotter to NT, 15 June 1836.
7. Ltr., NT to James Wilson, 25 Dec. 1840.
8. Henrietta M. Larson, "A China Trader Turns Investor: a Biographical Chapter in American Business History," *Harvard Business Review* (Apr., 1934), p. 356.
9. Kenneth W. Porter, *John Jacob Astor: Business Man* (Cambridge, 1931), I, chaps. iv, ix; II, chaps. xvii–xxii.
10. N. S. B. Gras and Henrietta M. Larson, *Casebook in American Business History* (New York, 1939), Case XXIII, "Cornelius Vanderbilt, 1794–1877," pp. 363–366.
11. Information about the *Pacific* venture is taken from the daybook, 21, 22, 23, 24, 31 Mar., 5, 6, 8, 11, 20 Apr., 1, 4, 8 May, 20, 23 June, 1815, 21 May, 30 July, 16 Aug., 31 Dec. 1816; ledger for 1815–1816; ltrs., James Sterling and William Brown to NT & Co., 13 Apr. 1815.
12. Information about the *Kensington* venture is from the daybook, 3, 6, Apr., 9 May, 26 June, 25, 30 July, 25, 28 Dec. 1816; and ledger for 1815–1816.
13. Kenneth Scott Latourette, in *The History of Early Relations between the United States and China, 1784–1844* (New Haven, 1917), p. 64, states that in the early years the Canton commerce "had been in the hands of a comparatively large number of firms and individual investors, small for the most part, and scattered among nearly all the seaports of the North Atlantic States. Beginning about the time of the war [the War of 1812] trade began to . . . be confined to the larger cities, New York, Boston, and Philadelphia, where it was concentrated in the hands of large firms."

These large firms are listed in *The Old China Trade* (Boston and New York, 1930) by Foster R. Dulles. He observes (p. 113) that "in 1825, it was reported that seven-eights of the China trade was in the hands of four firms: Perkins and Company of Boston; Archer, of Philadelphia; Jones Oakford and Company, of Philadelphia; and T. H. Smith, of New York." The two Philadelphia firms mentioned above and Matthew Ralston and John W. Rulon influenced Nathan Trotter to venture in the trade with Canton or Calcutta, since some of them were engaged in trade with both ports.

14. Daybook, 25 May 1836.
15. Nathan Dunn, Joseph Archer, and Jabez Jenkins advertised in the 13 Oct. 1830 issue of *The National Gazette and Literary Register* that they had "entered into Co-Partnership, under the firm of Nathan Dunn & Co. for the transaction of a General Agency and Commission Business at Canton."
16. Ltrs., NT & Co. to Thomas N. Richards, 8 Oct. 1838; to Morrison, Cryder & Co., 19 Aug. 1836: "our friend John W. Rulon sailed from here on 15 inst in the Washington for Calcutta and we handed him our Setts of Exchg: . . . on your House, amounting together to one Thousand pounds Sterling which we will thank you to protect Mr Rulon may or may not dispose of these Bills he will be governed by Circumstance."
17. Private ledger accounts and daybook items for (a) Adventure pr Ship *Washington* to Calcutta (b) Adventure to Canton (c) Adventure pr *George Gardner* to Calcutta and (d) Mdse. from Canton /Barings Credit/; ltrs., NT & Co. to J. E. Smith, 31 Mar. 1840; to Wm. Van Antwerp & Co., 19 Mar., 11 Apr.,

22 May, 23 June 1840, 8 June 1842; to Wm. F. Leggett, 1 Aug. 1842; to Wm. G. Bull & Co., 12 Aug. 1842; to Baring Bros. & Co., 29 Jan., 12 Mar., 6 Nov. 1841; to Wm. S. Wetmore, 4 Feb. 1841; to Wetmore & Co., 23 Feb. 1839.

The Oriental trade had changed in another respect, to quote Dulles (*op. cit.*, p. 123): "about six American companies in Canton carried on the trade there for American merchants" and he mentioned Russel and Company, D. W. C. Olyphant, Augustine Heard, and the firm used by the Trotters—W. S. Wetmore.

In one respect Trotter's experience does not bear out Dulles. He stated that "By 1841 the China trade was the tea trade pure and simple" (*op. cit.*, p. 118). Oakford and Trotter imported both teas and silks. Neither was very profitable.

18. Although commercial-paper discounting belongs more logically in the following chapter, I shall mention a few instances here since they concern the India and China traders, also. The Trotters—both the firm and Nathan with private money—discounted the notes of men who traded with the Orient. One entry reads "Pd. Billy O[verman] for Jones, Oakford & Co. notes 5 mos.," and the same firm, on 1 Jan. 1826, requested Nathan Trotter & Company to send a check "for money he can conveniently spare today." Throughout the 1830's Nathan Trotter & Company were loaning fairly large sums—$18,000 and $21,000—to Samuel and Joseph Archer and Richard Oakford.

19. Brig *President* to LaGuira, ledger, 1828, and daybook entries; ltrs., NT & Co. to Collin K. Davis, 3 Mar. 1828; C. K. Davis to NT & Co., 2 Apr. 1828; J. G. A. Williamson to NT & Co., 19 Apr., 15 Aug. 1828.

Shipment pr *Ontario* to South America, ledgers for 1821 and 1822 and daybook items; ltrs., Benj. C. White to NT & Co., 26, 30 Jan., 24 Feb. 1822.

Brig *Clio* to South America, ledger, 1823–1824, and daybook items.

William Wallace to Rio Janeiro, ledger, 1826–1827, and daybook entries; ltr., NT & Co. to Daniel T. Haines and Isaac Burkhard, 18 Sept. 1826.

Brig *Ontario* to Bahia and a Market, ledger, 1827, and daybook entries.

Brig *Rose* to Monte Video, ledger, 1829–1830, and daybook entries; ltrs., NT & Co. to D. T. Haines, 12 Oct. 1829; Daniel T. Haines to NT & Co., 8 Jan., 6 Feb. 1830.

20. Private daybook, 30 Jan. 1819: "Purchased of Geo. Tellman & wife 2 lots of ground with the appurtenances."

21. Private daybook, 12 Feb. 1830.

22. In Coates Alley the brothers had purchased a carpenter's shop and lot (13 May 1826) for $337.50, repaired it, and sold it for $879 (17 Mar. 1827 and 28 Jan. 1832).

Daybook, 30 Oct. 1830. Stables must have been a problem to Philadelphians with their houses side by side. Between the period when Nathan Trotter sold his Front Street place and built the Crown Street stable (Jan. 1830–July 1831), he rented a stable of Powell Stackhouse in Keys Alley (daybook, 14 July 1831).

23. Purchase price was $5,014.87 (ledger, entry for 22 Nov. 1828).

24. Daybook, 31 Dec. 1832. Purchased of George Thomas for $21,000, "deduct subject to a mortg of $7,000 $14,000."

25. NT & Co., private ledger, 25 Apr. 1833. Purchased for $1,513.35; Minutes, Northern District Monthly Meeting, 1830–1838, 3d mo. 24th 1835. Purchased from Monthly Meeting for $1,350 (NT & Co., private daybook, 7 Apr. 1835).

26. NT & Co. private daybook, 18 June 1849. Accounts of the stable John Rice built are scattered through the daybook from Dec., 1849, to Apr., 1850.

27. NT & Co., private daybook, 22 Dec. 1838; NT private daybook, 14 Aug. 1839.

28. NT & Co., private daybook, 26 May 1838, "house & lot adjoining our store" (31 Oct. 1838).

29. NT private daybook, 31 May 1842 states: "6 Dec 1841 purchased property of Th. H. Sickels at sheriffs Sale . . . got possession of 25 inst."

30. NT private daybook, 23 Sept. 1843: "Paid for lot 21 ft x 126 ft $4080, M. Randolph for his right of purch[ase] 220 $4,300   Said lot leased me for 99 years at $30 p year."

29 Aug. 1844, "agreed to pay John Rice for Bldg & materials for new House 5200   Total Cost 9,500."

31. NT private daybook, 1 Jan., 4 Apr. 1851.

32. Franklin Square was glowingly described in the guidebooks of the day; see *The Stranger's Guide in Philadelphia and its Environs* (Philadelphia, 1852), p. 55.

33. NT private daybook, 31 Dec. 1852.

34. The New Jersey farm was purchased 7 Dec. 1832 for $12,895.54; sold 28 Mar. 1837 for $14,177.07 (NT & Co., private daybook).

The Oxford farm was purchased of Timothy Paxson (NT & Co., private daybook, 7 Aug. 1839).

35. NT & Co., private daybook, 31 Mar. 1843: New dwelling house on farm in private ledger for 1844–1847 and daybook entries.

36. Trotter-Newbold papers, 8 Aug. 1844.

37. NT & Co., private daybook, 31 Dec. 1833.

38. M'Elroy's *Philadelphia Directory* for 1842 mentions among the "Agencies" at the Bank of Pennsylvania that of the Planters' Bank of Tennessee and the Sandy & Beaver Canal Co.

The Sandy & Beaver Canal formed "an important connexion between the two great works already completed—the Pennsylvania and Ohio Canals from Bolivar on the latter to the mouth of the Little Beaver in Pennsylvania." *The National Gazette and Literary Register*, 28 Apr. 1835.

39. Nathan Trotter wrote his son Edward, 15 Feb. 1836, as follows: "Another question has also made a great excitement here— the Chartering the United States Bank by our Legislature with a capital of 35 millions! it *has* passed the House and *will* pass the Senate and become a Law without doubt—the Globe has written against it and many other papers with great bitterness, but all wont do— Pennsa cant consent to the transfer of such amot of capital to another State and lose with it a bonus of Several Millions."

John Jay Knox, *A History of Banking in the United States* (New York, 1900), p. 75.

40. *Ibid.*, pp. 76–77.

41. NT private daybook, 31 Dec. 1839, the following losses were written off:

Chesapeak & Delaware Canal	$ 400
Philadelphia Steam Tow Boat Co.	100
West Chester Rail Road	350
Loan to Sandy & Beaver Canal	4,500
	$5,350

19 Sept. 1845 he paid $230, or 5 per cent on $4,600, a new subscription to Sandy & Beaver Canal stock, "being with others a united effort to resusitate it." 28 Mar. 1848 entry: paid $1,000 for bonds of Sandy & Beaver Canal Co.

42. Jules I. Bogen, *The Anthracite Railroads: a Study in American Railroad Enterprise* (New York, 1927), p. 35.

43. Published in Philadelphia in 1854.

44. James M. Swank, *History of the Manufacture of Iron in All Ages* . . . (Philadelphia, 1892), p. 352.

45. Ltr., NT & Co. to Jevons Sons & Co., 3 Oct. 1838.

46. *Ibid.*, 15 Jan. 1839.

47. *Ibid.*, 31 July 1839; Swank, *op. cit.*, pp. 360–362.

Jevons Sons & Co. also informed Nathan Trotter of the progress of anthracite smelting in England. On 14 November they wrote:

The great difficulty which we meet with in smelting with anthracite is that we cannot make quantity—the most that has yet been run from any

Furnace on this side the Water in one week is 52 Tons, & with the same labour at the Furnace some of our coke Furnaces yield three times that quantity.

16 Nov. 1844 they had their "Anthracite Furnace in blast again making about 50 Tons a week which is sought after by all the Tin plate makers in our neighbourhood."

48. *Souvenir History. Philadelphia Stock Exchange* (Philadelphia, 1903).

CHAPTER X. Commercial-Paper Discounting

1. Kent, *The story of Alexander Brown & Sons*, p. 141.
2. Dallas 92. *An Abridgement of the Laws of Pennsylvania . . . with References to Reports of Judicial Decisions in the Supreme Court of Pennsylvania*, John Purdon, Jr. (Philadelphia, 1811).
3. Ralph C. H. Catterall, *The Second Bank of the United States* (Chicago, 1903), p. 484.
4. For example, Condy Raguet in *A treatise on currency and banking* (London, 1839), pp. 110–111, states that many banks got more than the legal rate by giving preference in their discounts to customers who agreed to leave in the bank, never to be drawn on, a proportion—20 to 40 per cent—of the money borrowed.
5. Walter Bagehot, *Lombard Street: a description of the money market* (new ed.; New York, 1910), pp. 284–285.
6. Minutes of the Northern District Monthly Meeting, 5th mo. 25th. 1841.
7. *Ibid.*, 8th mo. 1st day 1842 Haines was "treated with for contracting debts which he is unable to pay," and when he was treated with further the following month he was "not in a disposition of mind to condemn his conduct in contracting debts that he is unable to pay," and the Meeting concluded that "further delay will not be attended with benefit" and directed the committee "to prepare a testimony of disownment against him, for consideration at our next meeting."
This was done, as the Minutes of 11 mo. 1st 1842 show: Ephraim Haines "who had a right of membership with us, has contracted debts which he is unable to pay; on which account he has been treated with, but our labor proving ineffectual we testify, he is no longer a member of the Religious Society of Friends."
8. *The Report of the Committee Appointed to Examine into the State of the Bank of Pennsylvania and Philadelphia Bank* (Harrisburg, 1829) gives considerable information about the reasons discounting needs were not being met. One statement was: "The want of means to discount business paper in the bank of Pennsylvania has been attributed to the large loans made to brokers. In one year $189,000 was discounted for one broker" (p. 8).
John T. Sullivan reported (pp. 51–52) that the business paper rejected at the Bank of Pennsylvania in 1828 was "principally occasioned by the large amounts of stationary loans [accommodation paper?], held by the bank which crippled its resources." The discounts of the bank at one time that year consisted of about $301,244 in "accommodation some of which has been running for several years; about 918,025 is business, in addition there is about 58,867 secured by mortgages" (p. 32).
William Sansom, in answer to the question "Were you present at the meeting of the board of directors on the 16th of April last [1828] when a certain auction house offered for discount 3 notes?" replied: "I was present. The notes were objected to as the offerers were discounters at the bank for 38,124 and they kept a poor account and the Commonwealth would soon require a temporary loan and the bank ought to furnish" part of the loan to the Commonwealth (p. 101).
Director Tobias White defended the bank, concluding: "I have understood that in times of pressure, other banks have been obliged to reject large sums of the best business paper, and that on an average, I think the bank of Pennsylvania has accommodated its customers about as well as most other banks."

Some of the state-appointed directors were hostile and the bank-appointed were favorable in their statements.

9. Over a long period of years there seems to have been considerable uniformity as the following material indicates:

Minutes of the Proceedings of the Stockholders of the Bank of Pennsylvania for 19 June 1793 read: "Resolved, that the President and Directors of the Bank of Pennsylvania be and they are hereby authorized . . . to discount Notes or Bills at the rate limited by Law, for any term, not exceeding sixty Days."

Benjamin Davies in *Some Account of the City of Philadelphia* . . . published in 1794 states: "At all the banks, bills or notes may be left, at any time, to be collected; which will be done free of expense; but, in cases of non-payment and protest, the person leaving the bill or note must pay the expense. Three days grace are allowed on all bills or notes payable. Discounts are made on personal security only, and for not longer than sixty days."

And the Bank of Northern Liberties of Philadelphia, as I have already mentioned, resolved in 1822 to discount no note having a longer time to run than 60 days, unless, "under peculiar circumstances, the Board decide otherwise."

10. Mease, *The Picture of Philadelphia* . . . , p. 108.

11. Catterall, *op. cit.*, p. 54.

12. Willard L. Thorp, *Business Annals* (New York, 1926), pp. 118–120.

13. In *The National Gazette and Literary Register* (Philadelphia) they advertised "cotton yarn from Woodville, Phoenix, Little Falls, Blackstone, and other approved factories" (25 Aug. 1825); "shirtings, sheetings, plaids, stripes, from Blackstone, Scituate, Sterling, and Williams Factories"; also "Peterboro Shirtings received from Boston" (2, 30 May 1825).

14. It seems never to have been the practice of Nathan Trotter, or of William Trotter in using the money of Daniel Trotter's Estate, to put the money to work and give the minors the full return on the investment, except in the case of bonds or mortgages which brought in 5 or 6 per cent and were considered, seemingly, the safest forms of investment.

The Trotter papers contain material on Trotter's efforts to obtain safe investments. In 1825 he arranged for a "bond & mortgage" for $3,440 on a farm near Burlington, N. J., stressing in every letter the necessity of seeing that this property is "free of every kind of incumbrance when our Mtge. is given so that ours is the *first* and *only claim* against it—" Since the property was "represented" to Trotter as being worth $7,000, he therefore considered it "a sufficient security for the present loan" (ltrs., NT to Abraham Brown, 3, 12 Jan. 1825).

15. August 16, 1830

Bills Rec Dr to Sundries

To Cash—pd Jennings, T[homas], G[ill] & Co			
Stryker & P	5 Aug. 6 mos	$ 987.74	
Lippincott & W	"	723.16	
Ashmead & A	"	486.92	
Wm Norris Jr	"	805.31	
Busby & Spngel	"	2409.33	
B. Eytinger	"	668.05	
Trevor & B	"	249.55	
Geo: Riston	"	967.41	
Martin & H	"	993.17	
N Thomson & Co	"	1301.—	
C & M Cope	"	763.38	
Wood & A	"	1443.93	
		$11798.95	
	disct 5½	322.12	11476.83
To Int a/ct			
disct 5½%			322.12

16. Thorp, *op. cit.*, pp. 121–123.

17. Catterall, *op. cit.*, pp. 296–298. See also Davis Rich Dewey, *Financial history of the United States* (10th ed.; New York, 1928), pp. 205–206.

18. Ripka paid high discount rates for years—higher than that paid by merchants. Of a lot of 12 notes which Trotter purchased 28 Nov. 1851, discounts were 9, 10, and 12 per cent. The only one higher, 1¼ or 15 per cent, was Ripka's note. It is amazing that he survived financially until the Panic of 1857.

The manufactories and manufacturers of Pennsylvania of the nineteenth century (Philadelphia, 1875) gives the following information about Ripka (pp. 411–412):

Joseph Ripka (1788–1864) was born in Silesia. At the age of 16 he went to Vienna, then to Switzerland, and to Lyons in France. In France he learned the silk-weaving business. In 1815 he came to Philadelphia, and in 1828 built the Ripka Mills at Manayunk, Philadelphia, for the manufacture of cottonades in which he was the pioneer in America. He later became owner of a spinning mill at Chandlersville, of the City Mills in Philadelphia, and of the Pennypack Print Works near Holmesburg.

"In 1837, the great crisis in the commercial world found him, by his capital, credit and business integrity, able to continue the operation of his many industrial establishments; and this was uninterrupted until the financial panic of 1857, when he was obliged to succumb. It may be said of him that he was the pioneer and founder of the 'Lowell' of Philadelphia [Manayunk]. . . . As a manufacturer, in his line of business he had no superior in the thorough knowledge of every branch connected with it in this country."

19. Jules I. Bogen, *The Anthracite Railroads* (New York, 1927), pp. 22–35.

20. "Jay Cooke's Memoir," typescript copy in Baker Library, Harvard University.

21. The note was signed (although the signature was probably a forgery) by Foster & Co. in favor of and endorsed by Key & Biddle. Trotter consulted Charles Chauncey, a counsellor and director of the Bank of Pennsylvania, as to whether the endorsers were liable for the payment "admitting the drawers name to be forged."

Chauncey replied: "I have no doubt of the liability of the indorsers to pay the note on the facts stated in the foregoing case. It is not necessary for the holder to prove the maker's signature, to recover from the indorser; because the indorsement is a new contract; and it is considered as affirming the genuineness of the maker's signature. Supposing the endorsement by one of the Copartners to be in the usual way of their business, there can be no doubt of the liability of the Copartnership.

Ch Chauncey
Jany 28, 1837"

In five notes, dated 12, 18, 24, 30, and 36 months, Trotter received the amount, commenting that this arrangement was the best he could make.

22. Henry Simpson, *The Lives of Eminent Philadelphians* (Philadelphia, 1859), p. 20. The article on Samuel Archer was by William D. Lewis who appeared to know Archer well.

23. *Report of the Committee Appointed to Examine into the State of the Bank of Pennsylvania and Philadelphia Bank*, pp. 51–52, gives the following amounts *rejected* each month by the Bank of Pennsylvania in 1828:

Jan.	$ 50,097
Feb.	76,902
Mar.	334,822
Apl.	213,319
May	176,667
June	170,032
July	90,188

Aug.	$ 45,545
Sept.	52,391
Oct.	211,669
Nov.	122,872
Dec.	165,237
	$1,709,741

24. Dunlap's *Pennsylvania Packet*, 12, 13 Jan. 1791.

25. *Ibid.* In the issue of 13 Jan. Samuel Hays advertised at no. 119 Front Street, six doors below the Post-office, "where *money* may be immediately obtained for good *notes*."

In the 26 Feb. 1791 issue, Andrew Summers, Jr., a broker, advertised that he "Discounts notes, and procures money on a Depost of Public Securities."

26. Poulson's *American Daily Advertiser*, 14 Dec. 1803.

27. A broker whom Nathan Trotter used occasionally in the 1820's was "Billy" Overman. He was, doubtless, the William Overman mentioned in 1813 as one whose "list of subscribers to the Sixteen Million Loan, whose deposits will be made in Stephen Girard's Bank" amounted to $398,500. McMaster, *The life and times of Stephen Girard*, II, 250.

Index

INDEX

TECHNOLOGY AND SOCIETY

An Arno Press Collection

Ardrey, R[obert] L. **American Agricultural Implements.** In two parts. 1894

Arnold, Horace Lucien and Fay Leone Faurote. **Ford Methods and the Ford Shops.** 1915

Baron, Stanley [Wade]. **Brewed in America:** A History of Beer and Ale in the United States. 1962

Bathe, Greville and Dorothy. **Oliver Evans:** A Chronicle of Early American Engineering. 1935

Bendure, Zelma and Gladys Pfeiffer. **America's Fabrics:** Origin and History, Manufacture, Characteristics and Uses. 1946

Bichowsky, F. Russell. **Industrial Research.** 1942

Bigelow, Jacob. **The Useful Arts:** Considered in Connexion with the Applications of Science. 1840. Two volumes in one

Birkmire, William H. **Skeleton Construction in Buildings.** 1894

Boyd, T[homas] A[lvin]. **Professional Amateur:** The Biography of Charles Franklin Kettering. 1957

Bright, Arthur A[aron], Jr. **The Electric-Lamp Industry:** Technological Change and Economic Development from 1800 to 1947. 1949

Bruce, Alfred and Harold Sandbank. **The History of Prefabrication.** 1943

Carr, Charles C[arl]. **Alcoa, An American Enterprise.** 1952

Cooley, Mortimer E. **Scientific Blacksmith.** 1947

Davis, Charles Thomas. **The Manufacture of Paper.** 1886

Deane, Samuel. **The New-England Farmer,** or Georgical Dictionary. 1822

Dyer, Henry. **The Evolution of Industry.** 1895

Epstein, Ralph C. **The Automobile Industry:** Its Economic and Commercial Development. 1928

Ericsson, Henry. **Sixty Years a Builder:** The Autobiography of Henry Ericsson. 1942

Evans, Oliver. **The Young Mill-Wright and Miller's Guide.** 1850

Ewbank, Thomas. **A Descriptive and Historical Account of Hydraulic and Other Machines for Raising Water,** Ancient and Modern. 1842

Field, Henry M. **The Story of the Atlantic Telegraph.** 1893

Fleming, A. P. M. **Industrial Research in the United States of America.** 1917

Van Gelder, Arthur Pine and Hugo Schlatter. **History of the Explosives Industry in America.** 1927

Hall, Courtney Robert. **History of American Industrial Science.** 1954

Hungerford, Edward. **The Story of Public Utilities.** 1928

Hungerford, Edward. **The Story of the Baltimore and Ohio Railroad, 1827-1927.** 1928

Husband, Joseph. **The Story of the Pullman Car.** 1917

Ingels, Margaret. **Willis Haviland Carrier, Father of Air Conditioning.** 1952

Kingsbury, J[ohn] E. **The Telephone and Telephone Exchanges:** Their Invention and Development. 1915

Labatut, Jean and Wheaton J. Lane, eds. **Highways in Our National Life:** A Symposium. 1950

Lathrop, William G[ilbert]. **The Brass Industry in the United States.** 1926

Lesley, Robert W., John B. Lober and George S. Bartlett. **History of the Portland Cement Industry in the United States.** 1924

Marcosson, Isaac F. **Wherever Men Trade:** The Romance of the Cash Register. 1945

Miles, Henry A[dolphus]. **Lowell, As It Was, and As It Is**. 1845

Morison, George S. **The New Epoch:** As Developed by the Manufacture of Power. 1903

Olmsted, Denison. **Memoir of Eli Whitney, Esq.** 1846

Passer, Harold C. **The Electrical Manufacturers, 1875-1900.** 1953

Prescott, George B[artlett] **Bell's Electric Speaking Telephone.** 1884

Prout, Henry G. **A Life of George Westinghouse.** 1921

Randall, Frank A. **History of the Development of Building Construction in Chicago.** 1949

Riley, John J. **A History of the American Soft Drink Industry:** Bottled Carbonated Beverages, 1807-1957. 1958

Salem, F[rederick] W[illiam]. **Beer, Its History and Its Economic Value as a National Beverage.** 1880

Smith, Edgar F. **Chemistry in America.** 1914

Steinman, D[avid] B[arnard]. **The Builders of the Bridge:** The Story of John Roebling and His Son. 1950

Taylor, F[rank] Sherwood. **A History of Industrial Chemistry.** 1957

Technological Trends and National Policy, Including the Social Implications of New Inventions. Report of the Subcommittee on Technology to the National Resources Committee. 1937

Thompson, John S. **History of Composing Machines.** 1904

Thompson, Robert Luther. **Wiring a Continent:** The History of the Telegraph Industry in the United States, 1832-1866. 1947

Tilley, Nannie May. **The Bright-Tobacco Industry, 1860-1929.** 1948

Tooker, Elva. **Nathan Trotter:** Philadelphia Merchant, 1787-1853. 1955

Turck, J. A. V. **Origin of Modern Calculating Machines.** 1921

Tyler, David Budlong. **Steam Conquers the Atlantic.** 1939

Wheeler, Gervase. **Homes for the People,** In Suburb and Country. 1855

LIBRARY OF DAVIDSON COLLEGE

Books on regular loan may be checked out for **two weeks.** Books must be presented at the Circulation Desk in order to be renewed.

A fine of **five cents** a day is charged after date due.

Special books are subject to special regulations at the discretion of library staff.